History and Computing III

Historians, Computers and Data

Applications in Research and Teaching

Edited by
Evan Mawdsley, Nicholas Morgan
Lesley Richmond *and* Richard Trainor

Manchester University Press
Manchester and New York
Distributed exclusively in the USA and Canada by St. Martin's Press

Published by Manchester University Press
Oxford Road, Manchester M13 9PL, UK
and Room 400, 175 Fifth Avenue,
New York, NY 10010, USA

Distributed exclusively in the USA and Canada
by St. Martin's Press, Inc.,
175 Fifth Avenue, New York, NY 10010, USA

British Library cataloguing in publication data
History and computing III
1. Historiology. Applications of computer systems
I. Mawdsley, Evan, 1945–
907.2

Library of Congress cataloging in publication data
History and computing III / edited by Evan Mawdsley ... [et al.].
p. cm.
ISBN 0-7190-3051-X - ISBN 0-7190-3211-3 (pbk)
1. History – Data processing - Congresses. I. Mawdsley. Evan. 1945– II. Title: History and computing 3. III. Title: History and computing three.
D16.12.H59 1990
902'.85—dc20 90-36568

ISBN 0 7190 3051 X *hardback*
0 7191 3211 3 *paperback*

Printed in Great Britain
by Dotesios Ltd, Trowbridge

Table of Contents

IV. Teaching

V. Research

VI. Conclusion

Introduction

In recent years there has been an astonishing upsurge in the use of computers by historians in the United Kingdom. Encouraged by the availability of cheap dedicated word-processors, scholars have paddled in the waves of technology and found them sufficiently pleasant to be lured further into the surf. It is now by no means unusual to find historians in 'traditional' history departments engaged in research projects which rest heavily on computers as tools of analysis, as well as of authorship; and computers are increasingly being used by them in the classroom. The entry of this new group of historians into the deeper waters of historical computation has been accompanied by a change of methods. There has been a significant shift away from the cumbersome statistical packages and the number-crunching techniques employed in the 1960s and 1970s (by 'social science historians'), to a greater dependence on the text-searching capabilities provided by sophisticated yet easy to use hierarchical and relational database management systems. Historians are also looking towards the methods employed by literary and linguistic computationalists, so long the mainstay of 'humanities' computing, in order to find tools to analyse documents themselves. With these moves has come a refreshing concern for the nature and integrity of sources, and a reawakened acknowledgment by computer-minded historians of the primacy of place held by the raw materials, rather than the tools.

In a modest way the Glasgow conference of April 1988 offered an opportunity to assess these developments. Although something less than a complete image of the conference, the papers published here represent a 'state of the art' summary of historical computing in the UK in the late 1980s. That the state of the art will undoubtedly have advanced by the time this volume is published reflects the pace at which technology - and our methods — are changing.

Anyone coming to the Glasgow conference after even two or three years away from history and computing would be astonished by the range of hardware and software now available to the scholar, even to the scholar with modest resources. It is easy to forget that microcomputers, now increasingly powerful, portable and affordable, were once none of these. At Glasgow the first Superbrain microcomputer was delivered to the University Archives in 1981; it was a double-disc drive machine (each disc with 340k of storage), with 64k of RAM, and running under the clumsy CP/M operating system. Users soon learned that whatever 'user friendly' meant it was not synonymous with ease of use. No software existed that met the needs of inexperienced historians with little free time to learn new concepts or complex skills. Microcomputers were still not far enough advanced to process large quantities of data and, at around £2,750 for

10Mb of storage, Winchester discs were uneconomic compared to mainframe disc-space. The same money today would easily buy what is an increasingly common historian's workstation, a 80806 or 286 machine with between 20 and 60 megabytes of hard disc storage, at least a megabyte of memory, and running at a clock speed of somewhere between 7 and 12 MHz. With this sort of power readily available on a desk-top (at home or in the office) it is hardly surprising that many historians have increasingly chosen to base their work on microcomputers. In 1981 the response to the inadequacies of the microcomputer at Glasgow (as elsewhere) was to confine its use to data entry and data-transfer, in effect to use it as a sort of glorified punch card machine. The real work was done on an unfriendly and slow VME driven ICL 2988 mainframe. By contrast, as the papers here show, now only those projects with extensive filestore requirements, or occasionally with special software or hardware requirements, really need recourse to mainframes.

Distributed computing is a strategic feature of all current Computer Board procurements in British universities, and a similar philosophy is underpinning the creation of computing environments in polytechnics and colleges. For many this need be no more than the local area network - a desk-top microcomputer driven by a powerful fileserver and bringing essential shared software and peripherals within the reach of everyone connected to a piece of cheap co-axial cable. But the increasing ability of machines to talk to each other also allows the scholar to move up from the desk-top through a range of more powerful machines (possibly to a Sun workstation or a minicomputer) until an appropriate work place is found. Increasingly (particularly with the continuing improvement in operating environments) the division between machines is becoming transparent; equally transparent, in consequence, are the arguments of those who insist on the supremacy of one machine type or manufacturer over another.

Similarly paper-thin are claims that historians have to restrict themselves to one or two particular software packages in order to get the best from their data. The packages extolled in the past were those that placed the heaviest burden on the scholar's original information in terms of coding, standardisation and classification. Although some of those who gave presentations at Glasgow could still be put in this camp, one of the clearest points of agreement seemed to be that information came first, software second. The software had to suit the information, and the problem.

Reflecting this, a wide variety of concepts can be found in the papers that follow: artificial intelligence; hardware-orientated solutions (to facilitate high-speed text-retrieval); relational and hierarchical databases; spreadsheets and statistics programs; mapping and graphics packages; text-searching and hypertext applications; business packages; educational software; and even the schools-level data handlers. There were also hand-written programs, and some of the teaching software demonstrated at the conference was of the highest standard. This range demonstrates the imagination with which scholars have tried to tackle traditional (and some not so traditional) problems in a machine-mediated environment. Some of these problems are simply defined, and simply answered, with the computer still acting as nothing more or less than a workhorse. It takes the drudgery out of re-working figures or re-sorting index cards in order to ask the same simple question from different standpoints. Computing does not have to be complicated; indeed there is a danger that those who insist that it is so are losing the focus of their initial historical enquiry, replacing it with a technology-dependent methodology. As many of these papers show, conformity to 'industry standards' (i.e. over-sophistication) is often not necessary if the researcher has a sufficiently clear view of the problem and of how the machine can either help solve it, or more often than not, help define it more clearly.

Realistically, of course, few historians have an unrestricted choice of tools; most departments are under-resourced, and most computing services are still either ill-equipped or temperamentally unsuited to help or advise arts-based users. It is not that arts or humanities problems are uninteresting to computer professionals; often quite the reverse is true. At the moment, however, arts-based computing within universities - and historical computing in particular - does not have the income-generating potential that might win it the sort of resources devoted to Interdisciplinary Research Centres or externally-funded research projects. This situation need not persist. One relevant point was made at the Glasgow conference, both in formal sessions and informal conversation: arts computing is often based on problems concerning information about the past, and these problems share all the complexity and ambiguity of information about the present. Historical computing in particular offers an opportunity for the joint development, with public or private sector collaborators, of tools and techniques of organising, storing, analysing and presenting information that would be equally useful to both parties. Novel tools for textual analysis, innovative applications of expert systems, imaginative uses of graphics tools for plotting or storing historical data - all these areas featured at the Glasgow conference. They have clear applications in the 'real' world that is alleged to exist outside the university cloisters. Given the current lack of resources available to UK historians for software development, it is unlikely that any significant progress will be made in this area unless such collaborations are forthcoming.

An overview of the Glasgow conference might make one see an unbroken sequence of progress - in true Whig tradition - towards a better end. However, it is clear that methodological problems still persist to plague the computer-aided historian with self doubt about the validity or appropriateness of the approach chosen. This uncertainty was most clearly expressed at Glasgow in relation to two areas: data collection and storage, and data classification and coding. The utility of the computer is that it allows large amounts of information to be processed, and reprocessed, according to a variety of criteria, or sets of instructions. But how is that information to be captured in the first place? What role have repositories to play in the computerisation of the materials they hold? What rules should be followed to preserve the integrity of an original source? What are the tensions between funding bodies interested in a quick turnover of projects and associated publications, and the scholar determined to create a database that will both lead to publication *and* serve as an enduring resource for others?

And what do historians need to do to their information in order to help the machine make sense of it? Is the obsession with classifying and coding data a hangover from the days when historical computing was dominated by often inappropriate quantitative research techniques - techniques that can be dispensed with in the era of the sophisticated text-orientated database? Or is classification an essential prerequisite for the historian to comprehend fully the data being used, and to appreciate the complexities that lie behind simple descriptions (for example, of occupations)? For it is often only when classification is attempted that these complexities come to light. The Glasgow conference showed that for the most part historians have rightly been concerned less to please the social or computer scientist, or the database designer, than to achieve (as far as possible) a replication of the content and structure of original record sources in simple data formats. So sampling a fraction of the information is increasingly rejected in favour of the capture of the whole. Scholars have been driven by a concern to record data warts and all: to reject standardisation (typically of personal names, place names or job types), to be cautious (if not intolerant) of using coded values in place of original items, and to accept duplication of data items (again, typically of personal names, place names or job types) within a record or file.

So much for the development of the method. How does it relate to research and teaching? As virtually all historians who use computers would agree, information technology is only a tool, albeit a tool exceptional both in the power that it confers on the profession (opening up sources which could only be dipped into without excruciatingly laborious analysis) and in the demands for precision that it imposes. Moreover, the computer is likely to function best when used in conjunction with conventional historical sources and on questions whose importance does not depend on their suitability for machine analysis.

Yet if these precepts command almost automatic agreement, there is less consensus concerning the range of activity to which the computer is relevant. In particular, it is only beginning to be appreciated that in history the computer can and should be applied both to research *and* teaching. Too often, historians view the role of information technology in these spheres as quite distinct: the computer acts as an inspired analyst in advanced research but as a drill-and-practice tutor in rudimentary teaching.

The increased sophistication of teaching software, even of packages presenting basic facts and concepts, makes the denigration of computer-aided learning seem increasingly out of touch. Meanwhile historians are ever more aware that the use of highly complex programs to analyse huge volumes of research data can be more befuddling than illuminating. As software comes to be seen increasingly as a way in which historians and their students *explore* historical materials, the processes of computer-based learning and computer-based research are drawing closer together. For in history, as in other humanities and social science disciplines, the computer fosters the analytical skills toward which all good teaching is directed; it also breaks down the traditional division of labour between information-producing academics and information-receiving students without encouraging anarchy. Looked at in this way, computer-based teaching and computer-based research reinforce each other. Students gain from the insights and enthusiasm of teachers who are actively engaged in research on materials which also feature in the classroom; teachers find that the task of adapting computerised materials for use in courses sharpens their thinking in both research and instruction.

The close and fruitful interaction between teaching and research can be illustrated from this volume. All the contributors to the research section are engaged in computer-based teaching, either directly or through the activities of others using their data. In many cases the research materials analysed in the essays have been adapted for teaching. Most of the contributors to the teaching section who are located in higher education are also involved in computer-based research. And, as the contributions to the section from the school sector show, the painstaking preparation of computer-based teaching materials involves, as in higher education, a considerable degree of research, much of it original.

Interconnected as they are, research and teaching each have their validity. As the essays in the research section demonstrate, when the sources and the questions involved are suitable the computer can be an invaluable part of the historian's research armoury. Its utility stretches across the full range of historical themes, periods and countries — (contrary to the suspicions of some, the computer has not been, and could not be, monopolized as a research tool by economic historians or by modernists). And given the similarities between computer-aided research and teaching, it is not surprising that the teaching essays show the same wide spread. They also indicate that the computer's value for teaching is not restricted to databases: textual material, simulations and tutorial instruction are equally valid applications.

As Charles Harvey's concluding essay reveals, historical computing in Britain is not an isolated pursuit. Just as the methodology of British history as a whole has influenced, and been influenced by, that of historians in many other countries (notably France, Germany and the United States), so historical computing in Britain is part of a general, and increasingly closely knit, movement. The four international conferences of the Association for History and Computing have demonstrated this cosmopolitanism. Although this volume is the product of the first conference of the United Kingdom branch of the Association, it too indicates the ways in which historical computing refuses to be contained within neat political boundaries.

To argue for the broad-ranging usefulness of the computer in the four areas of sources, methods, teaching and research is not to suggest that information technology is a panacea or even an easy process. As has been mentioned, historians often lack ready resources. The practice and the practicalities of computer-assisted history are still far short of maturity. Nevertheless, this volume, like its predecessors, aims in part to show that the field *has* grown from infancy to a rapidly developing childhood. Only individual readers can decide if this 'snapshot' is fair to the child, or if they wish to continue to follow its progress into adolescence.

N.J.M., R.H.T.

* * *

The following is a short outline of the volume:

Burnard's article, originally presented at the conference dinner of the 1988 AHC meeting, provides a light introduction to the nature of the 'database' which, it turns out, goes back as a concept some time before the invention of the computer.

The section on '**Sources**' ranges widely. The article by **Moss** - appropriately the archivist at the conference's host institution - lays out Glasgow University's experience and his vision of the close connection of the University's archives with the DISH Project. **Wilson**, from the experience of a municipal archive (Edinburgh), shows the potential, even the necessity, of applying computer techniques to the modern search room. **Foster/Bowman** move from the general to the specific with a discussion of the management of medical sources. Finally, **Parker** opens the topic out with a paper on the computerisation of the National Register of Archives.

In the '**Methods**' section **Jeacocke** introduces the general potential of computers and databases for the historian, and also presents the challenge involved in achieving cooperation between historians and computer scientists. The potential of hypertext in the history of art and elsewhere is outlined by **Dyer**. **Bourlet/Minel** show the use of an expert system to make conclusions about a difficult source, medieval Parisian tax rolls. **Greenstein** focuses on the value of another increasingly common tool, the relational database, in one area in which it is commonly used, collective biography (in this case, of Oxford graduates).

The last three authors in this section turn to data structures and information in general. The problem of categorisation of British census data forms the basis of the paper by **Higgs**. **Schurer** provides more detail on a much discussed but still central question, data coding, and stresses the benefits of standardisation. Finally, **Blumin** raises technical questions of data classification, with examples from American nineteenth-century urban directories.

The final two sections are about the use of sources and methods. Of the articles on '**Teaching**', Blow, McArthur and Munro deal mainly with current and future trends in secondary schools. **Blow** stresses the importance of pupils' own discoveries using computer methods. A similar argument is advanced by **McArthur**, based on the Scottish experience. Some of McArthur's expectations for the future are fleshed out by **Munro**, with his vision of a multi source visual database for a rural case-study.

Of the six articles about higher education, **Phillips** is a useful starting point for newcomers, as he recalls the decision to get involved in computer-based teaching at Manchester University. **Trainor** might be looked at last, as he discusses future perspectives. Those authors in between lay out the use of computing in university courses. **Ayton** takes the discussion of the survey course (at Hull) one step beyond the Manchester experience, while **Newton** looks at the development of tutorial software at Rhode Island College. **Munck** and **Mawdsley/Whitelaw** describe the application of computer techniques to more specialised courses at Glasgow.

Although all '**Research**' papers are concerned with the history of the British Isles, the range of topics is considerable. Three are on Scotland (Dupree, Macinnes and Morgan) and one on Ireland (Collins), and the time period ranges from the seventeenth century (Spaeth) to the twentieth-century frontiers of nominal census records (Collins). The papers also contain a wide diversity of approaches, and will give a lead to historians working on other societies and periods. **Spaeth**, while focusing on seventeenth-century parish history, raises a number of important issues concerning the uses of small databases, in ways that would be of interest to historians who think that computing is not relevant to them. **Macinnes's** work on the Scottish Estates at the beginning of the following century suggests a straightforward approach for other political historians. **Lloyd-Jones/Lewis** provide an approach for looking at economic growth, taking the example of nineteenth-century Manchester. **Morgan** explores the usefulness of a large-scale study of property ownership in Scotland from rating documents. **Collins** shows the power of relational databases in looking at census data (Londonderry in 1911). **Dupree's** article is on medical history, but looks at a number of questions about collective biography which can be broadly generalized. **Nenadic**, with her text-based research, shows the great potential beyond the database; she uses diaries to examine personal networks in eighteenth-century Britain.

In the concluding paper **Harvey** surveys the general situation of historical computing and shows that the gap between historical computing and traditional British perceptions of the historical discipline is not as wide as it sometimes seems. He also outlines the great potential for the profession of the Association for History and Computing.

The Association for History and Computing

The Association for History and Computing (AHC) is an international organisation which aims to promote and develop interest in the use of computers in all types of historical study at every level, in both teaching and research.

The Association was proposed at a large conference at Westfield College, University of London, in March 1986. At a second conference at Westfield, in March 1987, it was formally founded and its constitution approved. A central co-ordinating body, the Council, organises the Association's international activities, including an annual conference (this was held in Cologne in 1988 and in Bordeaux in 1989; the 1990 conference will be in Montpellier, the 1991 conference in Odense). Sub-groups dealing with specific aspects of computing, such as the standardisation and exchange of historical data, have also been formed. Within 30 months of the Association's official foundation its membership grew to over 850 from 27 countries.

A vital part of the AHC's work is its publication policy. It distributes free to members an international magazine, *History and Computing*, published by Oxford University Press. Having replaced the newsletter *Computing and History Today* in 1989, *History and Computing* publishes research and educational news, reviews of hardware and software, and a variety of articles and comments. Other publications are available to members at a discount on the published price. A series of Research Reports has been inaugurated, and the publication of introductory material is also planned.

The Association has a particular commitment to the dissemination of computing techniques among history teachers. Courses and summer schools are organised both internationally and in various countries, and publications directed specifically at teachers are in hand.

Further details of the Association's activities, and membership application forms, are available from Dr Veronica Lawrence, Membership Secretary, Association for History and Computing, 4 Nunnery Close, Blackbird Leys, Oxford OX4 5EG. On general matters relating to the Association contact Dr Peter Denley, Secretary-General, Association for History and Computing, Department of History, Queen Mary and Westfield College (Hampstead Site), Kidderpore Avenue, London NW3 7ST.

National associations within the AHC, which organise activities at a local level, have been or are being formed for countries or groups of countries where a large membership exists. Among these is the UK Branch; *History and Computing III* arose out of the papers given at its first annual conference, which was held at the University of Glasgow in March 1988. The second annual conference was held at the University of Durham in March 1989 and the third at Wolverhampton Polytechnic in April 1990. The fourth conference in the series will be held at the University of Southampton in March 1991. Questions relating to the UK Branch should be referred to its Secretary, Dr Kevin Schurer, ESRC Cambridge Group for the History of Population and Social Structure, 27 Trumpington Street, Cambridge CB2 1QA.

List of Contributors

Andrew Ayton *Department of History, University of Hull*
Frances Blow *Centre for History Education, Trinity and All Saints College, Leeds*
Stuart Blumin *Department of History, Cornell University, Ithaca*
Caroline Bourlet *Institut de Recherche et d'Histoire des Textes,CNRS, Paris*
Marion I Bowman *Medical Archives and Manuscripts Survey, Wellcome Institute for the History of Medicine, London*
Lou Burnard *Computing Service, University of Oxford*
Brenda Collins *Institute of Irish Studies, Queen's University, Belfast*
Marguerite Dupree *Wellcome Unit for the History of Medicine, University of Glasgow*
Alan Dyer *Department of Art History, Coventry Polytechnic*
Janet Foster *Medical Archives and Manuscripts Survey, Wellcome Institute for the History of Medicine, London*
Daniel I Greenstein *Department of Modern History, University of Glasgow*
Charles Harvey *Department of History, Royal Holloway and Bedford New College, London*
Edward Higgs *Public Record Office, London*
John Jeacocke *Department of Computer Science, University of Glasgow*
M J Lewis *Historical and Critical Studies Department, Sheffield City Polytechnic*
Roger Lloyd-Jones *Historical and Critical Studies Department, Sheffield City Polytechnic*
James M McArthur *Strathclyde Regional Council Education Department, Glasgow Division*
Allan I Macinnes *Department of Scottish History, University of Glasgow*
Evan Mawdsley *Department of Modern History, University of Glasgow*
Jean-Luc Minel *Institut de Recherche et d'Histoire des Textes, CNRS, Paris*
Nicholas Morgan *Department of Scottish History, University of Glasgow*
Michael Moss *Archives, University of Glasgow*
Thomas Munck *Department of Modern History, University of Glasgow*
Robert K Munro *Computer Education and Business Studies Division, Jordanhill College of Education, Glasgow*
Stana Nenadic *Department of Economic and Social History, University of Edinburgh*
Jeffrey L Newton *Office of Corporate and Foundation Relations, Johns Hopkins University, Baltimore*
James Parker *Royal Commission on Historical Manuscripts, London*
Colin Phillips *Department of History, University of Manchester*

Kevin Schurer *ESRC Cambridge Group for the History of Population and Social Structure, University of Cambridge*
Donald A Spaeth *CTI Centre for History, University of Glasgow*
Richard Trainor *Department of Economic History, University of Glasgow*
Stephen Whitelaw *Computing Service, University of Glasgow*
Arnott Wilson *Archives, City of Edinburgh District Council*

I.
Foreword

1 *Lou Burnard*

The Historian and the Database

Hwaet! we Gar-Dema in gear-Dagum
theod-cyninga thrym gefrunon,
hu tha aethelingas ellen fremedon.
Oft Scyld Scefing sceathena threatum
monegum maegthum meoda-setla ofteah;
egsode Eorie, syththan aerest wearth
feasceaft funden; he thaes frofre gebad:
weox under wolcnum, weorth-myndum thah
oththaet him aeghwylc thara ymb-sittendra
ofer hron-rade hyran scolde,
gomban gyldan: thaet waes god cyning!

These are the opening words of the Old English epic *Beowulf*, the earliest literary masterpiece of our language, probably composed in eighth-century Mercia. When its unknown Christian author affected the imagined manner of the scop in the ancestral mead-hall, he was of course largely ignorant of living conditions in the fifth-century pagan courts of Hrothgar or Hygelac, where the poem's action is set. He may even have been, like modern readers, somewhat skeptical about the objective existence of the underwater monsters and dragon-guarded treasure-hoards which provide the poem's hero with so much excitement. Yet he and his audience still felt the need to take an ancient story and use it as a vehicle for articulating a contemporary opposition: the tension between atavistic pagan fatalism and optimistic Christian perfectibilianism. This clash is marvellously condensed in the much-quoted line 'Wyrd oft neriath unfaegne eorl thonne his ellen deah.' (Fate will often spare the undoomed man whose courage is good enough — though the ancient Germanic notion of fate is not at all the same as the ancient Greek notion now inextricably bound up in the modern English word).

But reading *Beowulf* today is not entirely an exercise in hermeneutics; to appreciate this poem, as to appreciate any epic, we need only to recognise its historical purpose. *Beowulf* was composed as a history book, even a historical database: we do it an injustice to treat it as anything less. Its language is not that of everyday eighth-century Mercia, as far as other evidence shows, it is formally arranged; it uses the metrical device of alliteration; it contains some phrases that seem to be fossilised metaphors (such as 'hron-rade', — whale-road — for sea) and others that are clearly formulaic ('gomban gyldan', gift-giving); it is rich in near synonyms (there are many different words for weapons and armour; the poet remarks that he 'deprived many princes of their mead-stools'). The artifice of this language has two crucial functions: firstly it serves to mark this text as belonging to a specific body of linguistic productions, to categorise it, to locate it in another imagined world; and secondly, precisely because it is so different from the everyday tittle-tattle of eighth-century Mercia, to make the text itself memorable. The heroic style seems to have a pragmatic function in pre-technological, pre-literature as a way of preserving speech.

In a somewhat mind-boggling book called *Worlds of Reference*[1], the distinguished linguist Tom McArthur proposes that, provided we take a sufficiently broad perspective, we shall see there have been four great communicative shifts in human history: each mediated by its characteristic enabling technology: that of speech, of script, of print and of electronics. Each of these technologies represents a better attempt to satisfy the same fundamental human desire: not to be forgotten, to step outside of time.

In the beginning, he argues, there was only functional speech — 'Pass the burnt root, dear' kind of stuff. But then, stuck as human intelligence is with a strong sense of things not-having-always-been quite as bad as they are now (not to mention the dour suspicion that they may well get quite a lot worse), there evolved the concept of 'Storage Speech' — language with quite another type of function: that of preserving information. Special techniques, such as the alliteration and kennings in the passage from *Beowulf,* were invented for this purpose, to ensure the accuracy of what was passed on. Other techniques, such as the shamanistic use of fetishes, beads, knots and other non-verbal signifiers, seem to have been less successful, at least in the European context, than that satisfyingly recursive method of changing the nature of the medium itself. And so, McArthur says, the database came into being, long even before writing, as a formalised narrative, an oral repository of that information by which a culture defines itself. And the claim is that successive paradigmatic shifts have not served to dislodge that primary atavistic function, of tying down the here and now, locating it in a temporal nexus, giving us a past, a present and a future. Instead they have emphasised or facilitated different aspects of that primary urge to a greater or lesser extent.

We have not yet drunk deeply enough to be overwhelmed entirely by this sort of rapid canter through world history, There comes a point of elevation (whether metaphorical or actual) from which all details blur into one cosmic whole. And surely there are at least as many differences between the secret language of a priestly elite and the demotic of the electronic bulletin board as there are similarities. Quite a good case (but perhaps a bit too Marxist for this occasion) could be made for the view that the shift from oral to written to printed to electronic communication is a necessary consequence of the progressive alienation of the individual: the whole paraphernalia of copyright and ownership, the notion of authorship itself, seem to be inextricably intertwined with a particular political system rather than with any evolutionary necessity.

But it does no harm to look for similarities: indeed, it is a very seductive notion, that of McArthur's that 'We have been this way before'. I wish I had some explanation to offer for the pleasure with which I draw a parallel between the writer at his word-processor cutting and pasting choice phrases from previous compositions on the one hand, and the bard of yore picking and recombining kennings and genealogies from his word-hoard on the other. Is it an innate human charcteristic, this desire to step outside of time? Is it a peculiarity of some times rather than others? Is it related to other phenomena? Before this audience I will not presume to provide answers to these essentially historiographical questions.

Instead, let me focus more precisely on the topic of this conference: the use of this latest version of 'storage speech' in making sense of the products of earlier versions of the same. When a new technology emerges, an undervaluing of its predecessor is commonplace. Thus, we are told that some Renaissance printers, having set Carolingian manuscripts into type, tended to use the originals as firelighters. And the metal plates from which the last edition of the *OED* was printed proved such an embarrassment to the Oxford University Press that many of them have been given away as trendy ornaments. To be sentimental about steam trains or red phone-boxes is no less an intellectual weakness because it is an officially sanctioned one. Let me parenthetically remark on how frequently we find various forms of sentimentality being officially sanctioned these days. As good historians, I hope you will all be on your guard against the current insidious attempts to manufacture national memory as a means of fuelling the xenophobia on which Governments such as the present one depend. The word has gone out somewhere in the corridors of power that Britain is ripe for 'theming-up' and we look to the professional guardians of the past to thwart it: please read Robert Hewison's *The Heritage Industry*[2] for further information.

Surprisingly perhaps, the computer might just provide you with the tools to do it. Sentimentality is a form of storage speech in which all the rich awkwardnesses of actuality have been conveniently smoothed away, to serve some polemical end. It is typified by the artefact-free museum, the theme park, the digest. It avoids controversy and thrives on passive acceptance. But we don't have to be sentimental in our attitudes to the past. The past is actually still there to be discovered, encapsulated in all those other undervalued forms of storage speech, buried in local archives and other forms of distributed database such as human memory. What the computer gives us is a new way of gaining access to that information, efficient ways of storing it, of searching and re-presenting it. It enables us to combine information from a variety of sources in ways so quantitatively different as to approximate a qualitative change. And it enables us to add interpretations to the store of information, automatically or mediated by as many editorial processes as there are editors, without however significantly changing the original stored form of the data. Simply, it lets us form our own conclusions from the available data. As such, it is as potent and as subversive a tool as ever the printing press was.

This may sound implausible to those whose view of this technology was formed in the days when the machine was called a 'giant brain' and was tended by serious people in white coats. It may also sound absurdly optimistic to those who fear (perhaps justly) that deprivation of access to information will become a new instrument of class oppression. But the cat is already out of the bag. The micros are already in the classrooms — perhaps small, under-funded and over-used, but they are there; and what has once been learned cannot easily be unlearned.

My title, 'The Historian and the Database', suggests an opposition, but my theme is one of synthesis. Whether or not we accept the Californian millenarianism which loudly proclaims the death of the printed book, it is clear that the written word has at least found a new home. As a way of marshalling concepts and modelling our understanding of them, the formal structures of language have served us very well for centuries. But it has become necessary to define a new sort of storage speech. Now, the most productive way of processing a text by computer turns out to entail additional interpretative information about it, either separately in some sort of database structure, or embedded within it as markup or tagging. It looks as if we are making up for the computer's lack of innate intelligence by supplying rules for interpretation and categorisation, sometimes of the most rudimentary sort, such as where one word stops and the next begins. But what we are actually doing is representing both data and meta-data: storing both information and guidance on its interpretation. Let me conclude by suggesting that this double focus has always characterised what I earlier called 'storage speech' and that consequently to perceive it as a limitation is to miss the point — in rather the same way as it would be to miss the point to say of the storage speech with which I began that it is repetitive or cliche-ridden.

Notes

1. Tom McArthur, *Worlds of Reference: Lexicography, Learning and Language from the Clay-tablet to the Computer*, Cambridge, 1986
2. Robert Hewison, *The Heritage Industry: Britain in a Climate of Decline*, London, 1987.

II.
Sources

Jubilant and Joyful or Distraught and Disillusioned — Computer Applications in the Searchroom: The Experience of Glasgow University Archives

For almost 15 years archivists have been beguiled by the potential computers appear to offer in retrieving information from their catalogues and holdings. There have been many experiments and many failures. Disillusioned archivists reflect sadly on piles of punch cards and printouts slowly gathering dust amongst the rest of their uncatalogued collections. Some have persevered and there are a few mainframe and micro-based prototype systems in operation. These range from simple stock control applications for records management purposes, to ambitious projects like that on the Wellington papers at the University of Southampton. Many of those who have either toyed with computers or considered the option, have been put off by the apparently high costs of hardware, software and staff time. The cost has often seemed far to outweigh the benefits. Much of the disappointment has resulted from the unrealistic expectations that one application can be used to address every archival problem, from the cataloguing of mediaeval documents to the sophisticated manipulation of modern files.

At Glasgow University Archives, when the use of computers was first explored some nine years ago, the nature of the available technology and the allocation of computing resources tended to dictate a single solution. At this time, when microcomputers were in their infancy, the University mainframe was the only vehicle for such experiments, and the number of packages capable of dealing with alphanumeric data was limited. Unlike many public authority archives, access to the mainframe computer was not restricted, either by financial penalties or by the low priority assigned to archives in the administrative structure. On the contrary, there was tacit encouragement for a humanities development which might have a beneficial effect on arts-based computing more generally. Yet, despite the absence of hardware constraints, many obstacles remained.

Initially, data in alphanumeric form was entered using punch card operators, but it was soon found that the error rate was unacceptable, principally because it was difficult to see what had been entered and one record often required several cards. At this stage, a microcomputer was purchased through a Manpower Services Commission (MSC) scheme,[1] in the mistaken belief that this would solve the problem. It soon emerged that no data-entry program was available. A programmer in the University Computing Service, feeling sorry for these dejected pioneers, came to the rescue by writing a simple program named Famdata — so called because it was recommended that the Famulus package, produced by the Canadian equivalent of the Forestry Commission for stock control, might suit archival needs. When the initial batch of data was ready to be loaded on to the mainframe, it transpired that Archives was the first department in the University to attempt such an operation. Famulus, likened by one programmer in the Computing Service to 'trying to fly with pieces of wood strapped to your arms', soon proved cumbersome and far from adequate. As data began to accumulate on the mainframe, Archives was notified that there were constraints on filestore which could only be resolved by purchasing space using the department's external income. When large amounts of data were manipulated the whole mainframe slowed dramatically, to the annoyance of science departments that had been accustomed to unfettered use of central computing systems. In the depths of despair, we were lucky to recruit a well qualified programmer to our MSC scheme, who was able to write software tailored to our requirements. Under the direction of Arnott Wilson, then assistant archivist, this software formed the basis of the PARCH suite of programs, designed to provide a mainframe solution to archival problems.[2]

During our incursion into computing, we came to a number of important conclusions about our objectives. It soon became obvious that computer techniques were not applicable to all classes of records. For example, nothing is to be gained from constructing datasets from catalogue entries of long series of repetitive records of the same type, like volumes of case notes from a hospital or accounting records from a business house. These can just as easily be catalogued normally. On the other hand, much is to be gained by making the contents of such records machine-readable.[3] This observation was translated by Arnott Wilson into our first article of faith, that the computer should be used to solve specific problems in unlocking previously unapproachable records and accumulations of historical data. We had already hit on an archival group that precisely fitted this criteria — the records of sequestrations (bankruptcies) in Scotland held, not in the University Archives, but in the Court of Session series in the Scottish Record Office.

This source and the accompanying processes had been used for some time by scholars as a sort of historical lucky dip. In 1979/80, John Hume and Michael Moss made more systematic use of bankruptcy material in their study of the Scotch Whisky industry,[4] forming the basis for the creation of an index of all sequestrations in Scotland from 1839-1914 (some 40,000 cases in all) by Glasgow University Archives.[5] For the purpose of this paper, the experience of building this database yielded the important lesson that even with improved enabling technology, large-scale database construction will inevitably be time-consuming. This conclusion was enshrined in a second article of faith that, even if no direct cost is attached to the labour of data entry, all viable historical databases must be multi-functional. The sequestration database fulfilled this second commandment. It can be used in the searchroom by readers with little training, to locate precisely individual bankruptcies or groups of bankruptcies in one location, but it can also be used in an aggregate way to examine the performance of the economy as a whole or individual sectors.

While the sequestration database was under construction, other smaller datasets were being assembled, either to provide answers to particular difficulties or as experiments in general cataloguing problems. One such dataset related to detailed drawings from the North British Locomotive (NBL) Company. Unlike many engineering companies NBL had not prepared separate sets of drawings of components for each contract, because components were used in a great many different contracts. The component drawings were stored by type with a master index. Unfortunately, the index had become detached from the drawings before deposit. Although it is not normally necessary to retain all the detail drawings for an engineering product, in this case the number of locomotives still in service, and the demands of model makers, made it necessary. This was a natural application for database techniques. Our experiments with general cataloguing, while of limited success, suggested that the programs we had devised were not yet sufficiently flexible to access such a disparate archival grouping efficiently.

These further investigations, together with the experience of Dr Nicholas Morgan in the Department of Scottish History in constructing a large database relating to property ownership in Glasgow between 1861 and 1911, confirmed two further observations that have come to characterise our general approach — the need for flexible structures and respect for the integrity of the sources.[6] In compiling our datasets we found repeatedly that after work started it was necessary to add further fields and that field lengths larger than eighty characters were essential as archival descriptions cannot conveniently be compressed within that limit. For example, when we came recently to extend the sequestration database back to the 1790s, a further field had to be added to differentiate between the different types of legal processes in use. Respect for the integrity of sources may be second nature to archivists and sometimes historians, but computer database specialists scarcely gave it a thought, however desirable their clients may deem the appearance on the screen of an approximation of the original documentation.

We reached these conclusions about five years ago and were convinced that, in the current state of the art, progress would only be made by substantial programming effort to improve data entry techniques and interfaces to existing software. We realised that there was little chance of raising the necessary funds unless a community interest was formed with the four history departments at Glasgow where there was increasing interest in the use of computers in the classroom, sparked off by the pioneering efforts of Nicholas Morgan. Our decision to take this route rather than to collaborate with another archival institution was not just a matter of *realpolitik*, but the outcome of careful consideration of the place of archives within the teaching of history. In common with other archives offices, we had witnessed an exceptional growth in our readership, mostly from enthusiasts such as local historians, genealogists and model ship and locomotive builders, but at the same time we were aware that history, as an academic subject, was under severe pressure. Never before had the past been so popular as a leisure pursuit, but never before had it been so out of fashion as a classroom subject, largely because it had no apparent utility. It required little imagination to appreciate that the introduction of computing into the history classroom could meet much of the criticism.

Our first efforts at fund-raising, which were conceived more from an archival standpoint than a teaching application, failed. Unable to retain our MSC programmer under their regulations, no progress could be made in writing the PARCH software. Despite this setback, we remained committed to our cause. In the meantime there had been more general developments in database programs and microcomputer technology, allowing micros to be linked together in a network, sharing data in common. These technical gains were in our favour as they created a demand amongst employers for graduates who had some understanding of the problems associated with real data and methods of using computers for their interpretation. The Government, recognising this requirement, commissioned a report on the use of microcomputers in higher education and on the basis of its findings made funds available to universities on a competitive basis through the Computers in Teaching Initiative.[7] In collaboration with the departments of Economic History, Modern History and Scottish History, the Archives was successful in the second round of the Initiative in the spring of 1985, securing funds for the establishment of a teaching laboratory and the employment of a programmer for two years.[8] Fundamental to the success of this application was the existence of substantial historical datasets, created by the Archives and the Department of Scottish History, from which subsets could be downloaded for teaching onto a local area network. This project, christened the 'Design and Implementation of Software in History' (DISH) Project, immediately became the focus of the Archives' computing activity. The participation of the Archives has helped to ensure that sources have been at the heart of the Project from the outset and that as a group DISH has remained steadfast to the concepts derived from our long incursion into the application of computers in our searchroom.

Since 1985 the Archives' approach to computer application has inevitably been modified by the teaching objectives of DISH and access to the more powerful microcomputers that now link the four departments together in a large local area network (LAN). It is now possible routinely to carry out procedures locally that five years ago could only be achieved remotely and often unpredictably on the University mainframe. Like our colleagues in the history departments, we have benefited from DISH software developments and a level of technical support not available previously. There have been more subtle, and perhaps more significant gains — the outcome of the interaction between the archivists/historians and the programmer, which has brought the historians' methodology sharply into focus.[9] A direct consequence of a long commitment to source-based research at Glasgow, this close scrutiny of the content of primary sources has given cohesion to our collective endeavour, confirming that individual cases are as important to the student in the University classroom as to the untutored reader in the archivist's searchroom. The disentangling of individuals with all their often inexplicable characteristics from an aggregate pudding has begun to break down the artificial barriers between the teaching of history at different levels from the primary school to University and between research at different levels from the academic to the genealogist. In addition, by bringing sources into the computer laboratory, there has been an increase in the number of students wishing to use our holdings in an imaginative way for dissertation work. Similarly, in the Archives we have been able to begin introducing our more enthusiastic readers to new ways of approaching and interpreting their sources.

Despite our comparatively early start in harnessing the potential of the computer to the needs of our readers, there is still a long way to go to achieve our initial objectives. The advent of textbases, employing such software as HyperCard and Guide, offers a potential solution for general cataloguing that defied early pioneers. The integration of software into total packages with databases, statistical and graphical facilities will make such catalogues far more multi-functional than they have been since the days of the great Victorian series of record publications. Similarly the increasing use of electronic mail, using national and international networks, will permit the remote interactive interrogation of historical texts and databases even across national boundaries. These developments will change the archival and historical landscape more profoundly than database applications in the next decade, making much of what we do now seem crude and simplistic. What is certain is that the new technology will not go away, either at Glasgow or elsewhere. If it has not yet arrived in other archive offices, it is only as far away as the next decision to replace an electric typewriter. It is our ambition that our experience as part of the DISH team will ease the path of others. Although we have and will write software that must, under the terms of our funding, be employed elsewhere on different equipment, we do not pretend that our software will provide all the answers to every archival or classroom application. Increasingly we consider our role in the archival world is to pioneer a methodology that can be adapted to suit different circumstances and objectives. We believe that the new technologies offer the exciting opportunity to cut across the historical divide. As in mastering any new craft, there will be times of distress and disillusion when the instructions in the manual seem totally opaque, but providing objectives are well defined, joy and jubilation should outweigh despondency.

Notes

1. A British government unemployment relief scheme. Since the West of Scotland had high rates of unemployment, large funds were available in Glasgow.
2. Claire E Findlay, Khosrow Hejazian and Arnott Wilson, 'PARCH — A Package for Archivists, Researchers, Companies and Historians', in C Keren and L Perlmutter (eds.), *The Application of Mini- and Micro-Computers in Information, Documentation and Libraries*, Holland, 1983.
3. See for example Nicholas Morgan and Michael Moss, 'Urban Wealth-holding and the Computer', in Peter Denley, Stefan Fogelvik and Charles Harvey (eds.), *History and Computing II*, Manchester, 1989, pp. 181-192.
4. M S Moss and J R Hume, *The Making of Scotch Whisky — A History of the Scotch Whisky Distilling Industry*, Edinburgh, 1981.
5. M S Moss and J R Hume, 'Business failure in Scotland 1839-1913: A Research Note', *Business History*, xxv, 1983, pp. 3-10.
6. ESRC Grant D0023216 'Property Ownership in Victorian and Edwardian Glasgow'.
7. *Nelson Report on Computer Facilities for Teaching in Universities,* 1983.
8. N J Morgan, M S Moss, R H Trainor and A T Wilson, 'The Design, Implementation and Assessment of Software for Use in the Teaching of History' in *Historische Sozialforschung Quantum Information*, 38, 1986, pp. 105-11.
9. R H Trainor, 'Implementing Computer-based Teaching and Research: the Need for a Collaborative Approach', *Computers and Education*, 12, 1988, pp. 37-41.

3 *Arnott Wilson*

Liberating the Historical Record

The computer has presented the archives profession with a great opportunity. Most people have very little idea of what is meant by the word archives and know even less about what an archivist is or does. Where a popular image exists at all it tends to be that of the eccentric white haired octogenarian, festooned in cobwebs, presiding over dusty old books. Archivists are fond of sniggering about newspaper extracts and books describing their profession along such lines, and certainly the popular label is somewhat unfair. But a set mould is hard to break and it will become impossibly so unless the developing power of the computer is harnessed where it can do most good — in the public search room. Here the computer can be used both to unlock and disseminate the sources for the future and at the same time help to preserve inviolate the original record of the past.

The first main objective may seem very obvious. It is simply that computers should have a physical presence in search rooms. Considering that even word-processing has yet to make significant inroads in record offices this may take some time.[1] But if it fails to happen the increasingly computer literate user of the next decade and beyond will simply go elsewhere and the misconceived antiquarian curatorial image will be reinforced and vindicated.

Once installed in the search room, machines must be simple to operate with the minimum of support either from staff or separate written instruction. Eventually, it should become possible even for the first time user to sit at a terminal and obtain sensible answers to questions, or information about records, within a very short time. It is true that increasing numbers of future users will know more about the inner workings of a computer than the archivist on duty, but a machine which is more of a barrier than a guide to, or medium of, archival information will soon lose credibility. Icons, mice, touch, colour and split screens — everything seen to promote, rather than inhibit, access should be applied as far as possible. The second main objective therefore is ease of use. Users must not have to think about the computer, its operating system and resident software but rather the information at their disposal through the window of the terminal.

The third objective may be less obvious and might be regarded as controversial among archive professionals. It concerns the needs of users.

Targetting what is on offer towards the customer may appear to be a very natural goal but a recent issue of the newsletter of the Society of Archivists revealed some interesting general attitudes. The public relations working party had been scrutinising leaflets providing introductions to record offices. They commented, 'Some were clearly intended to attract people to the record office. Others seemed not to be, and indeed on occasions seemed positively to discourage.'[2]

In some quarters, therefore, changes will be necessary if the computer is to be given the chance to take up what may become one if its main roles in the search room of the future — the medium through which faithful electronic versions of selected original sources may be searched, scanned, analysed and manipulated in an infinite variety of ways. To achieve this third objective the conversion of historical source data into machine-readable form must have greater emphasis in record offices — eventually perhaps just as great an emphasis as the descriptive listing process. In this way the quality information in archives will reach wider audiences, establish greater relevancy, ensure its survival in the age of information and bury its popular image. There is great potential for this type of development as the following examples from Edinburgh City Archives will demonstrate.

Despite adopting a policy of benign neglect towards its historical records throughout much of the twentieth century, Edinburgh City Archives is blessed with some magnificent examples of information collected by the plethora of bodies responsible for local government since the medieval period. There are particular strengths in records of property and taxation reaching as far back as the seventeenth century and even building plans dating from the mid eighteenth century.

From about 1750 the Edinburgh annuity tax, which was levied on householders for the upkeep of the clergy and poor, provides information in tabular format comprising the equivalent of an address, householder's name and occupation, the valued rent, amount due and date of payment. Beyond supplying outside dates for the series, most archival listings would not provide much more useful information for the benefit of the user. Much more could be delivered if the source data contained in each annuity tax volume was available in machine-readable form. Even with a very small number of variables the user could wield enormous intellectual power over the source. Genealogists would be able to search for nominal data not necessarily included in the printed burgess roll since householders need not have attained burgess status. Local historians interested in obscure closes and pockets of old Edinburgh, would be able to build up pictures of who lived where, and what they did for a living. The possibilities for all levels of educational user are also exciting, allowing more accurate conclusions to be drawn about relative wealth, social mobility, demographic trends and many other avenues of approach.

Clearly, higher education will benefit if archivists use the computer to present some of their holdings in this way, but so too will schools who are already creating further demands, reflecting the emphasis on investigation of original sources in the new Scottish Standard Grade and English 'O' Level history syllabuses. Even primary school children could be introduced to computerised versions of records, provided the presentation is imaginative and makes full use of graphical facilities. With the potent combination of building elevations and local tax records it takes little imagination to think of the varied assignments a teacher could set. Pupils could be asked to explore the streets of eighteenth-century Edinburgh: how are things changing? — what has happened to Monsieur La Mole, the dancing master? — is he staying in the same close? — what is his valued rent? — how does it compare with his neighbours? None of this type of questioning will be possible if the only teaching resource is a bare listing of each annuity tax volume. Without such computerisation, only manual perusal would be possible and the effort on the part of the archivist, teacher and pupils to utilise the source would be prohibitive, quite apart from the physically damaging effect on the records themselves.

There are many other sources in Edinburgh City Archives which suggest themselves as being suitable for similar treatment. There is, for example, a series of shore dues which becomes very elaborate in the eighteenth century. Like the annuity tax it is arranged in tabular fashion, thus lending itself to the model of the hierarchical or relational database. In each case it provides a running number, date of arrival, name of master and vessel, home port, last port of call, name of merchant, whether merchant was a burgess, quantities and types of goods, tonnage, beaconage and anchorage dues and, finally, shore dues complete with date of payment. This type of quality data has to be regarded as prime source material for all kinds of user, but most record offices would probably not consider creating a database and would still tend to concentrate on listing. The eventual effect of such a policy will be to limit very seriously the potential for widespread usage.

Much of the trade recorded in the shore dues series is domestic — movements within the Firth of Forth and off the east coast. In 1753 '210 bolls of barley' from Burntisland, Fife, were unloaded from a vessel called the *Dispatch*.[3] In the same year the *Lucky John* skippered by William Scotland, arrived from Limekilns, Fife, with coal owned by David Scotland.[4] The intrepid Jonathan Swinton appeared in 'ane open boatt' all the way from Newcastle-upon-Tyne with miscellaneous goods.[5] The island of Incholm in the Firth of Forth seems to have been quarried extensively at this time, judging by the number of vessels which arrive laden with stones for 'the London Ships'.[6] Foreign trade although less frequent is also present. In 1753 the *Thistle* arrived from Virginia with a huge cargo of tobacco owned by Alexander Brown and Company.[7] The *Olive Branch* came from Hamburg carrying oak.[8] The *Betty* sailed in from Bordeaux carrying a very good year of just what one might expect to arrive from that part of France.[9]

Another Edinburgh City Archives source suitable for computerisation is an eighteenth-century ledger series of brewers liable for payment of the 'tuppeny tax' on each pint of ale produced. Each volume has a very convenient index, reinforcing the case for providing merely a general description of the series in a list. But it can also be argued that more detailed treatment is justified, thus opening up the entire contents of the source.

The record consists of the monthly output of each brewer measured as barrels and 'firkins', together with tax levied and date of payment. A glance at one volume reveals some interesting patterns. Although some brewers are clearly small concerns, many others are producing several hundred barrels a month. There are also significant numbers of women brewers. In July 1736, Violet Johnston produced 69 barrels while Thomas Younger could manage only 34 barrels.[10]

Apprentice registers, poor lists, army muster rolls, caution books and court and jail registers are some examples of other sources which are strong contenders for conversion from paper to electronic media. There are also the more unusual items. In the 1790s the High Constables of Edinburgh were particularly anxious about the foreigners in their midst so they kept an aliens register, thus providing present day search room customers with a fascinating record of foreign influence at work in Edinburgh at that time. The unfortunate aliens had to appear before one of the Edinburgh baillies and account for their presence in the City. Jean Bretier had only just arrived when he was marched in front of the presiding baillie declaring that he had come, 'Via Southampton and intended to remain twelve months for the purpose of studying physic'.[11] There are even detailed physical descriptions presumably of those regarded as highly suspicious. Not surprisingly these are usually citizens of France. Bretier was 30 years old, 5 feet 11 inches, thin made, had a swarthy smooth complexion complete with a mole on his left cheek. His hair was dark brown and at some time in the past he had lived on Jersey.[12]

Edinburgh may be more fortunate than most cities in the range and depth of raw data held for a comparatively early period, but all archive repositories hold unique records generated by their parent authorities and their antecedents. There must be many records series described very adequately in a list but with little hope of really widespread usage. Even that keenest seeker after truth, the indefatigable genealogist, can be put off by the daunting prospect of wading through several volumes of information. Given current day pressures of work it is doubtful whether the old fashioned practice of calendaring, producing verbatim copies of originals, still exists. Where it did, the tendency was to concentrate on records belonging to a definite diplomatic form such as early charters, or to correspondence relating to events of some historical significance.

Commendable this may be, but it does not cater for the present day market place. Many users are interested in individuals who were not particularly important to anyone but their latter day descendants, and there are at least some historians interested in quantitive analysis of sources. With the prospect of a guaranteed user market and the enabling facilities of the computer, the calendaring of those records can now be justified.

There is a burgeoning interest in nominal data. In his annual report for 1985 the Keeper of the Records of Scotland stated, 'Both search rooms saw the highest numbers and attendances ever, approximately 50 per cent above the comparable figures for 1975. On several occasions every available seat in the Historical Search Room was occupied for a substantial part of the day. Over half the increase was accounted for by Scottish users, ...overseas readers increased by nearly 20 per cent with the USA and Canada again predominant. Genealogy retained its primacy as a research topic with 41 per cent of the readership.'[13] The report went on to state that local studies was the next most popular research topic, accounting for 16 per cent of users.[14] So a massive 57 per cent of Scottish Record Office (SRO) business in 1985 emanated from the two predominant categories of genealogy and local history. To place these figures in context, the fact that the SRO holdings do not include the most obvious genealogical sources such as baptismal, marriage, burial and census records should be borne in mind.

At present we are constantly being bombarded with the need to respond to the demands of the market place. Computerising records most obviously suitable for the user community will certainly help in this direction, but it seems likely that user expectation in the future will demand additional points of entry to more awkward data such as several centuries of council minutes. In the case of Edinburgh this source can only be described as an historical treasure trove of information on virtually every aspect of life in the city over the past 400 years. It contains much nominal and localised data stretching far beyond the closed circle of city politicians. In 1736 Treasurer Young was ordered to pay John Inglis, merchant in Glasgow, the price of ruinous houses Inglis had owned in the poetically described 'Nether Stinking Close'.[15] In 1765 Patrick Ogilvy was saved from the noose by courtesy of a respite sent by the Duke of Grafton.[16] Clearly Grafton must have been interested in Ogilvy's welfare but would an interest on the part of a twentieth-century descendant meet with the same degree of success? If the essential information is to remain hidden in a listing such as 'Minutes of the Town Council of Edinburgh, 1764-68' the chances are slim indeed. A computerised index to the minutes series would deliver so much more to the user and might be linked very effectively to the original using emerging digital image processing technology.

Quite apart from the technical problems which would be posed by such large-scale computerisation projects, there are undoubtedly major resource implications. Cost is a huge barrier, but there can be a marked tendency to hide behind the fence rather than make a serious effort to break it down. There are ways of raising the finance necessary to carry out the sort of database construction already mentioned. Local authority record offices and universities might pool resources, agreeing to own resultant data jointly. Employment Training (ET) schemes, evening classes, private funding, other types of grant aid, and even voluntary labour are other possibilities. Direct charging for access to databases would be contentious, but may also have to be examined seriously in the present economic and political climate. The awesome enormity of database construction is daunting, but provided clear objectives are set, effective management and quality control in place, growth rates might be faster than expected. Moreover, given the advances in computing over the past thirty years it may be dangerous to predict we will never have a machine which will record, retrieve and analyse unstructured seventeenth century Scots hand. Clearly defined manuscripts are already definite contenders for such treatment.

Notwithstanding technological advancements, there will always be a place for professionally produced listings of archive holdings. There has been much activity within the archive profession in recent years on the subject of writing archival descriptions, with the main impetus coming from the archival description project at the University of Liverpool. Copious manuals known as MAD have been produced and will undoubtedly stimulate archive professionals to think more clearly about the complexities of the listing process. The extent to which MAD will affect record offices on a practical level remains to be seen, but with so great an emphasis on listing practices, there is perhaps a danger that little time will be left to undertake projects which would deliver original source data direct to the user and release the potential inherent in prime record series.

It can be argued that this is not the remit of the archivist, but the archive profession should not deny all responsibility for this type of work. Having preserved archival material successfully, the realities of present day economics demand that it should be put to good use. More and better quality lists will help in this direction, but will the users of the twenty-first century be satisfied with mere representation files? There are also conservation implications. The needs of users and the needs of original records are diametrically opposed. Given that increasing numbers of users will be satisfied with authenticated computerised versions of source material, the computer may come to be seen as a kind of window in the wall of the stack room through which information can be viewed and manipulated without recourse to the original. The prospect of reducing wear and tear will be difficult to resist for the archivist whose most fundamental professional duty is preservation of archival material.

In the future, search rooms in the computer could become just as important as computers in the search room. Accessing data via national networks is already commonplace. As more data become available it may become increasingly difficult to tempt historical computer buffs into infidelity with another PC. However, there will always be researchers who will need to assess the full physical context of, or check, the paper record, carry out group research, or prefer to work with the original. Casual, recreational and tourist customers may attend more frequently, particularly if the goods on offer are attractively packaged. Finally, the advantages of the interpretative skills and personal knowledge of an experienced archivist are of most benefit at close range.

If we are to witness the demise of the traditional search room it will not be due to the introduction of computers, but rather because of a failure on the part of archive professionals to make the leap into the realities of the information age. It is imperative that the computer is introduced more widely, becomes increasingly straightforward to use, and adequately satisfies user demand. Otherwise the great opportunity to achieve credibility as information professionals will be lost. The Canongate Jail record of 10 December 1785 reveals that William Dickson, a distiller from Lasswade, had been imprisoned until payment of a £225 debt.[17] In contrast to the other entries in the record it appears Dickson was never released. A 200 year sentence for a debt of £225 is long enough. Dickson and many others like him, literally incarcerated in the records, must now be released.

Notes

1. See J Walford, H Gillet and J B Post, 'Introducing Computers to the Record Office: Theory and Practice', *Journal of the Society of Archivists*, 9, 1988, p. 21.
2. P Methven and A Nicol, *Newsletter of the Society of Archivists*, 44, 1988, p. 9.
3. Edinburgh City Archives (ECA), Register of Shore Dues 1752-1753, p.15.
4. Ibid, p. 9.
5. Ibid, p. 11.
6. Ibid, p. 9.
7. Ibid, p. 11.
8. Ibid, p. 39.
9. Ibid, p. 27.
10. ECA, Impost Ledger, June 1736 — June 1737, p. 51.
11. ECA, Aliens Register, Declarations of Foreigners, 1794, p. 53.
12. Ibid, p. 53.
13. *Annual Report of the Keeper of the Records of Scotland*, 1985, p. 9.
14. Ibid, p. 10.
15. ECA, Council Record (Town Council Minutes), Vol 56, 1735-1736, p. 240.
16. Ibid, Vol.81, 1756-1766, pp. 223-4.
17. ECA, Canongate Jail Record, Vol 2, 1784-1793, entry for 10 December 1785.

The Medical Archives and Manuscripts Survey: Three in One: Surveying, Publishing and Creating a Database

The Medical Archives and Manuscripts Survey was established, with a staff of two, in October 1986, at the Wellcome Institute for the History of Medicine in London. The idea for the Survey had been germinating for several years previously, and the original intention was to produce a book which would provide a guide to primary sources throughout Britain, relevant to the history of medicine in its widest sense. The aim, therefore, was to cover all aspects of health and disease from 1600 to 1945, recording the professional and personal papers of individuals and institutions concerned with medical and nursing practice, research and education; local and central government records relating to public health and the provision of health care; and personal papers with a significant medical content, whether as patient, practitioner or observer.

From the start it was envisaged that the project would be computer-assisted and we were fortunate in having the Institute's newly-appointed data processing analyst, Helen Gibson, working closely with us from the beginning. Our discussions with her quickly established that it would be most beneficial to record the Survey information in a database rather than simply word-processing it. The contents of the book could then be drawn from the database which would, moreover, provide a permanent research tool in the Institute which could be utilised for a variety of purposes, thereby making the best use of the information gathered. Also, as we would be working primarily from catalogue entries or descriptions taken from varying types of repository finding aids, it was important to avoid enforced manipulation of the information. Therefore we decided to create our own database structure rather than use any of the existing models which at that time were mainly oriented towards printed books.

The database was developed on an Olivetti M28, with dBase III plus software and the MS-DOS operating system. dBase III plus was decided upon for a variety of reasons, not least because it is well supported and tried software which has become virtually an industry standard. We now operate the database on both an Olivetti M280 and an Opus PC2 with 40 megabyte hard disks, partitioned 30/10 because MS-DOS can only address 32 megabytes; the 30 Mbs are used for the main database, with the remaining 10 for the permanent program.

Devising and perfecting a database for recording and manipulating the Survey information took roughly three months, time well spent trying to anticipate the demands that would be made of it in its different capacities, and learning from Helen Gibson how the software's potential could be maximised in this task. It was clear that the facility of linking the main database to subsidiary databases could be most usefully exploited for our purposes. This initial planning stage was vital for the success of the project, as we knew that once we embarked upon inputting it would be counter-productive to have to revise the structure of the database in any major way.

As we would be doing our own inputting, and there would be a huge amount of data to handle, we were keen to minimise time-consuming repetition and unnecessary length. We were also adamant that the description of the manuscript material should not deviate from the archival norm by being manipulated to fit a structure to which it was not suited.

These underlying principles are clearly demonstrated in our main input form. It was deliberately designed to be compact, taking just one screen, to ensure clarity and efficiency. We have made extensive use of codes, for the name and address of repositories, for types of manuscript material and for subjects. We have used a memo field for the actual description of the item(s) recorded. This is a free text field of unlimited length and is beneficial in a number of ways: it cuts out manipulation into a set field length or artificial form; it provides a 'ready-made' book entry; and it gives a 'user-friendly' piece of information to researchers querying the database. However, memo fields cannot be directly queried so index fields must be provided. These are the types, persons, institutions, places and subject fields which not only provide an impressive range of querying tools, making swift and sophisticated on-line searching possible, but ensure that indexes for the book can be easily generated.

The input form for the main database (see Figure 1) contains the following fields:

> PIECE NUMBER: This obviates the problems of computer-generated record numbers changing by providing a permanent reference number for each computer record. It is also the link field for the index fields of the relational databases described below.
>
> TOWN CODE: Consisting of the first five letters of the place name. The book will be arranged alphabetically by town and the database can also be queried for repositories or types of documents within a particular town.

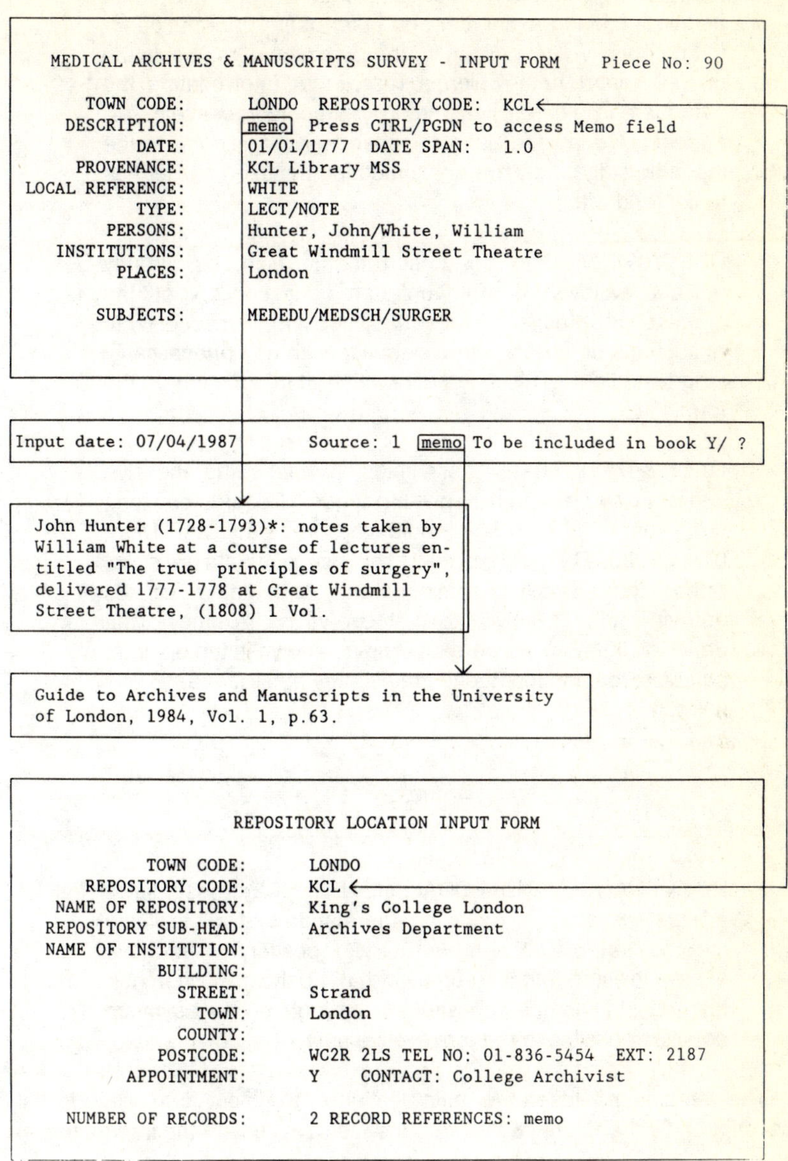
MEDICAL ARCHIVES & MANUSCRIPTS SURVEY - INPUT FORM   Piece No: 90

TOWN CODE: LONDO REPOSITORY CODE: KCL
DESCRIPTION: memo Press CTRL/PGDN to access Memo field
DATE: 01/01/1777 DATE SPAN: 1.0
PROVENANCE: KCL Library MSS
LOCAL REFERENCE: WHITE
TYPE: LECT/NOTE
PERSONS: Hunter, John/White, William
INSTITUTIONS: Great Windmill Street Theatre
PLACES: London

SUBJECTS: MEDEDU/MEDSCH/SURGER

Input date: 07/04/1987   Source: 1 memo To be included in book Y/ ?

John Hunter (1728-1793)*: notes taken by William White at a course of lectures entitled "The true principles of surgery", delivered 1777-1778 at Great Windmill Street Theatre, (1808) 1 Vol.

Guide to Archives and Manuscripts in the University of London, 1984, Vol. 1, p.63.

REPOSITORY LOCATION INPUT FORM

TOWN CODE: LONDO
REPOSITORY CODE: KCL
NAME OF REPOSITORY: King's College London
REPOSITORY SUB-HEAD: Archives Department
NAME OF INSTITUTION:
BUILDING:
STREET: Strand
TOWN: London
COUNTY:
POSTCODE: WC2R 2LS TEL NO: 01-836-5454 EXT: 2187
APPOINTMENT: Y CONTACT: College Archivist

NUMBER OF RECORDS: 2 RECORD REFERENCES: memo

Figure 1: Medical Archives and Manuscripts Survey - Input Form

CODE REPOSITORY: Each repository has a code which relates to the location database containing the full name, address, telephone number and other useful information for the prospective user. Both for the purposes of the book and on the report from which a researcher interrogating the database would receive, the full name, address etc. will appear. Codes are used for speed and efficiency at the inputting stage; they are not something the user/ reader has to contend with.

DESCRIPTION: The description memo field, as already outlined, allows for the unfettered description of the manuscript item(s), without imposing unacceptable restrictions or wasting the disk space with an unnecessarily long fixed field. This is the core piece of information on the form.

DATE & DATE SPAN: These fields allow for comprehensive searches by year and for given periods. Records covering the years 1780-1820 would be entered as Date: 01/01/1780, Date Span: 40. The use of the date span, rather than simply beginning and end dates, makes querying fully inclusive, so that everything relating to the period 1780-1820 will be picked up as shown in the diagram below, even though those dates may not appear in the fields:

PROVENANCE AND LOCAL REFERENCE: These fields are self-explanatory, providing information that will facilitate the location of the item(s) at the repository. We have always insisted that the survey aid, not only the researcher, but the staff at the repositories, through giving as much detail as possible to the prospective user.

The remaining fields in the main section of the input form relate to the description field and provide various means of access to the information in it:

TYPES: The types field was envisaged primarily as a tool for interrogating the database, but it will be used to a lesser extent in indexing the book for items such as lecture notes, photographs, clinical records, etc. The use of codes again minimised the space taken by this field.

PERSONS: Personal names are entered in the inverted form and separated by a backslash. The field allows a maximum string of 200 characters. A program extracts all the entries in this field, with their piece number as an identifier, in order to create a subsidiary database of personal names in alphabetical order. This can then be set in relation to the main database, via the piece number field, to provide a speedy search facility.

INSTITUTIONS: A similar field and program are provided for institutional names.

PLACES: Again a string field with a program and resultant database. If within Britain, but outside London, a placename will be entered with its county, so that regional searches may be made. Where a place outside Britain is referred to, the country name only will be entered.

SUBJECT: A string field using six letter codes and allowing for up to six subject entries. The codes are derived from a thesaurus, comprising 134 terms, contained in a relational database. The compilation of this thesaurus was among the most difficult and time-consuming tasks we undertook in the initial stages of the project. It has, however, created a comprehensive finding aid and indexing tool.

The main section of the input form deals with the surveyed material. Beneath this there is administrative information, relevant to the long-term future of the database and the creation of the book:

INPUT DATE: If, as we hope, the database continues to be used and updated, it is important that the researcher knows the age of the information he/she is receiving.

SOURCE: A code number indicating the source of the information contained in the description field, so that 1 = printed catalogue; 2 = repository finding-aid etc. The accompanying memo field provides space to give an exact reference where appropriate; this ranges from lengthy bibliographic details to simply 'card catalogue'.

TO BE INCLUDED IN BOOK: A true/false logic field to identify entries to be used when compiling the book.

By combining the professional experience and concerns of archivists sensitive to the form as well the content of the Survey material, with the expertise of a data processing analyst having knowledge of dBase III plus, software applications have been created which serve our immediate needs for the Medical Archives and Manuscripts Survey. Moreover we have a database of immense value for future research in the history of medicine. Finally, we believe that these applications have the potential to satisfy the obvious need for sympathetic computer applications for cataloguing archives.

5 *James Parker*

Computerisation of the National Register of Archives: Designing a System for Staff and Public Use

Introduction

The National Register of Archives (NRA) is maintained by the Royal Commission on Historical Manuscripts and can be consulted in the Commission's search room in London.[1] The aim of this paper is to provide an introduction to the computerisation of the NRA and to report on the current stage of its development. The eventual system will provide live access for Commission staff and members of the public to the NRA. Those parts of the database that have been fully loaded and checked have only recently been made available to the public. Thus the Commission has not yet had sufficient time to evaluate public use of the system. This paper, however, is intended to give some idea of how the public will be expected to use the NRA's computerised database and how the information will be presented.

The Commission was established in 1869 to enquire into the nature and location of manuscripts of importance for British history, to inspect them and publish details of them. As a result, during the first 70 years of its existence — to the outbreak of the Second World War — the Commission concentrated on producing reports on, and calendars of, collections of privately-held papers in the United Kingdom. In all, 236 volumes have been published describing over 600 collections. Since the War, however, the Commission has for various reasons been seeking other ways of identifying and making available information about manuscript sources for British history. This can be seen most clearly in the establishment and development of the National Register of Archives.

The NRA was set up in London in 1945 under the auspices of the Commission to record the location and ownership of manuscripts of relevance to British history. From its first beginnings the NRA comprised lists and catalogues of manuscript collections sent in from record offices and libraries throughout the country as well as reports on papers remaining in private hands. The lists are stored centrally in London and made available to scholars in the Commission's search room. They include material of relevance to every aspect and every period of British history with the exception of records of central government which remain the preserve of the Public Record Office. Thus the lists describe papers of politicians, diplomats, soldiers, writers, societies, business firms, churches, landed estates, political parties and a multitude of other individuals, families and organisations.

The NRA has grown steadily over the past 40 years and its maintenance has been taking up more and more of the time of the Commission's small staff. The most dramatic developments have taken place in the last five years following a number of information-gathering projects in this country and abroad. Lists are now flowing in at a rate of 2,000 a year. The total number of these in the NRA now stands at 32,200 and they represent material held in 5,600 institutional and private locations in the UK and overseas.

From an early date it was realised that to make the information held in the NRA more accessible indexes to the lists would have to be compiled. The approach to indexing has been modified at various times over the years but the result is a two-tier system based on fairly selective indexing criteria. At the first level there is a central register recording three basic pieces of information about each list:

(1) Its number in the NRA sequence (e.g. 30,600, 30,601 etc.)
(2) Its title (the name of the individual, institution etc. whose papers are described)
(3) Its location (where the papers described are held)

As the register is arranged by NRA reference number, staff traditionally have had to compile separate indexes arranging this information by title (Short Title Index) and by repository (Locations Index). To provide more information about the contents of lists — particularly in the case of large or diverse collections of papers — a second tier of indexes has been developed.

These are, first, a personal index which identifies substantial groups of correspondence and papers of individuals of historical importance. The arrangement is alphabetical and includes information on over 33,000 politicians, diplomats, soldiers, explorers, writers and others. Secondly, a subject index which comprises 31 subject groups including the army, churches, landed estates, societies and political parties. Some subject groups are broken down further into subgroups to enable researchers to identify relevant material: for example, 'societies' is subdivided into friendly, literary, charitable bodies etc. The political parties section includes details of the records of 700 branches of all the major British political parties. Entries in the landed estates section note deeds, family, estate, legal and household papers for some 12,000 estates in every part of the British Isles. In all the index has 45,000 main entries. Thirdly, a companies index provides summary details of the records of business firms. Before computerisation the index was in two parts: an alphabetical arrangement by firm's name and a classification of the firms by business activity, for example, textiles, chemicals and mineral extraction. The index has entries for 14,000 firms.

All the subsidiary indexes include additional information about papers from sources outside the NRA, for example, record office annual reports, published surveys, guides and catalogues. With the expansion of the NRA in recent years the indexes have had to assimilate a growing volume and range of material. By 1987 the register and indexes held in the region of 200,000 entries. It was therefore decided to explore the possibilities of computerising them with a view to facilitating the maintenance of the NRA's data and providing a wider range of options for retrieving information.

System Development

Advice was taken from the Treasury's Central Computer and Telecommunications Agency (CCTA). Various options were considered and applications in related institutions investigated. An in-house system was felt to be more appropriate than a 'bureau' approach where the NRA's indexes would be stored on computer by a host institution elsewhere and to which NRA users would have access by telecommunication link. The advantages of direct control of an in-house system were felt to outweigh any savings in maintenance costs and enhanced performance that might accrue from using a more powerful external system. Applications development was undertaken by the CCTA's Small Systems Unit and a Prime 2350 supermini computer with a 240 megabyte fixed-media disk purchased. Several software packages, allowing the creation of indexes from free text, were examined but were felt to be too simplistic to meet the needs of the Commission to pose difficulties for coping with the volume of data in the NRA indexes. Prime's own Information software, enhanced by a PACE system generator supplied by Ampersand Systems Ltd, was selected as the most appropriate to the NRA's requirements. Similar systems are in operation at the British Museum and the National Army Museum.

The system was installed at the Commission's offices in London in June 1987 and on-line input of new material for the register began on 1 July. Following extensive preparatory and editorial work by Commission staff, temporary keyboarders were employed to load the register details (i.e. NRA reference number, title and location) for the 30,000 existing lists. The companies index was loaded in the same way. The personal index, which has been held on a mainframe computer by HMSO since 1970, was transferred automatically to the Commission's own system by means of a specially written conversion program. The principal tasks now remaining are the preparation and loading of the subject index, and editing the many entries in the personal index that were corrupted during conversion from the HMSO mainframe.

Structure of the System

The Commission's system was designed to reflect the existing structure of the NRA with its register and subsidiary indexes and to enable the introduction of further options for data retrieval not previously possible. Underlying this was the need to cope with access to the database by three groups of users: firstly, dedicated use by those members of staff with responsibility for the maintenance of particular indexes or parts of the system. This group had to be able to search, retrieve, display and amend information, and have access to printout facilities; secondly, use by staff not directly concerned with maintenance but who needed to have display (but not updating) access to the whole database and with printout facilities; and thirdly, use by the public who needed display access to most of the database, with the exception of confidential information which will be masked, and direct access to printout facilities.

Access to the system has been set up via a hierarchy of menus leading onto search screens. The main menu at the top of the system, which is seen by Commission staff, is as follows:

(1) Display register and indexes
(2) Amend register and indexes
(3) Output reports
(4) Public access
(5) System administrator

It can be seen from this list that from the three user groups, group 1 (dedicated users) will need access to options 2 and 3, other staff (group 2) will go in through options 1 and 3, while the public will be confined to 4. The search room terminal is set up with the public access menu already on display, enabling users to go straight into their search screens. The fifth option will be used exclusively by the system administrator.

The main public access menu displays the following options:

(1) Register
(2) Locations index
(3) Companies index
(4) Personal index
(5) Subject index
(6) Locations file

Options 1 and 2 enable the user to search the register in various ways for details of lists held in the NRA. These include searches for lists of particular collections by title, NRA reference number and location of documents, or combinations of these. Whereas separate title and locations indexes had formerly to be maintained, this information is now generated automatically by the computer from the register. Options 3, 4 and 5 on the public access menu provide access to three subsidiary indexes — companies, personal and subject.

The companies index (see Figure 1) allows searches to be made on each of the fields, from Sort Name down to Co Location and Dates. As with the manual index, each firm has been classified by the nature of its work. This information is now entered in the Code field. Advantage has also been taken during computerisation to subdivide the Codes into smaller sections or Sub-Codes to facilitate identification of related material. As an example, the Code for chemicals now includes Sub-Codes for refining, synthetics, explosives etc. By using combinations of search fields the user can search for one firm, or for several firms, which operated in a particular county or town, which did the same sort of work, or whose records fall within a given date span.

```
                 COMPANIES INDEX  :  DISPLAY & UPDATE SCREEN
                 -------------------------------------------

  COMPANY REF  : 103           SORT NAME : Mcfarlane
  COMPANY NAME : McFarlane, Marshall & Co, tanners


  BUS CODE     : 10  LEATHER
  BUS SUB-CODE : 1   leather curing and tanning

  COMPANY LOCATION - TOWN/PARISH : Glasgow
                     COUNTY      : Lanarkshire

                                                 (SUB-RECORD 1 OF 1)
  DESCRIPTION  : business corresp

        DATES  : 1778-80

      NRA REF  : 22009   Glasgow: Dreghorn
   NRA DETAIL  : TD 465/27
 DOCUMENT LOCN : Strathclyde Regional Archives
    OTHER REF  :
```

Figure 1: NRA Companies Index

The personal index (see Figure 2) allows individuals to be retrieved by surname. Further qualification by forenames is also possible. In the example below, for convenience, Palmerston's own papers are dealt with first, followed by his correspondence with other individuals arranged alphabetically. In each case there is a reference to a NRA list or to a published source from which the information has been extracted. Options for the future include searches by the occupation of individuals and their dates of birth and death.

Report PRINT.PI

Page 1
21 JUL 1989

PERSONAGE DETAILS REPORT

TEMPLE, HENRY JOHN, (1784-1865) 3RD VISCOUNT PALMERSTON, STATESMAN

corresp and papers
. HMC, Papers of British cabinet ministers 1782-1900

1801-66: political corresp and papers
NRA 12889 Temple. Southampton Univ L

1806-65: letterbooks, letters to, accounts
NRA 11930 Temple. British L

1840-64: letters from his wife; c1800: notebook and mathematical notes
British L. Add MSS 45553-54, 59853

1830-55: corresp with 4th Earl of Aberdeen
British L. Add MS 43069

political letters to Sir TD Acland
NRA 14687 Acland(p41). Devon RO

1831-35: letters (c150) to Sir Robert Adair
. HMC Prime ministers' papers 1801-1902, 1968

1830-52: corresp with JD Bligh
British L. Add MSS 41268-85

nd: corresp with Sir John Bowring
Essex Inst, Mass, USA NUC MS 67-1252

1832-61: letters (14) to Sir John Bowring
NRA 20033 Bowring. Houghton L, Harvard Univ, Massachusetts, USA

1861-65: corresp (13 items) with Speaker Brand
NRA 6114 Brand. House of Lords RO

1826-63: letters to Lord Brougham
Univ Coll London.

1831-61: letters to Lord Broughton
British L. Add MS 46915

corresp with Sir Henry Lytton Bulwer
NRA 6790 Bulwer. Norfolk RO

1831-51: corresp with Stratford Canning
NRA 23623 Canning. PRO, Kew

1853-59: corresp (15 items) with Sir Edwin Chadwick
NRA 21653 Chadwick. Univ Coll London

Figure 2: NRA Personal Index

The entry for the subject index (see Figure 3) shown below notes estate records of the Campbell family of Craignish, Argyllshire, which are described more fully in NRA list 29202. As this is a more complex index than the companies index there is a facility for a second Sort Name which, in the estate papers section, might be used if the NRA list includes papers of another family in connection with the same estate. Searches can be carried out on one field or a combination of fields. Thus, in the estate papers section the user could search for the Craignish estate, or could search under County, Dates and Code to list all estates in Argyll with records in a given period.

```
                    SUBJECT INDEX : DISPLAY & UPDATE SCREEN
                    ---------------------------------------

  SUBJECT REF    : 8248         SORT NAME : Campbell
                      SUBJECT SORT NAME :
  SUBJECT NAME       : Campbell family of Craignish
  SUBJECT CODE       : 12  ESTATE PAPERS
  SUBJECT SUB-CODE :

  SUBJECT LOCATION - TOWN/PARISH : Craignish
                     COUNTY      : Argyllshire
                                                    (SUB-RECORD 1 OF 2)

  DESCRIPTION    : deeds, legal and estate papers 1590-19th cent, household
                   papers 1779-85


          DATES  : 1590-19th cent
        NRA REF  : 29202   Campbell
     NRA DETAIL  :
  DOCUMENT LOCN  : National L of Scotland
      OTHER REF  :
```

Figure 3: NRA Subject Index

All the indexes can cope with a variety of date formats, from single dates such as 1812 to periods such as 1812-1880. They can also interpret combinations like '18th-19th cent' or 'early/mid/late 19th cent' where 'early' is taken as the first 30 years of a century, 'mid' as the middle years (e.g. 1830-70) and 'late' as the last 30 years. It can also cope with 'c' (circa) and 'fl' (flourished).

Returning, finally, to the public access menu, option 6 (Locations file) provides information about the 1,000 institutions which have sent lists of their holdings to the NRA. Once the researcher has consulted a list in the NRA and wishes to see the original papers he can turn to the locations file for information such as the address, opening hours and copying facilities of the repository holding the papers.

There is still some way to go before the NRA computer system can be made fully available on-line in the Commission's search room. However, the register, companies index and locations file have been accessible for some time now and early feedback has been encouraging. The principal problem encountered so far has been devising guidelines for the public user that are both helpful and brief. There is clearly scope for further development of Information's on-screen 'help' facilities. We remain optimistic that in the future we will be able to offer an enhanced service to the public in terms of improved accuracy and consistency of information, a wider range of ways in which data can be retrieved and faster availability of newly received information.

Note

1. Quality House, Quality Court, Chancery Lane, London WC2A 1HP. The search room is open Monday-Friday 9.30-17.00.

III.
Methods

The Computer Scientist and the Historian: Problems — Yes: Solutions — Pending

The Inheritance of the Past

Computing science is a young discipline and history is an old one; it is only recently that the special problems of the historian have begun to be looked at by computer scientists. The pioneers among the historians have had to use what was there already. What was there had been produced largely at the behest of two groups: business, commerce and administration was the greater, but science was the earlier, influence. The majority of historians had their interest awakened with the advent of cheap micros and easy-to-use software.

The major characteristic of the business community's use of computers has always been large volumes of regularly structured data. These data have been arranged into homogeneous files with processing requirements that can be accurately predicted. Typical data values have been numbers, dates, amounts of money and textual strings such as names and addresses. The view of reality that is being modelled is essentially simple. There may be a large amount of detail (say a file with 250 different fields in each record) but there is rarely much debate over the meaning of any given data item.

The presentation style of the data has fallen into two classes, tabular and form-based. In the tabular style each row of the table describes the properties of a single instance of an entity (such as a customer or a spare part). The form-based style uses a two-dimensional area to display one entity with each property individually labelled. Both of the styles have been in use from earliest times and their introduction to computer systems was natural.

More recently (starting in about 1970) the data in the files has been integrated into a single collection called a database. The chief advantage has been that applications software can be made largely independent of the way the data is actually stored in the database. This makes it possible to transfer the data from machine to machine and keep the software more or less the same.[1] The databases have themselves been built around models of data. The three models that dominate in the commercial market are hierarchical, network and relational. These all share the assumptions that data will be regular in structure and that there is no doubt about the meaning of any of the values: most of the subtlety of real life information is lost.

The world of science is obsessed with quantification so numbers and calculation predominate here. Often the underlying mathematics is sophisticated and the original data is of very low volume. The main exception to this is the analysis of experimental data using various statistical techniques. The social sciences also produce large volumes of data for statistical analysis. However, whereas social scientists and the self styled 'social science historians' (who shared the obsession with quantification) of the past were confined to mainframe computers, historians have instead adopted the microcomputer, perhaps better known today as the personal computer. This has emphasised above all else ease of use. This enhancement of the interface between the user and the computer has been used to sell the products (both software and hardware) in a competitive market place.

Some genuinely new tools have been developed for this new desk-top environment, most notably the spreadsheet which supports a flexible form of calculation. However, the most widely used applications packages have been for word-processing: the production of documents of all kinds. These are not restricted to text; diagrams and illustrations can also be included. Two other facilities are often provided in so-called integrated packages: data management (improperly called database management) and communications. The data management packages are usually not true database management systems because they do not support certain key ideas. In particular they lack the idea of a single unified description of the data structure and relationships (usually called a schema) that is itself 'data' that can be processed in the same way as other data. They lack the idea of sub-schemas, that is partial views of the database suited to particular users who write programs and perform queries in terms of these sub-schema. These ideas support the independence of the programs both from the detail of how the data is stored and from the schema. This allows changes in how the data is organised (to make access more efficient, say) and what kind of data is stored (adding new properties of an entity) without requiring any change to existing database application programs or queries.[2] The communications facilities make it possible to connect to other computers, both locally and remotely.

A more recent development is that of hypertext. The term hypertext was coined by Ted Nelson in the 1960s, though the idea can be traced back 20 years earlier.[3] Soon after Nelson's use of the term a working system was demonstrated, but widespread awareness only came with the arrival of cheap micros and Apple's decision to push its hypertext product. Hypertext breaks away from the idea of linear text and so allows easy associative referencing of information. The text (supplemented by pictures, sound and video sequence) can be accessed in different sequences equally easily. Instead of having to go away and consult an article or source referenced in a text the relevant content is available immediately on-line. The cross-referencing can be made dynamic so that users can personalise a hypertext document or suggest routes through the material for others to follow.[4] These allow the possibility of putting much more structure into the data that is stored in the computer.

All the above products were produced for either the business community or the home user. If they are of use to historians that is really accidental. With the exception of hypertext there is little attempt to come to terms with the complexity of data in a typical historical source. The danger with this inheritance from the past is that it will distort what the historian does with the computer. It is easier to change the problem to fit the computer solution than to produce a proper computer-based answer. This is hard to resist because it can be relatively easy to take the first few steps and the returns seem considerable. It has some of the dangers of addiction!

The Preoccupations of the Present

The most significant source of help for the historian should come from the database area. However this topic has become stuck in a rut in recent years; there are four reasons why.

Firstly, the cost of producing a database management system (i.e. the software product) is very high and so only a few are commercially available. It is hard for anyone with new ideas to build products that can compete. Current suppliers are naturally concerned to protect their investment. Secondly, all major products are being extended in a number of areas. Distributed systems deal with data and processing shared between different sites. Other data types (notably graphical data and better text-handling) are being supported. Fourth generation languages are being added to increase the productivity of programmers. These are in some cases over-extending the development teams.

Thirdly there is no agreed direction for databases. For a time the relational model held the field but now there is no accepted model of data. There are a number of contenders: functional, object-oriented, semantic network and so on, but no single one is obviously 'right'. Another area of debate is that some claim that conventional programming languages should be extended to include database manipulation but others say the way to go is to extend existing database languages to meet the needs. Fourthly the most fashionable area in which to innovate at the moment is the human-computer interface. This makes systems much nicer to use but does not necessarily make an inapplicable tool any more useful. It is now more fun to solve the wrong problem!

It is accepted that there is a seven to ten year lag between research maturity and software product availability. The lack of focus in database research in the early 1980s means that we are now only starting to get commercial products based on data models that can deal with the complexity of content and relationships of much historical data.[5]

We will now look at a couple of examples to see why historians need something more than what is on offer or is in sight.

Occupations

We suppose that a database is to include data concerning the occupations of individuals. The source has the occupations expressed in hand-written text with a certain amount of abbreviation and inconsistency. For ease of subsequent processing it is decided to encode the occupations numerically so a list of numeric codes is drawn up.

The usefulness of such coding schemes has long been recognised, and the computer can be harnessed to aid this task. It can be used to sort into numerical or alphabetical order, print out such lists, search for a given entry with a full or a partial match and so on. The list of codes can be automatically updated. But care is still needed: one person's rat catcher is another person's rodent operative. The coding scheme itself may distort the data. Indeed some historians may want to know what people called the occupations rather than what the other people called them. Coding may lose this information by forcing an artificial uniformity.[6]

A further difficulty arises where there may be multiple values; in this case multiple occupations may be listed for an individual. The classical database approach to multiple values is through a technique called normalisation but this introduces extra relations and increases the cost of reconstituting the original data. If it is decided to use a fixed length group, say three occupations per individual, then for many there will be a lot of wasted space and for the occasional entry there will be more than three.

If the set of occupations is made of variable length this complicates the specification of the processing. For example, we must decide how the values should appear on any output. Should the occupations field have a variable width or number of lines? Should it be truncated or abbreviated?

Finally there is the problem of meaning. For example, the query 'Find all the father-son pairs with the same occupation' will produce different results depending on the definition of 'same'. At least three definitions can be given:

(1) strict set equality, i.e. precisely the same set of occupations must be present in each (and is the order in which they appear significant?)

(2) non-empty set intersection, i.e. at least one occupation is common to both sets

(3) equality of singleton sets only, i.e. 'same' is only defined if there is a single occupation in each

Even this is not the end of the matter: are two empty sets equal? Do we require transitivity, i.e. does it matter if 'A is the same as B' and 'B is the same as C' do *not* imply 'A is the same as C'? This property is satisfied for meanings 1 and 3, but not for meaning 2. Most existing systems give no choice in such matters so the historian loses some control over the meaning of the derived data.

Genealogical data

The idea here is to support the processing of genealogical data in a graphical manner. We need to determine what the operations are that will allow the diagrams to be manipulated in a natural manner. Some possibilities are: to be able to move around in a large tree displaying just part of it on the screen, adding new individuals and new relationships, changing existing relationships or orderings of siblings, highlighting all the individuals with a common attribute, merging together two trees, identifying two individuals.

We need to be able to add data about any individual. We need to decide on the structure of the data, for without structure we shall not be able to use the power of the computer to process it. The data is made up of facts about the person but what is a fact? Should each fact be tagged with the historical source used? Should decisions made about the interpretation of source data or deductions made from it be supported by a justification?

This application seems to be well matched to hypertext systems, but they will need to be developed so that they can connect to conventional database systems where much of the source data is already being stored.

The Challenges for the Future

It is clear that the historian needs to proceed circumspectly at the present time. The allure of the computer must not blind him or her to the inadequacies of existing software. For there to be a fruitful outcome from the coming together of the historian and the computer scientist both sides must contribute.

The historian must think. It may be necessary to ask some basic questions like: what is history? how do I do history? how do I use sources? These questions must not be discussed solely within history circles. The debate must draw in the computer scientist who needs to understand the problem before knowing what to do to help. It will be very good for computing to have actual problems to regulate its growth and problems of a different kind from those traditionally tackled. Within the computing community those who specialise in office information systems are as close as any to the needs of historians.

A good place to start would be to have both sides read and discuss *Data and Reality: Basic Assumptions in Data Processing Reconsidered* by William Kent.[7] Parts of it will need a fair bit of explaining for the historian but the effort on the part of the computer scientist will help to establish a common language. I am sure historians could suggest a suitable work on the nature of history for the computer scientists to struggle through![8] Patience will be needed since it can take several years to move from a research prototype to a supportable product. Impatient historians will only 're-invent the wheel'. Computer scientists who are unwilling to listen will invent tools that no one can use.

Notes

1. There are other gains — and losses, such as the increased size and cost of the software, the increased difficulty in performing, testing and the backup and recovery of data, the overheads of supporting concurrent access to the data, but they are not relevant here.
2. These issues can be explored in C J Date, *Databases: a Primer*, Workingham, 1983, and J Martin, *An End Users Guide to Database,* London, 1981.
3. Ted Nelson, 'Getting it out of our system', in G Schecter (ed.), *Information Retrieval: A Critical review*, Washington, 1967, pp. 191-210.
4. For a further introduction see *Communications of the ACM*, 31, 1988, (special issue on hypertext); and E J Conklin, 'Hypertext: an introduction and survey', *IEEE Computer*, 2, 1987, pp. 17-41.
5. See R Elmarsi and S B Navathe, *Fundamentals of Database Systems*, London, 1989, chapter 2.
6. For more on coding see the chapters in this volume by Stuart Blumin, Edward Higgs and Kevin Schurer.
7. William Kent, *Data and Reality: Basic Assumptions in Data Processing Reconsidered*, Oxford, 1978.
8. A basic starting point for computer scientists might be standard historiographical works by G Elton, Fogel & Elton, and E H Carr.

7 *Alan Dyer*

Hypertext and Art History in Art Design: Education at Coventry Polytechnic Faculty of Art and Design

Introduction

In the early days of art and design degree courses the History of Art Department was seen primarily as describing the successive development of movements and schools of art and the lives of major artists. It helped to bring the student practitioner into contact with a wide range of images and enabled the young artist or designer to locate himself or herself within a cultural tradition. During the 1970s art history departments gradually changed their character and began to incorporate contributions from a wider range of disciplines — subject areas which provided new theoretical perspectives on art and design practice. Art history departments began to appoint staff to teach subjects such as sociology, philosophy, anthropology, psychology and literature.

The resulting new courses in art history and complementary theory were designed to enable students to widen and deepen their intellectual life within the Faculties. Their objectives were to help students better understand their chief study area in a wider historical and theoretical context, to develop their powers of critical thinking, and to increase their visual and formal awareness of works of art. In addition they aimed to give undergraduates a deeper insight into the social, political and ideological factors which influence our understanding and interpretation of art and generally to introduce them to the knowledge and perspectives derived from a wide range of humanities disciplines.

The interdisciplinary nature of what might in this context be described as historical and humanities teaching has presented many difficulties for tutors wishing to introduce computers into their courses. Up to the present time the major developments have been in the use of computers for data-handling and word-processing. Such systems have enabled students to manage research and essay presentation more efficiently and to create small, in-house databases. Often course designers have had to maintain caution when introducing art and design students to the hardware and software which might be of value to history, English, philosophy, or psychology undergraduates. Frequently such tools are inappropriate to the theoretical studies courses in an art and design context where teaching is devoted primarily to studio and workshop practice.[1]

Within the field of art education the manipulation of visual imagery in relation to perception, appearances and the representation of reality has been extensively explored over many years. The picture is both a window onto a world of appearances and at the same time an interface between the artist and audience, and various models of reality. Theoretical work at Coventry over some fifteen years has included the modelling of graphic and pictorial imagery for representing conceptual worlds. Unlike the conventional pictorial realisms, the new representations function as models or maps. They are lights onto an abstract world of knowledge structures. However throughout this period of work at Coventry it became increasingly clear that although paper-based graphic maps could function as strong and informative images, as interfaces they were often inflexible and limited. Concurrent developments in computer systems and low cost hardware and software increasingly enabled staff and students to extend the modelling of such interfaces beyond the limitations of conventional paper-(or canvas-) based media. The software which seems to lend itself most readily to this modelling has come to be known generally as hypertext.

This paper describes a research project funded by Coventry Polytechnic Learning Systems Development, and conceived in the Department of Art History. The aim of the project is to examine three such hypertext systems together with a rationale for their introduction into student projects. It will also briefly describe some of the intellectual and educational issues with which the systems deal and which the projects seek to foster.

The introduction of hypertext systems into the art history curriculum at Coventry is designed to introduce students to aspects of computing which are relevant to theory-based projects situated in an art and design faculty where courses are predominantly devoted to the teaching of practical, image manipulation, skills. The case for introducing hypertext into the art history curriculum is that it might enable students to manipulate information and concepts in a way that makes use of graphic imagery and visual modes of thinking. In this context students would be encouraged to relate theory to graphic media and visual communication. Students at Coventry use hypertext applications where text is arranged, not in ordered linear narratives, but in interrelated networks which permit multiple pathways through bodies of information. The construction of such documents calls upon and develops students' design and visualisation skills in ways that are not encountered in the more traditional sequential essay or thesis structures.

In the past departments of art history have usually requested that art students present their theoretical research in the form of the standard essay or thesis. Nevertheless, opportunity has always been available for developing approaches to knowledge manipulation and presentation which can draw on visual image manipulation skills. For many years, then, particularly at Coventry, the ground has been prepared for the advent of image manipulation systems which would operate in conjunction with theoretical text-based research and information systems.

It is an implicit feature of art and design education at undergraduate level that struggling with a painting, sculpture or design project is not simply a struggle to craft a usable, functional and ultimately marketable artifact. Studio practice presents the student with a medium and a set of problems associated perhaps with giving visual form to a set of technical and theoretical problems or with giving formal expression to personally held belief systems or perceptions of reality. Ideally the particular medium will be flexible enough to play its part in an ideas-processing dialogue with the student or practitioner. A tutor is able to observe, comment on and influence the nature of the dialogue by observing its progression both in the development of the picture and through conversation with the student.

In art education this is a well-established process of creative authoring as part of conceptual development and educational practice. The traditional essay format is less rich in its manipulative characteristics because of its strict formatting rules and its essentially linear nature. New forms of knowledge manipulation and presentation employing hypertext can offer a middle ground between studio-based image manipulation skills and the text-based theoretical components of courses.

At present there is much speculation about hypertext and its potential. However research at Coventry seems to suggest that it might be a system which allows theoretical material to be manipulated in ways which have much in common with the techniques of pictorial and sculpture representation. The most obvious application of hypertext in historical and theoretical studies in the art and design context is where ideas and information can be represented or organised graphically. This involves not simply the use of visual images for illustration but necessitates the creation of maps or models which may describe a particular theory or create and plot multiple pathways through a knowledge structure. Figure 1 shows ways in which the hypertext document might bring together manipulative skills from both practical and theoretical components of art and design courses.

Clearly in an educational environment where students are exposed to a wide range of visual media and where courses are involved in the development of creative design skills, the construction of graphic models provides students with images of wholes that might otherwise not be perceived. This makes students' graphic constructions valuable aids to perception, learning, data organisation, concept manipulation and communication. These are also processes fundamental to the construction of hypertext documents. An advantage to the student in the devising of graphic models is their potential explanatory function, in that they can present (in simplified form) information which might otherwise prove ambiguous and too complicated to manage. This clearly gives the model a heuristic function in that it can guide the student researcher to key points in a process or system. Further it can enable the student to engage in a dialogue between the concepts and data with which he or she is dealing, and an external malleable representation of that material. On a more intuitive level this is what happens in other areas of the Art and Design Faculty. The use of such teaching and learning techniques in the context of art history and theory allows students to engage in and develop techniques and processes which have many formal similarities with their studio-based practical projects.

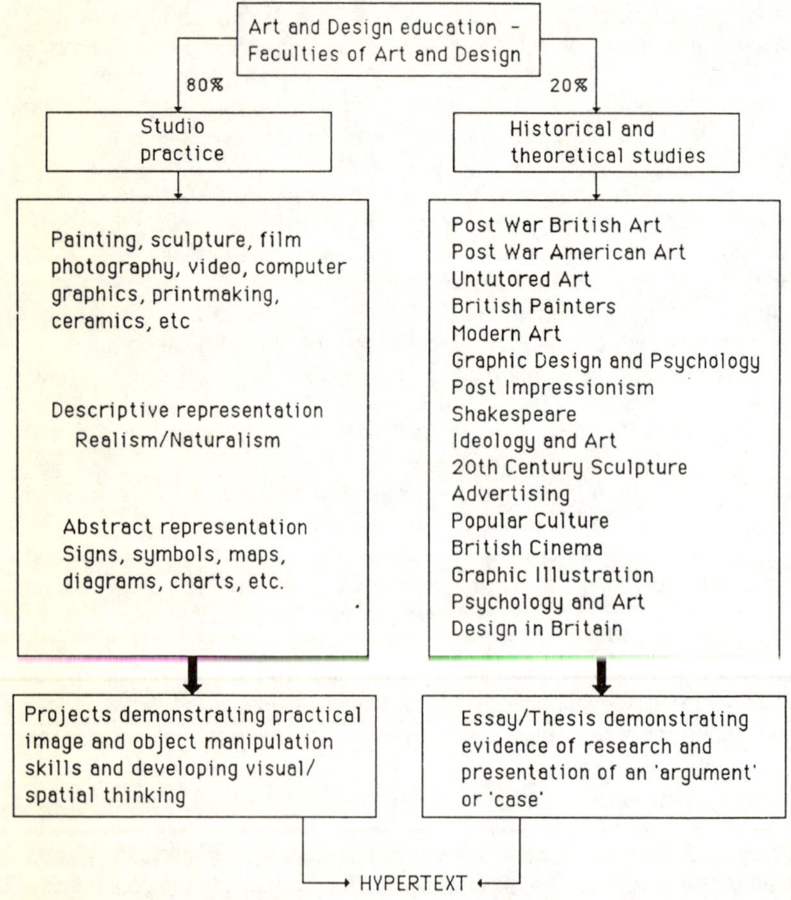

Figure 1: Essays and Theses Written in Non-linear Form for Theoretical Components of Courses Can Call Upon the 2D and 3D Skills Encouraged in the Workshop and Studio Context.

Problems of navigation, mapping management of multiple pathways which are intrinsic to hypertext systems, are also central to art and design practice. The ability to create pictures, three dimensional constructions, diagrams, symbols, graphic signs, even simple box and arrow structures should give art and design students a ready purchase on the processes by which theoretical material is organised in hypertext systems. Furthermore it should enable tutors to approach students' theoretical material in ways which form the point of view of critical discussion and have much in common with critical tutoring in studio and workshop contexts.

Hypertext systems

Filevision[2]

Filevision is a flexible graphics-based database package designed for use on the Apple Macintosh. The system's special feature is that it allows the user to put pictures and diagrams together with attached data fields. It thus encourages the user to organise data by means of graphic displays making it highly appropriate for students who are dealing with theoretical material and who are also operating within a visual arts and design context.

Filevision helps the user to visualise ideas and bodies of information. It integrates graphics and information management. The Filevision system enables the user to create, manipulate, store and retrieve information through a picture or symbol of what that information means in visual terms. Students learn to design a networked database or filing system through a picture diagram or visual model of that information. The data is thus structured in the system in a way which represents to the author a recognisable aspect of the real world.

Guide[3]

Filevision demonstrates clearly the potential for integrating theoretical research with graphic image manipulation. What is less clear is the potential of text-based hypertext systems in the art and design context. Guide is essentially a text based system which runs on the Macintosh, on IBM PCs and compatibles under Microsoft Windows, and on Sun workstations. It has been described as a 'three dimensional outliner'. Although Guide allows a user to browse through documents following individually determined routes, the student/author must pay considerable attention to the design and construction of the document. Potential meaningful routes have to be structured in advance of text production in order to allow the user to browse through the finished document. Guide can be used to create research presentations, proposals, instruction manuals, reports, works of fiction, poetic and dramatic narratives or any document where information needs to be communicated in some structured form. It is this process of designing and structuring which, from an educational project point of view, can provide insights into the conceptual and intellectual problems associated with the development of an idea into some communicable end product.

Constructing a hypertext document from scratch, then, is a challenging design problem. As with any complex communication system it will be necessary to work out beforehand how the finished product might be structured and the ways in which it might function in the hand of a user. This process of constructing a document might well mean creating a visual or diagrammatic design which will give an overview of the potential routes and interconnections between the elements in the document. Such a schematic overview will have similar characteristics to the graphic models and maps which are produced in other areas of the art and design curriculum.

HyperCard[4]

HyperCard is an authoring system and an information organiser designed by Apple for the Macintosh computer. The author generates stacks of information. HyperCard can be used to create, store and retrieve information — words, diagrams, charts, pictures, digitised photographs, statistics etc.— on any subject the author decides. The stack consists of any number of electronic cards. The card is screen size and can hold graphics or text. Any of the elements of information on a card can be connected to any other piece of information (another card in the same stack, a separate stack or a document produced in a different application — MacWrite or MacPaint etc.) by means of buttons. It is through the use of buttons that the author designs and generates the network of routes and pathways through the information system.

It is possible for users to plot their own routes through a body of information making whatever connections they choose and finding out what they want to know in as much or as little detail as they decide. They key to HyperCard's authoring environment is HyperTalk. This is a simple programming language built into the HyperCard system. HyperTalk will permit students who have little or no programming skill to design and build information systems which meet their particular needs or research requirements. In this way HyperCard can draw upon and develop the non-computing expertise of the author. It allows the student or author, trained in visual image manipulation skills, to construct elaborate knowledge structures relating to both visual and theoretical research projects.[5]

Notes for Guidance

Having looked at the institutional and educational context within which hypertext systems might fruitfully operate, and having looked briefly at three current software packages, it remains to describe the way in which these systems are currently being made available in the Art History programme at Coventry Polytechnic as part of the Art and Design curriculum. The following extract from the course *Notes for Guidance* provides a guiding framework within which students who wish to use hypertext can author their final year thesis as part of their degree presentation.

> *Computer-Based Presentation*
> It will be possible for students to present their research in the form of computer based structures. This will depend upon the availability of equipment and staff expertise, and on the students' own understanding of the appropriate technology.
>
> A computer-based presentation of theoretical research is not simply a matter of typing a normal thesis into a word-processor and having a reader access it from the screen. There should be good reasons why the material needs to be authored and accessed electronically. There are a number of systems currently available which permit text and images to be manipulated and presented in ways which conventional print on paper does not allow. The general term hypertext has been attached to such systems, several of which could be appropriate to research presentation in the art and design context.
>
> In general terms, hypertext refers to the handling of electronic information in particular ways. The handling of information in such systems extends beyond conventional information structures which employ linear narratives, lists, indexes and sequential card systems etc.
>
> Hypertext systems do not require either the author or the user to follow predetermined structures and access routes through bodies of information. The body of data within the system can be repeatedly cross-referenced. Topics that might have relationships either for the author or the accessor can be directly connected even though in a conventional thesis they might be many pages apart.
>
> Elements of data within this type of presentation, then become networked in such a way that fixed linear routing becomes unnecessary. The information system is 'designed' by the author in such a way that routing can be

controlled by the user. If the information system has been organised appropriately then multiple pathways and therefore multiple meanings can be created according to the disposition or needs of a reader. Thus, what might best be described as a three-dimensional knowledge structure is constructed allowing information to interact in an almost fluid way, depending upon the number of links and connections which the author builds into the system.

Hypertext systems can be particularly useful where an author wishes to establish links across traditional subject and discipline boundaries. For example, when studying a period in the history of art, where reference is made to a particular philosophical theory, a user might want to examine in more detail the philosopher referred to. One hypertext link could connect the historical period to the philosopher's biographical information. This information might be located in a separate document dealing with the history of philosophy as distinct from the history of art.

Similarly, other documents might be created which describe technical details of painting processes, social and political events, etc. These can be 'stand-alone' documents so far as their location within the computer system is concerned. The effort on the part of a student/author would be interested in the design of the networked structure which permits the user to become an author through the possibility of generating multiple-pathways.

Finally, it should be emphasised that preparing a body of information and building it into a hypertext system can be extremely demanding both intellectually and technically and should only be embarked upon for a research project after detailed discussion with a tutor who understands the system and subject proposed.

Summary and Conclusions

Besides the theoretical work which occurs at the level of studio practice in art and design degree courses, specific departments have been created in most art faculties for teaching theoretical studies. Students' research in this area of the courses is often presented in the form of the standard essay or thesis. However these methods can limit the extent to which students are able to manipulate and present their research material while drawing on the visual image manipulation skills developed in the studios and workshops. For many years now the ground has been prepared at the Faculty of Art and Design, Coventry, for the development of image manipulation skills which can work in conjunction with theoretical research and the construction of knowledge systems.

The *Notes for Guidance* describe the cross-referencing capabilities of hypertext. However it is well known among those engaged in hypertext research that problems of document design and navigation strategies arise out of hypertext's capacities for endlessly linking element with element within an information structure. It might be argued that even in documents which consist wholly of text-base information, the devising of navigation routes relating to potential meanings becomes a problem of overview or map-making. Although graphic images might not be included within the body of information, the design and manipulation of the system as a whole might be dependent upon the type of image manipulation skills described earlier which are an integral part of art and design education.

If it is the case that information management in hypertext systems necessitates plans, maps, charts or diagrams for navigational purposes, then clearly a fruitful relationship exists between theoretical research presentation in hypertext and the characteristics of an art and design practice which I described earlier. It remains to be seen, as more art and design students are introduced to this new medium, whether it will indeed form a bridge between two- and three- dimensional image manipulation practices in art education and the accompanying historical or theoretical research components of courses.

In the meantime it must be noted that the characteristics and potential of hypertext systems are not yet fully understood. It might be worth concluding with the comments of the external moderator for art history at Coventry Polytechnic regarding the introduction of hypertext into the undergraduate curriculum. He writes:

> A special problem may shortly arise for hypertext (and other) methods of presentation, of which there may be a small number (at most) in any year. Guidelines are needed which have the assent of the whole department, and which are then formulated in writing as part of the general notes for students... It may be, however that some caution is needed here, since hypertext seems to respond to certain information-handling needs and does not obviously lend itself to the concept of a thesis in its usual form of an argued, sequential, text about a defined subject. Hypertext needs a different rationale, and one that can be accepted. I look forward to hearing more of this discussion.

Notes

1. For more information about computers and Art History contact Anthony Hamber, Secretary, CHArt (Computers and the History of Art), Department of the History of Art, Birkbeck College, University of London, 43 Gordon Square, London, WC1.

2. Filevision is produced by Marvelin Corporation, 3420 Ocean Boulevard, Suite 3020 Santa Monica, CA 90405, USA. It is available from most UK Apple dealers.

3. Guide is produced by Office Workstations Ltd, Rose Bank House, 144 Broughton Road, Edinburgh EH7 4LE. It is available from OWL, and from NEOW (Windows software distributors).

4. HyperCard is produced by Apple Computers Ltd. It is currenty packaged with all new Apple computers and is available from Apple dealers.

5. For more information about HyperCard see Danny Goodman, *The Complete HyperCard Handbook,* London, 1987.

From an Historian's Know-how to a Knowledge-base: Using a Shell

Our basic material consists of seven Parisian tax rolls dating from 1292-1313.[1] The value of these sources in the study of the Parisian craftsman and tradesman during the reign of Philippe the Fair is well known. But, due to the lacunae of each of these registers and due to the particular nature of two of them, a quantitative analysis of social data cannot be done without building a meta-source which gathers information from all registers for each person. To build such a database is not a trivial task. Therefore, we decided to develop an expert decision support system for individuals' identification,[2] that is to say a system based on the historian's reasoning.

Knowledge Representation: General Principles

During the construction of a system based on reasoning, the two most important tasks are firstly, the construction of the fact base (i.e. the choice, between given information, of what will appear in the fact base and the values that will be attributed) and, secondly, the construction of the reasoning and the expression of all knowledge necessary to it.

The fact base must contain the description of the 75,000 mentions of individuals whom we want to identify. The information at our disposal is temporal (dates), spatial (location of persons in a parish, a street), fiscal (sums to be paid) and personal identity as follows:

> Jean le potier, fondeur de monnaie
> Pierre, Valet Jean le potier
> Nicolas, fils Robert des chans, talemelier

Six groups of information may be distinguished: the temporal data, the spatial data, the sums to be paid, the name and description of the taxpayer (firstname, surname, craft...), the type of relation between him and a next of kin, and the name and description of his next of kin.

Having established the facts, what kind of reasoning should be employed? In our case, it is a matter of comparison of information concerning two individuals mentioned in two (or more) registers with a view to deciding whether or not they are the same person. Does the reference to 'Pierre, fils de Aalis la normande' concern the same person who appears the following year as 'Pierre le normand' ? Are 'le fils Philippe de Vitry, drapier' and 'Etienne de Vitry' one and the same person ?

In order to facilitate the formulation of the reasoning, we followed the method of functional dependencies developed by P Levine.[3] This can be summarised as follows:

(1) definition of objects (i.e. information) on which the reasoning based, and definition of their values.
(2) setting up of the dependencies between the objects: construction of functional schemas and functional networks.
(3) setting up of reasoning rules.
(4) expression of contextual knowledge required by reasoning.

Objects are facts which characterise one individual. These facts are expressed in the fact base. Their values are the result of the comparison, and concern qualitative values such as: different, identical, uncertain, coherent, phonetically equal, compatible and so on. *Functional Schemas* indicate dependencies between information involved in the reasoning. The advantage of such a knowledge representation are that functional dependencies between facts can be used as rule schemas when one develops the reasoning. The following schema indicates that the object "taxpayer" depends on other objects which are his name and description, his relationship with a next of kin, the next of kin's appelation etc. It also indicates that the value of the comparison of two taxpayers depends on the value of the comparisons of their name and description, relationships with a next of kin and next of kin's appelation.

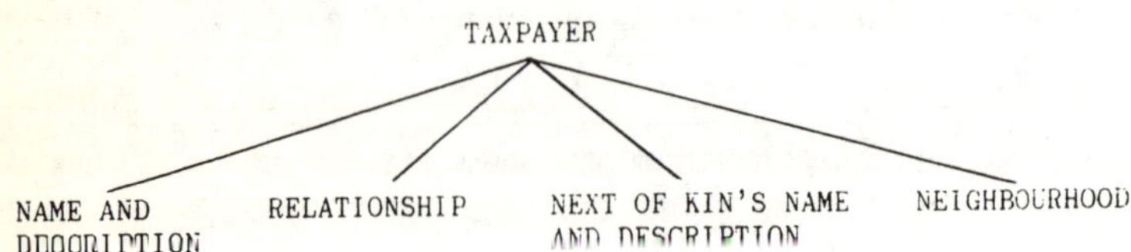

Figure 1: Example of Functional Schema

Functional Networks are branches which connect each schema to another on which it depends. They indicate the sequence of dependencies between the objects. *Reasoning Rules* indicate, for each schema, the values taken by the vertex of the schema according to the value taken by each object on which it depends. *Contextual Knowledge* is expressed either in specialised lists (frequent firstnames) or following the knowledge representation described (reasoning on different spellings of surnames).

Using a Shell to Validate and Test the Knowledge Base

While it is possible to record a functional network on paper and to control all its branches, controlling reasoning rules in the same way is quite impossible. Help in formulating and entering knowledge-base elements is, therefore, very precious. But help in managing the uncertainty is even more essential. Historical reasoning is what we could call 'qualitative estimations on uncertain facts'. On the other hand, we are frequently uncertain as to how to interpret the information with which we deal. For example: does a craft surname belonging to an individual refer to a craft practised by him ? On the other hand, our knowledge of the studied period is frequently lacunary: the comparison of crafts, to be very efficient would rely on an exact knowledge of legal rules concerning the practice of two crafts simultaneously (or succesively) and on a good knowledge of the enforcement of such rules. But the bibliography and the normative sources[4] dating from the thirteenth and fourteenth centuries give relatively little information on this. Furthermore what they suggest does not correspond with what can be observed from the tax registers. Testing the hypothetical basis of our reasoning is, therefore, fundamental.

For these reasons we have used a shell. A shell is an expert system which comprises, besides other tools, an editor which helps in entering objects schemas and rules, a development engine which permits us to process the reasoning and acts as an expert system on the knowledge base (detecting missing or incoherent rules, and allowing us to correct or complete them), and a trace command which permits a review of the reasoning. Such a tool is of great help in testing the accuracy of the knowledge base.

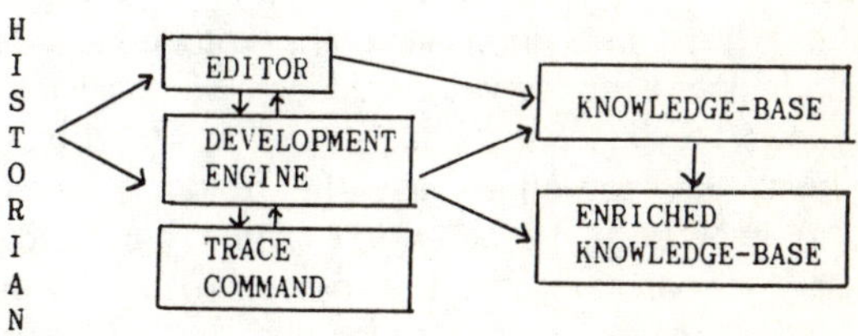

Figure 2*:* Using a Shell

The editor offers, through multi-windowing, a friendly environment for building the knowledge base. Crucially the development engine permits the verification of the coherency of the rules and their operational capacity. Checking is made on real examples by comparison between the reasoning of the system and of the historian. The development engine tries to apply the reasoning and asks the historian to supply the values for a comparison of two individuals. The reasoning is developed step by step under the control of the historian who can stop it, correct, delete or add rules, and (when rules seem to be correct) restart the reasoning until he is satisfied with the result.

The help provided by the tool during the modification is fundamental. The difficulty, when modifying a rule or a schema, is taking into account all the repercussions of these modifications. For each modification of a schema, the system detects the alterations which follow it in the rules-base and immediately asks the historian to modify all rules concerning the modified schema. In the case of the addition of an object to a schema, the system re-evaluates the coherency of the rules associated to this schema and asks the historian to choose immediately between those rules which have apparently become inconsistent. Nevertheless, even if the tool is a valuable help in the control of the coherency of the base, it is not capable of detecting the logical inconsistencies. It is the historian who judges the pertinency of the rules and decides what modifications are required.

Observing rules based on uncertain knowledge is a means of testing them. During development, the trace command constantly permits the review of the sequence of reasoning and its memorisation. The trace is a great help in optimising the strategy of reasoning. However not all the difficulties can be resolved at this stage: some of the historian's hypotheses will be validated only after a systematic processing of a representative part of the data. For example, we postulated that the wealthiest members of the population did not move frequently from one part of Paris to another. For this part of the population, the postulate led us to reduce the spatial area of comparison to the parish. Incomplete identification, after a systematic processing, would prove it to be false.

In conclusion, the advantages of such an approach are clear for at least two reasons. Firstly, as the method relies on the know-how of the historian and as the shell is a great help in building the knowledge base, the historian, using this method, acquires virtual autonomy in the construction of the system. It allows the historian to test hypothesis and to validate them. When he builds a knowledge base the historian employs his traditional skills and knowledge in order to acquire new knowledge. Secondly it permits the construction of a database which, although containing uncertainties, can identify cases as such through the formulation of schema that allow uncertain identifications. While admitting uncertainties such a database can also confess its lacunae.

Notes

1. Four of these tax rolls are published, for 1292, 1296, 1297 and 1313. See H Géraud, *Paris sous Philippe le Bel d'apres des documents originaux*, Paris, 1837; K Michaelsson, *Le livre de la taille de Paris l'an 1296*, Goteborg, 1958; K Michaelsson, *Le livre de la taille de Paris l'an 1297*, Goteborg, 1962; K Michaelsson, *Le livre de la taille de Paris l'an 1313*, Goteborg, 1951.

2. For more information about the reason why we opted for such a method, see: C Bourlet and J L Minel, 'A declarative system for setting up a prosopographical database', in P Denley and D Hopkin (eds.), *History and Computing*, Manchester, 1987, pp. 186-91; C Bourlet and J L Minel, 'Un systeme déclaratif d'aide à l'identification des individus dans un corpus prosopographique', *Informatique et Sciences Humaines*, 74, 1987, pp. 49-59.

3. G Benchimol, P Lévine and J C Pommerol, *Systemes Experts dans l'Entreprise*, Paris, 1986, especially chapter 5.

4. See particularly G B Depping, *Règlements sur les arts et métiers de Paris*, Paris, 1837; R Lespinasse and F Bonnardot, *Le livre des Métiers*, Paris, 1879; R Lespinasse: *Les metiers et corporations de la ville de Paris, Recueils, statuts et règlements depuis le XIIIe siecle jusqu'au XVIIIe siecle*, 3 vols., Paris, 1888-1897; G Fagniez, *Etudes sur l'industrie et la classe industrielle à Paris aux XIIIe et XIVe siècle*, Paris, 1877; B Geremek, *Le salariat dans L'artisanat parisien aux XIIIe — XVe siecles*, Paris, 1968.

Multi-sourced and Integrated Databases for the Prosopographer

Since Charles Beard's study of the economic interests of the United States' founding fathers, prosopography has been heralded as a means of getting underneath what historical actors said about themselves and explaining their behaviour with reference to their social, economic and political affiliations. The premise upon which such research rests is not, of course, above criticism. People with similar occupations or with common social backgrounds will not necessarily be conscious of themselves or behave as a coherent group. Despite this and other objections, prosopographical analyses have offered novel and convincing re-interpretations of historical events.[1]

In the 1960s the introduction of computing into historical research opened up new possibilities for collective biography. Larger groups could be analysed than was hitherto possible: so could non-elite groups for whom biographical information was only indirectly available in cumbersome census material. At the same time, the computer also threatened to reshape the course and content of prosopographical research by its insistence that data be highly structured and often numerically coded.[2] Consequently, prosopographers in the computer age ought to be far more conscientious with respect to methodology than their earlier counterparts. This essay aims simply to outline some of the strengths and weaknesses inherent in two kinds of databases that may be used for prosopography: flatfile and relational databases.

A flatfile database consists of one large table. In any prosopographical study, each row would represent one individual for whom biographical information has been collected. Each column would represent a variable

Figure 1: Coded Prosopographical Data

person	age	order of birth	place of birth	father's occupation
1	16	2	1	775
2	18	3	920	980
3	17	1	880	102

in the study, for example date of birth or father's occupation. Figure 1 shows part of a flatfile table prepared for a study of the social origins and career destinations of a sample of Oxford University's nineteenth-century students. The data have been numerically coded according to a scheme that was worked out in advance of data entry. The use of numeric codes is one way of overcoming problems that are inherent in sweating down complex data so that they may be organised within one matrix. It is also essential if the user wishes to conduct statistical analysis; commonly used statistical packages are flatfile databases that only handle numeric information. Insofar as the objectives of prosopography always contain a quantitative element — we want to know, for example, what proportion of any population achieves occupational or social positions higher than that attained by its parents — the flatfile database and the statistical facilities that they offer provide a useful methodological tool. There are, however, severe drawbacks involved in using the flatfile database. In short, the highly structured form which needs to be imposed upon the data before they may be analysed quantitatively may not accurately represent their richness and complexity. It may even be argued that the very meaning of one's data is altered in the process of its preparation for entry into a single matrix.

In collective biographies that are compiled from several different sources, it is almost inevitable that individual profiles will vary considerably in their coverage. Nonetheless, the flatfile database requires the imposition of standardised categories. Occupations, for example, must be classified, irrespective of whether they are culled from extensive listings in the *DNB* or *Who Was Who,* or from city directories which give only one-word citations such as 'merchant', 'chemist' or 'mechanic' with infuriating frequency.[3] Consequently, the process of categorising certain variables can be a highly inferential one. A problem with the flatfile database is that it reifies in the data those inferences that are made by the historian who, by coding data, treats individuals for whom he has extensive biographical information with the same level of certainty as those for whom his information is at best only minimal and at worst misleading.

A further problem with the flatfile database's insistence upon highly structured data is that it often mitigates against secondary and comparative analyses. The problem here, of course, is that the secondary analyst must operate within the framework of inferences and assumptions drawn by whoever collected and coded the data. These inferences and assumptions are intractable even when they are found to be wanting in any one of several respects. As data archives increase their holdings of social science and history datasets, and as funding bodies such as the ESRC take steps to ensure that prospective grant holders have exploited existing datasets, the problem of trying to interpret and use vastly complicated code books and inadequate classifications will be encountered more frequently by researchers.

A further drawback with the flatfile database is that it is not altogether easy to record the source of each piece of biographical information. To do so, two columns would have to be provided for each variable that was considered in a study: one for the information and another for its source. What, then would be entered next to an occupational code that was derived largely by inference and with reference to an individual's complete profile as it was compiled from several different sources?

So-called relational databases offer a genuine alternative to the prosopographer insofar as they do not require data to be so highly structured. The relational database appears to its user as a collection of tables each of which holds information of a very specific type e.g. jobs, schools, examinations or degrees. Others will join the information in the tables together. Figure 2 shows portions of three tables from an analysis of the social origins and career destinations of Oxford University's twentieth-century students.[4]

Figure 2: Portions of Three Tables

Table 1: Persons

NAMECODE	SURNAME	FIRSTNAME	SECONDNAME
1	Plates	Clifford	Lowe
2	Stones	Robert	Henry
3	Barnes	John	Arthur

Table 2: Jobjoin

NAMECODE	JOBCODE	JOBDATE	SOURCE
1	1	1910-11	Who Was Who
2	2	1920-21	DNB
2	3	1933	DNB
3	4	1918-28	Col Register
3	5	1928-32	Col Register
3	1	1932	Col Register

Table 3: Jobs

JOBCODE	JOBTITLE	FIRMNAME	JOBPLACE
1	Underwriter	Lloyd's	London
2	Journalist	The Times	London
3	Secretary	Church Assembly	——
4	Farmer	——	Tasmania
5	Businessman	——	NSW

Table 1 (Figure 2) Persons, consists of a row for each person who is included in the study and a column for each discrete piece of information about that person's name. Notice that each row is uniquely identified with respect to all other rows in the table by a number (namecode) in the first column. Table 3, Jobs, shows the jobs that the individuals listed in Table 1 held at various times in their lives. Here too, each record (or job) is uniquely identified by an assigned code and broken down into its component parts: title, name of firm, place of work — across the columns of the table. Table 2, Jobjoin, uses the name- and job-codes that identify the unique rows in Tables 1 and 3 respectively to join the names of the people listed in the Persons table with the jobs they held, and to give the source of this information. Notice that Table 2 contains more than one row for some of the people whose names are listed in the Persons table. John Barnes who was once a farmer, a businessman and then an underwriter at Lloyds, has three records in Table 2: one for each of the jobs that he held. Also notice that Table 2 shows that two people listed in the Persons table, Plates and Barnes, were both underwriters at Lloyds though at different times. The data in column two may also be repeated as many times as there are individuals who hold the same job.

Figure 3: Partial Database Model

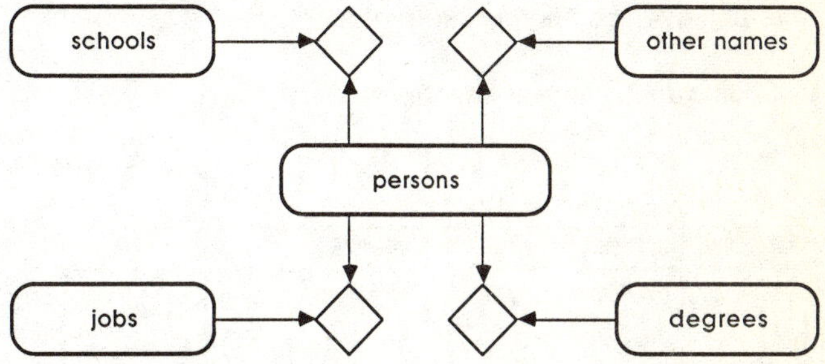

The value of the relational model in accurately representing biographical information of varying degrees of comprehensiveness is apparent. Biographical information is recorded precisely as it is found in the published record; no inference as to its meaning is imparted to it through the use of fixed numerical codes. The advantages for comparative and secondary analysis are self-evident. So is the promise that the relational model holds forth for those interested in building up archives of widely usable datasets. Less evident, perhaps, is the advantage that the relational database offers first or subsequent users interested in adding information that was not initially intended for inclusion. Figure 3 shows a partial database model used in the study of Oxford's twentieth-century students. The model, like the database, is not at all inflexible. New categories of information, say on religious affiliation, may always be appended simply through the addition of new tables.

Finally, the use of a relational database does not prohibit the subsequent use of flatfile databases to conduct statistical analysis. On the contrary, tables may be generated within the relational database containing data that are coded according to any number of different schemes. These tables may then be transferred into flatfile databases which provide the desired statistical facilities. Given the scope and purpose of this essay it is only possible to indicate the necessary procedure.[5]

Figure 4 shows once again the Jobs table together with another table called Codeocc. The Codeocc table classifies each of the jobs listed in the Jobs table according to some pre-determined scheme. Individuals' schools might be classified in another table according to whether they were institutions of primary, secondary or tertiary education, or whether they were privately or publicly funded. Additional tables might be created to designate degrees according to their subject, or to code geographical information. Together, subsidiary coding tables may be used to produce a matrix of numerically coded data that is suitable for use in a statistical package that depends on a flatfile format. Notice, however, that such coding procedures never alter the raw data themselves. The principal advantage of this approach is that data are stored in such a way as to support different, even competing interpretations.

Figure 4: Coding Jobs in the Jobs table

Table 1: Jobs

JOBCODE	JOBTITLE	FIRMNAME	JOBPLACE
1	Underwriter	Lloyd's	London
2	Journalist	The Times	London
3	Secretary	Church Assembly	——
4	Farmer	——	Tasmania
5	Businessman	——	NSW

Table 2 Occtype

JOBCODE	JOBTYPE
1	880
2	075
3	345
4	010
5	110

The problem with the relational database is that data entry is far more time-consuming than it is with a flatfile database. Quite simply, there is less information to be entered into the flatfile table because information is sweated down into a coded form. Admittedly, most relational database software comes equipped with facilities to develop 'user friendly' data entry and validation procedures which may be tailored to the particular needs of any project. So-called 'applications programming', however, is not something that researchers in history and the social sciences will specialise in and so may not be seen as an advantage by many.

In conclusion, the selection of a flatfile or a relational database for prosopographical research must be based on some serious consideration of the short- and long-term aims of the study itself. A useful rule of thumb might be as follows:

> Studies which compile relatively small amounts of data for the purposes of generating 'quick' results and which involve data that are unlikely to be of any wider interest should probably use a flatfile database. On the other hand, studies which involve large quantities of data, which will take some years to complete, and which comprise data which are likely to be valuable for secondary or comparative analysis should consider the relational model.

Whichever database one chooses, it is impossible to spend too much time modelling how it will work. This means paying careful attention to how computerised data will be organized and then analysed. With the flatfile database, modelling involves the use of limited datasets to test how different variables will be coded and analysed. With the relational database, modelling requires that some thought be given to the number and structure of the tables required by the data and their relationship to one another. It also requires the use of limited datasets to test whether different database designs can support the classifications that are ultimately desired. It is worth mentioning that the flexible structure of the relational database makes it relatively easy to recover if and when fundamental flaws or oversights in the research design are spotted even midway through the project. With the flatfile database, recovery from such mistakes is far more costly and may require that data be re-classified or even re-entered.

Notes

1. L Stone, 'Prosopography' in L Stone (ed.), *The Past and the Present*, London, 1981, especially pp. 47-8, 66-9; cf. R W Fogel and G R Elton, *Which Road to the Past? Two Views of History*, London, 1983, pp. 26-9; O Handlin, *Truth in History*, London, 1979, pp. 98-9.

2. F Furet, *In the Workshop of the Historian*, trans. by J Mandlebaum, London, 1981, pp.44-8; J M Kousser, 'Quantitative Social Science History' in M Kammen (ed.), *The Past Before Us*, London, 1980, pp.433-56.

3. See Stuart Blumin's contribution in this volume.

4. Lou Burnard, 'Principles of Database Design' in S Rahtz (ed.), *Information Technology in the Humanities*, Chichester, 1987; C J Date, *Relational Database: Selected Writings*, London, 1986.

5. Daniel I Greenstein, 'A Source-orientated Approach to History and Computing: the Relational Database', *Historical Social Research (Quantum)*, 14, 1989, pp.9-16.

Structuring the Past: the Occupational and Household Classification of Nineteenth-Century Census Data

Many of the controversies which arise over the use of quantification in history reflect, it can be argued, a confusion between quality and quantity. It is possible to quantify quantities but not to quantify qualities. One may say that ten pigs of iron happen to weigh the same as ten trees, but this does not mean that because of this numerical equivalence we experience a qualitative identity between iron and trees. The objects we meet in daily life are complexes or clusters of universal qualities; colour, shape, density, texture and so on. Our relationship with these is one of immediate experience. But this experience is different from one's discovery that these clusters of universals, which make up 'treeness' for example, can be replicated, the basis of our concept of number.

This distinction becomes still more important when dealing with human relationships. One cannot measure, for example, how people experience kinship. One can only measure the frequency with which they perform certain actions, which may give a clue to the subjective quality of what the family means to them. All one can legitimately say about statistical patterns in human behaviour is that they are consistent with a particular model of the human psyche, and are reliable for the purposes of prediction. An analysis of how people 'feel' subjectively about these actions and the reasons they performed them is necessary to substantiate such models.

Such problems are especially serious for historians as compared, for example, to sociologists. This is because qualities are constantly changing over time. The egg becomes a chicken, and the seed a tree. In the same way the range and quality of the relationships and experiences encompassed within the early medieval household, a productive unit within a subsistence economy, may have been very different from those within modern working-class families.

Historians also usually have to base their analysis on data created by others for quite different purposes to their own. The clues to the qualities they wish to study, the experience of family, status, the meaning of work, and so on, have to be derived by studying the frequency of entities or actions defined by others, or by creating their own units of analysis by aggregating other entities found in pre-given data. Problems arise here because the qualities addressed by others may not be appropriate to their own research, or because the nature of the underlying elements being aggregated is undergoing a qualitative change, or because modern linguistic signs used to signify certain qualities or entities were attached to different objects in the past, or to entities undergoing a process of mutation.

This final point needs to be amplified. Any act of linguistic expression is an exercise in classification and coding. When one says, 'This is a tree', one is assigning an object to a class on the basis of its qualities. One is also giving it a four letter code, 't-r-e-e', which identifies this conceptual category.

The documents which historians use, especially highly structured sources such as census returns, are in this sense already classified and coded databases. Some activities may not be classified and coded by contemporaries in ways one might expect today. Thus the productive activity of women was not within the Victorian 'coding frame' for 'work', and was therefore often excluded from the occupational returns in the census. Any further grouping or aggregation performed by the historian is merely another exercise in abstraction from historical reality. In order to use sources properly it is necessary for historians to understand the classifications and codings already inherent in them, as well as to understand the implications of their own structuring of the data.

The distinction between quality and quantity has not always been made by historians and this has led to much fruitless controversy. The standard of living debate, for example, has been so exasperating because the participants did not agree at the outset on what the 'Good Life' consisted of in qualitative terms.[1]

Similarly, any econometric analysis which treats the quality of what it measures as unproblematic runs grave risks. It is usually assumed by economic historians, for example, that growth in the production of goods and services is a 'Good Thing'. But if the kind of industrial growth, based on the consumption of non-renewable energy sources, which the world has experienced since the Industrial Revolution cannot be sustained, or leads to permanent and serious harm to the ecosystem, will succeeding generations come to see growth as a 'Bad Thing', and reverse all the signs in today's equations? Will rising levels of productivity and consumption cease to be considered as a sign of success and come to be regarded as evidence of accelerated destruction?

These general comments are, of course, as relevant to non-quantitative historians as to those using computers. However, the use of information technology forces such problems upon the historian with especial force because of the immense processing power of the computer. As yet computers lack a sense of irony; if one asks them to do something foolish they will do it without demur and to excess. This is what is meant by the old computer adage, 'Garbage In, Garbage Out', and its acronym, GIGO, aught to be constantly borne in mind by historians.

Some of these issues can be explored by considering the use made of census data by historians when examining economic and household structure. This is not because they have been particularly careless in their use of this source, quite the opposite, but because such a study shows clearly the problematic relationship between qualities and quantities in historical research.[2]

Charles Booth's attempts to make the nineteenth-century published census data on occupations consistent has been the basis of most subsequent attempts to show the changing structure of the British economy. Booth realised that the ways in which the 400 or so occupational titles in the *Census Reports* were grouped, varied from census to census. He attempted to rearrange these entities to make the occupational classification systems consistent over time. The numbers of persons attached to these occupational titles could then be rearranged to show the changing aggregate structure of work in the economy.[3]

But these titles were not in themselves entities of an homogeneous quality, they were merely headings under which other occupational titles given in the manuscript returns were grouped. In fact at least 30,000 occupational designations could be identified in the census returns, and these had to be grouped by the Census Office under their 400 headings using large occupational dictionaries. This was a level of aggregation and classification to which Booth did not penetrate.

According to Armstrong, one of the modern interpreters of Booth's work, this is no great problem since any misallocations of occupations in his system 'are likely to be of slight statistical significance'.[4] But this assertion, unsupported by evidence, cannot be accepted uncritically. The process of allocating activities to economic sectors was not simply a matter of juggling with labels. What those labels signified, could change. It is possible, for example to construct from the *Census Reports* a table showing the number of 'scientific persons' or 'persons engaged in scientific pursuits' from 1851 to 1901. But such a table is meaningless because what constituted a 'science' changed over the period. In 1871, for example, the clerks abstracting the occupational data were instructed to place antiquarians, genealogists, philosophers, phrenologists and topographers in the category of 'Scientific persons'. Such terms were gradually excluded in later years as the meaning of 'science' narrowed to exclude all but the experimental physical sciences. Also, if one looks at the individual census returns for leading Victorian scientists it is striking that they described themselves as anything but 'Scientist'.[5]

Another example is provided by the changing treatment of carters. In 1871 people simply designated as 'carters' were placed under transport only if they lived in 'large manufacturing or commercial towns'. Elsewhere they were placed under agriculture. In 1881 they were placed in agriculture only if they resided in a 'rural district or small town'. By 1891, however, all carters were to be placed under transport unless they were specifically returned as working on farms or in agriculture. It should come as no surprise that Booth's own figures show the numbers of 'Carmen, carriers, carters and draymen' increasing by nearly 100,000 between 1871 and 1891.

There was, in fact, a major shift in the 1870s and 1880s in the principles underlying the occupational classification systems used in the census. In essence the classification of occupations used in the mid-century was based on the type of materials being processed. This reflected the belief that disease was a chemical process, and that working with particular materials had a direct effect on life-expectancy. With the acceptance of the germ theory of disease, and growing interest in economic, social and eugenic research during the Great Depression, the occupational classifications used gradually came to place more emphasis on levels of skill, and the distinctions between making, dealing and administration. In the course of the last 30 years of the century a distinct tertiary sector came to be constituted in the classification systems, which gave, in part, the *appearance* of a tertiary economic revolution.

In his work on the occupations in the census, Booth also made certain assumptions about what constituted work. For Booth work was that set of activities which men performed to earn money to support their 'dependants' (i.e. wives and children). Women who worked at home, and in so doing contributed to the family income (farmers' daughters, the wives of lodging-house keepers and of shopkeepers and so on), had been included in the occupied populations of the early censuses but were removed in 1881. Booth chose to make the early censuses consistent with the later ones by simply removing these women to an 'unoccupied' sector of his classification. In so doing he introduced significant distortions into our picture of women's economic role in Victorian society.[6]

The census household is one of the more problematic entities found in the nineteenth-century returns. Tillott and Anderson, working on the returns of 1851 and 1861, have argued that the householder was defined as an occupier who rented space in a house. There was, therefore, considerable confusion over the status of boarders and lodgers. Single lodgers and lodger families are shown as forming separate households in the returns by the conventional marks used for this purpose but are still recorded as 'lodger' in the relationship to head column. In the absence of the sociological definition of the household as a group of people eating together such confusion was, Tillott argues, inevitable. Tillott and Anderson have chosen to ignore the conventional marks for households, and have defined the household as all those persons grouped under a person designated as a head in the relationship to head column.[7]

Although this may facilitate comparability across the same census, the convention does not, unfortunately, allow comparison between all censuses. This is because the definitions given to the enumerators after 1851 were quite specific, and changed over time. Contrary to Tillott's belief, enumerators were told in 1861 that lodgers boarding together separately from the rest of the people in a house should form a separate household, even though they should still be regarded as lodgers in relation to the principal occupier of the house. The separate lodger households found in the returns could quite correctly constitute definite social entities, although there was plainly still grounds for confusion. The Cambridge Group may well be justified, therefore, in excluding all boarders, lodgers and visitors from their analysis of household structures.[8]

Tillott was perhaps misled by regarding the enumerators' books as the sole source of instruction on this matter. But more extensive rules for defining the household survive at the Public Record Office in the instruction books given to enumerators.[9] These show a gradual progression after 1881 towards constituting the lodger, or lodger group boarding separately, as distinct households with household heads. This may lead, other things being equal, to an illusionary decrease over time in average household size, as the proportion of solitaries in society appears to increase.

Neither the Tillott/Anderson conventions, nor those used by the Cambridge Group, can deal fully with this problem because the people included in the household in the former case, and those excluded from it in the latter, changed over time. The solitary lodger in 1861 included in the head's household by Tillott and Anderson, and excluded from consideration by the Cambridge Group, would have been constituted as a solitary head in the returns by 1901, although his or her social position might not have changed. The Cambridge conventions might only give complete comparability across time for a comparatively brief period of twenty years in the mid-nineteenth century when the census definition of the household was stable. They do have the advantage, however, of concentrating analysis on 'clean' data. The Tillott/Anderson conventions, on the other hand, do neither.

In the field of research examined here, historians have given considerable attention to definitions. But the problems inherent in the source have still not been fully overcome. If historians are going to lay down conventions to facilitate comparability, they should be wary of doing so on the basis of one or two censuses, or in ignorance of the details of the classifications already inherent in the data. Granted, when historians first began to work with such material only one or two sets of returns were available for inspection. But sufficient material now exists at the Public Record Office to allow a detailed analysis of the conventions used at various dates. It is perhaps time to go back to basics in these areas, or at least to rework some past results to see to what extent the mutations outlined here affect them.

Historians need to pay still greater attention to the structure of documents, and to the complex and shifting administrative mechanisms which created them. More broadly, however, they might ponder on the nature of the changes in the past revealed by their quantification. Do these reflect trends in objective reality, or merely in the classification and coding systems used by those who created the historical sources they use? If the past is really that ironic archive of statements with shifting meanings which Foucault posited,[10] what are the conceptual or methodological tools which will allow historians to extract the objective kernel from the subjective meaning of their sources ?

Notes

1. It would be difficult, and indeed tedious, to give an exhaustive bibliography for this extensive debate but some representative contributions can be mentioned. R M Hartwell, 'The Rising Standard of Living in England 1800-50', *Economic History Review*, 13, 1961, pp. 397-416; E J Hobsbawm, 'The British Standard of Living, 1790-1850', in E J Hobsbawm (ed.), *Labouring Men*, London, 1968, pp. 64-104; E P Thompson, *The Making of the English Working Class*, Harmondsworth, 1968, pp. 347-84; H Perkin, *The Origins of Modern English Society, 1780-1880*, London, 1972, pp. 134-49; P H Lindert and J G Williamson, 'English Workers' Living Standards during the Industrial Revolution: a New Look', *Economic History Review*, 36, 1983, pp. 1-25; N F R Crafts, *British Economic Growth during the Industrial Revolution*, Oxford, 1986, pp. 89-114.

2. Much of the material outlined here is taken from a recently published Public Record Office handbook on the manuscript census returns; Edward Higgs, *Making Sense of the Census: the Manuscript Returns for England and Wales, 1801-1901*, London, 1989.

3. Charles Booth, 'Occupations of the People of the United Kingdom, 1801-1881', *Journal of the Statistical Society of London*, 49, 1886, pp. 314-444.

4. W A Armstrong, 'The Use of Information about Occupation', in E A Wrigley (ed.), *Nineteenth-Century Society*, London, 1972, p. 230.

5. Edward Higgs, 'Counting Heads and Jobs: Science as an Occupation in the Victorian Census', *History of Science*, 23, 1985, pp. 335-49.

6. For a general discussion of women's work in the census see Edward Higgs, 'Women, Occupations and Work in the Nineteenth Century Censuses', *History Workshop Journal*, 23, 1987, pp. 59-80.

7. P M Tillott, 'Sources of Inaccuracy in the 1851 and 1861 Censuses', in Wrigley, *op.cit.*, pp. 82-122; M Anderson, 'Standard Tabulation Procedures for the Census Enumerators' Books 1851-1891' in Wrigley, *op.cit.*, pp. 134-45.

8. This appears to be the convention implicit in P Laslett and R Wall, *The Household and Family in Past Time*, London, 1974; and John Knodel, 'An Exercise in Household Composition for use in Courses in Historical Demography', *Local Population Studies*, 23, 1979, pp. 10-23.

9. Public Record Office. Census Returns, Specimens of Forms and Instructions (RG 27): RG 27/1, pp. 18-35; RG 27/3, items 11-14; RG 27/4, item 29; RG 27/5, item 27; RG 27/6, item 6. Home Office, Registered Papers (HO 45): HO 45/3579. See also the examples in the enumerators' books which can be found in the relevant census returns for 1841 to 1881 (HO 107, RG 9, RG 10,

RG 11). Examples of the latter for 1891 can be found in RG 27/6, items 71, 73, 74.

10. M Foucault, *The Order of Things. An Archaeology of the Human Sciences*, London, 1970; M Foucault, *The Archaeology of Knowledge*, London, 1974.

The Historical Researcher and Codes: Master and Slave or Slave and Master

This article sets out to be deliberately provocative. It is written as an aid to those venturing for the first time down the path of computerisation, those who have before them a record, or series of records, and believe that there are clear advantages to be gained in turning toward automated methods of analysis, yet at the same time, are not sure exactly how one should go about it. It is written primarily as an introduction to the subject, and as such is intended for those fresh to the field of history and computing. The purpose of this essay is to help them on that initial journey.

The Use of Codes

In 1985, in a brief paper entitled 'Some Reflections on Coding', Konrad Jarausch opened his address with this perceptive remark: 'Coding seems to be one of the necessary evils of historical social research'.[1] However much we may dislike or disapprove of the practice, coding is a critical and usually unavoidable task which needs to be carried out in the process of analysing historical records via computer techniques. It is both evil and necessary.

Why should this be the case? First, it is perhaps easier to understand why codes are necessary. Even if we take a simple piece of information recorded in an historical record, for example, a person's marital status, we can see several good reasons why that piece of information would gain from being coded. Perhaps the chief reason lies within the general head of time, space and efficiency. Storage or memory space on computers is a lot more freely available now than in the past. However, for those working on microcomputers, the availability of disk space may still be a restricting factor. Consequently, storing a persons marital status as 'Unmarried', as opposed to simply '1' or 'U' may prove to be a critical factor. Equally, even if storage does not act as a constraint, when it comes to the writing of data entry and analytical programs, or the construction of logical query statements, there are not many who would choose to type in If Mar Eq 'Widowed' Or Mar Eq 'Married' in favour of If Mar Eq '3' Or Mar Eq '2', let alone if 2<=Mar<=3, especially if the expression has to be repeated several times. Lastly, the act of coding pieces of information, however simple, usually performs another task, that of standardisation. The same piece of information may be recoded several different ways over a series of historical records, or for that matter within the same record. To return to the example of marital status, individuals may be recorded in the record in question as 'Single', 'Unmarried', 'Unmarr' or simply 'Unm'. Due to our knowledge of the historical source we may conclude that each of these variants represents the same marital status. The computer, however, is not gifted with the same degree of intuitive judgment. To the computer each of these entries is little more than a string of characters, each of which is different. As such, when writing analytical programs, if we wished to refer to all those persons who were not married, we would have to let the computer know of each variation in spelling recorded for marital status in the dataset. By allocating a code to marital status we would tend automatically to standardise the entries as recoded in the source. Thus all persons we believe to be unmarried would receive the same code regardless of how the original entry was written down. The allocation of a simple code in the form of a single digit or letter therefore standardises all of the entries to a common form, making them quick and easy to refer to.

The reasons given above should make it clear why codes are necessary, but why are they also evil ? To understand this I think we need to look more closely at the way in which computer techniques first came to be used to investigate and analyse data in historical research. One of the first projects in this country to utilise computer resources for the purposes of historical analysis was that computerising the nineteenth century census enumerators' books for the London suburb of Camberwell.[2] When the project was started in the late 1960s, both data and programming commands had to be entered into the computer using punched cards. These were paper cards, 7 by 3 inches in size, with small rectangular holes punched in them to represent combinations of numbers and/or characters.[3] For the census books of Camberwell, Dyos and his team used five cards of 80 columns per every household. All of the information relating to the individuals recorded in a household were coded and entered onto the punch cards in a rigid fixed format fashion. Positions on the cards were allocated for data relating to the household head, spouse, up to 12 children, six relatives, 10 lodgers, six servants and two visitors. In all, a total of up to 38 persons per household. For each person codes for age, occupation and birthplace were entered; marital status was coded for heads, relatives, lodgers and servants; and a relationship code was assigned for relatives. The codes adopted provided for 21 occupational groups, 12 industrial groups, 36 birthplaces, 12 relationships to the household head, six marital statuses and six social classes.[4] Ironically the overall approach of this Camberwell study was little different from that which was used by the Census Office to analyse the national census of 1911. The census of that year was the first in the United Kingdom to be analysed using automated techniques, making use of the Hollerith card sorting and counting machine, adopted some years earlier by the Census Bureau in the United States.

At the time of the Camberwell study there was little alternative to the approach adopted. Yet since then there have been a number of technical advances. One obvious development is the fact that punch cards are now largely obsolete, data and programming commands are now usually entered via a keyboard and viewed on screen. Yet despite these changes the burden of the 80 column punch card still can be found hanging around our necks. This is because many of the software packages used by those working with historical material are designed and documented under the influence of a punch card mentality. Over the past 10 to 15 years the most widely used analytical software package throughout the social sciences has undoubtedly been SPSS. As far as data collection is concerned one need only quote from the opening section of the standard manual to see that the approach suggested is little different from that of Dyos:

> The measurements collected in a study (survey or otherwise) must usually be coded... before any analysis can be accomplished. As a rule, the variables are recorded so that each case occupied one or more eighty columns punched cards. Since it would be very cumbersome to actually punch onto the cards the names of the respondents or the alphabetic name of their race or political party preference, a coding scheme which equates numeric or alphabetic characters to each value of the variables is usually instituted... we *strongly* [their emphasis] urge users who are designing coding specifications for data to be input into SPSS to use only numeric codes.[5]

Although the SPSS package has been extended and upgraded in recent years, particularly in relation to the use of alphanumeric variables (character strings), the underlying concepts still appear to persist.[6] Equally, it is clear that despite good advice to the contrary in the text of standard works,[7] researchers creating machine-readable files, particularly newcomers, are still locked into the punch card mentality, squeezing their data to fit the recommended software and rigorously collapsing fields of information into bands of numeric codes. It is now time, if not a necessity, for researchers to break away from the restrictions of the punch card legacy.

When to Code

At this stage a newcomer to the subject matter may well have reached the conclusion that the message of this article is that we should not use codes at all. This is not the case. The key issue is simply one of timing. Following the text of software manuals and the standard advice offered by computing staff in the social sciences, researchers are often seduced into converting all, or some, of the items of information recorded in their sources directly into appropriate codes at the point of data entry. Thus, once completed, the machine-readable version of the historical record in question is not a transcript in the accepted sense, but rather an adaptation of the original record.

One could produce several arguments in support of such an approach. What is the sense, and how can one justify the extra time taken in typing entries such as 'Married', or 'Male' into the computer when the codes '1' or 'M' can be used adequately to convey the same meaning? It is true that in the case of items of information such as marital status and sex where the range of likely responses is limited it is not always easy to justify the practice of typing the information recorded in full, but where do we draw the line? Regardless of the records being created one does not have to search too far to find fields of information for which the range of entries recorded in the original document is as restricted: information on individuals' occupation is a classic case. The obvious answer, of course, is to devise a coding scheme incorporating appropriate occupational categories, so that when keying the record into the computer the various occupations can be assigned a code according to the classification being used. Or is it?

The chief problem with assigning codes during the process of data entry is that one automatically loses a measure of flexibility. Since the real or true piece of information recorded in the record is substituted for a coded value, the way in which that information can be analysed is ultimately dependent on the coding scheme or classification substituted in its place. This means that if the code is going to act as a satisfactory substitute, when devising the coding classification the researcher has to correctly identify and anticipate all of the ways in which the information will be used in the course of subsequent analyses. Clearly this is a very tall order, particularly in the early stages of a research project when theories and ideas are continuously being formulated. Unfortunately it is all too often that researchers find that their analyses are limited by the coding scheme they developed at the genesis of the research.[8] At the stage of data collection it is clearly both unrealistic, and to a certain extent undesirable, for a researcher to envisage all of the possible uses to which the data may be later put. Such an approach can only lead to mistakes and frustration at some point in the future.

This problem of inflexibility can be overcome quite simply by delaying the process or exercise of coding. If during the stages of data capture the researcher enters the information into the computer as recorded in the original record, rather than substituting this with coded values, then the resulting data file will be more of a machine-readable transcript than an adaptation of the source.[9] Once this information is safely stored on disk, codes can be applied as usual; equally, if needed, the original entries can be recalled to resolve difficulties or mistakes, or alternatively amend and develop the adopted coding scheme. The significant factor in this approach is timing. By the implementation of post-coding, as opposed to pre-coding (that is to say coding after the data have been entered into the computer rather than before or at the time of data entry) maximum flexibility is maintained.

How to code

If one has the ability to retrieve the form of the original record from the computer, the codes used are virtually irrelevant since the original entries can be used to verify, amend or totally redesign the coding classification scheme initially used. However, it is not particularly desirable to have to amend the coding classification every time one wants to ask another question of the data. Consequently, it is worthwhile taking care and spending adequate time designing a coding classification.

Perhaps the most straightforward of classifications is a simple list of values ordered alphabetically or sequentially, such as displayed in the first two columns of Figure 1. Although relatively easy to apply (such a code could easily be computer generated) its use as an analytical variable is limited. In the case of the example, such a code could be used to identify individual occupations, but would prove to be rather laborious for anything more complicated. However, it is perhaps interesting to note that when the Census Office collected detailed information on occupation for the first time in 1841, the published report took the form of a simple list of occupations in alphabetical order.[10]

Figure 1: Methods of Coding

Landowner	1	Agricultural lab.	1	Shepherd	1	Farmer	111
Shepherd	2	Basket maker	2	Farm servant	1	Tenant farmer	112
Farm servant	3	Basket weaver	3	Tenant farmer	1	Farm bailiff	121
Tenant farmer	4	Cattleman	4	Cattleman	1	Cattleman	131
Grocer	5	Cordwainer	5	Agricultural lab.	1	Shepherd	132
Shoemaker	6	Farm Bailif	6	Farmer	1	Agricul. lab.	141
Cattleman	7	Farmer	7	Farm bailiff	1	Farm servant	142
Agricul. lab.	8	Farm servant	8	Shoemaker	2	Cordwainer	211
Basket maker	9	Grocer	9	Basket maker	2	Shoemaker	212
Basket weaver	10	Landowner	10	Basket weaver	2	Basket maker	221
Farmer	11	Shepherd	11	Cordwainer	2	Basket weaver	222
Shopkeeper	12	Shoemaker	12	Grocer	3	Grocer	311
Cordwainer	13	Shopkeeper	13	Shopkeeper	3	Shopkeeper	312
Farm bailif	14	Tenant farmer	14	Landowner	4	Landowner	411

Most researchers will wish to code similar or related pieces of information together to form groups, by which the data can be examined and patterns of behaviour observed and compared. To return to the example of occupations, one may wish to subdivide the data by different groups of economic activity, or more dangerously, social class. The third column of Figure 1 illustrates a basic economic classification, grouping together agricultural workers, craftsmen, tradesmen and those of independent means. Clearly, depending on the nature of the research being undertaken, one may wish to focus the classification on particular sectors. For instance, if one was interested in studying miners, it may be appropriate to devise a detailed breakdown of this group by, for example, mineral mined, above or underground, cutters, hewers, getters etc., while compressing all other recorded occupations into one or two basic categories. Of course, if post-coding rather than pre-coding is being used then these miscellaneous categories can be expanded at a later date if need be.

A useful variation of the simple group-code classifications is the hierarchical coding scheme used in the final column of Figure 1. The advantage of this system is that it can be used to nest subgroups within groups, thus in the example all agricultural workers can be found in the range 100-199; farmers in the range 110-119; those working with animals 130-139; general workers 140-149; while individual occupation titles can be isolated by referring to the third digit. In this way the code acts like a telescope: viewed at full extension it can be used to focus on detailed information, while collapsed a broader, more overall, perspective is gained. Equally, one could focus on any one of a number of defined hierarchies or subgroups in between the two extremes. In this fashion one could also accumulate codes within the same general category. For example, the last digit of an occupation code could relate not to economic performance but to a suggested skill or training level required for the job, or alternatively, whether the information was recorded in the record unambiguously or inferred from a combination of factors. Clearly, there is much scope for the careful design and use of hierarchical coding classifications.

Lastly, when designing coding schemes it may often prove beneficial to refer to similar work previously undertaken. Clearly if one wishes to compare results with a previous publication then one needs to ensure that the two classification schemes are the same. If the results are to be strictly comparable then one needs to be satisfied that each separate entry has been allocated to exactly the same categories. Due to the failure of many researchers to provide this level of information, it is often impossible to know with certainty that individual entries have been assigned to the 'correct' categories. Along similar lines, it may be appropriate to use classification schemes devised and used by contemporary observers working with the data source. For example, for those working with local communities in the second half of the nineteenth century, to facilitate comparison with broader geographical areas one could adapt one of the occupational classifications used in the published census reports of the period.[11] However, in doing this one must be aware of how and why the original classification was developed. In this respect the occupational classification used by the Census Office in the mid-nineteenth century may prove to be inappropriate for the investigation of economic activities since it was developed primarily to investigate differences in mortality and to calculate occupation specific life expectancy rates rather than to examine economic structures.[12] Equally, the social class classification which was first introduced in the reports of the 1911 census, and has subsequently been much used by historians as well as social scientists working on contemporary populations,[13] was originally devised by eugenists to portray the effects of fertility decline.[14] Consequently, it may not be the most appropriate classification with which to examine interaction between social classes or class conflict.

This points to another problem which, unfortunately, is all too often overlooked by researchers. In designing or applying classificational groupings, the researcher wishes to compare the behaviour of one group with that of another. To return again to the example of social class, in allocating individuals to social classes, the logical assumption is that those within the same class will display common behavioural characteristics. Results or findings are then usually 'averaged' across the class in order to compare one class with another. Yet such practice may hide any variation in behaviour within the class, perhaps between different occupations, with the occupation in one class having more in common with an occupation in a different class rather than those which share the social class category. There is not always a simple answer to these problems, but if maximum flexibility is maintained through the practice of post-coding, then the search for a solution will no doubt be easier.

Reflections

The number of researchers using automated techniques to analyse historical material has grown markedly over the last decade, and continues to grow. Associated with this development is an increased trend for academics to work with secondary datasets, that is, files of data produced by others, for both teaching and research purposes. This practice adds a new dimension to the problems of coding. If pre-coding has been carried out and the codes are all that the secondary researcher has at his disposal, then the data file will only be as good as the codes that have been used. Even if the coding classifications are relatively elaborate, it is doubtful if they would be robust enough to fulfill the requirements of all secondary researchers. It is true that if post-coding has been adopted the situation can always be remedied by returning to the original values and starting the coding process again, yet this may prove to be a rather laborious task for the purposes of a simple calculation. This conundrum points toward two proposals. The first is the need for a central archive where historical material in machine-readable form can be deposited, stored, documented and distributed again in a form suitable to secondary users. Secondly, it would be of use to researchers if certain areas of 'common ground' in relation to coding were established. Standard procedures for the coding of various central types of information could be proposed, perhaps under the guidance of the Association for History and Computing, for researchers to refer to and use as appropriate. The aim of this would not be to restrict or standardise analytical exercises, but rather to facilitate the exchange of data and the comparison of results. In technical terms the age of the punch card is over. It is now time to look to the future and meet the challenge that the 'evil of coding' presents.

Notes

1. K H Jarausch, 'Some Reflections on Coding', in M Thaller (ed.), *Datenbanken und Datenverwaltungssysteme als Werkzeuge Historischer Forschung*, St Katharinen, 1986, pp. 175-8.

2. H J Dyos and A B M Baker, 'The Possibilities of Computerising Census Data', in H J Dyos (ed.), *The Study of Urban History*, London, 1968, pp. 87-112; see also H J Dyos, *Victorian Suburb: A Study of the Growth of Camberwell,* Leicester, 1961.

3. Illustrations of punch cards can be seen in R Floud, *An Introduction to Quantitative Methods for Historians*, London, 2nd edition, 1979, p. 199.

4. Dyos and Baker, *op. cit.*, p. 100. As far as I am aware the cards that were punched for this project still lie in a cupboard at the University of Leicester.

5. N H Nie, *et al.*, *Statistical Package for the Social Sciences*, New York, 2nd. edition, 1975, pp. 21-2.

6. See for example M J Norusis, *SPSS/PC+ For the IBM PC/XT/AT*, Chicago, 1986, pp. B10-B13.

7. R Floud, *op.cit.*, see especially pp. 208-10. However the previous pages of this text appear to adopt a punch card/coding approach.

8. Another problem of coding at the stage of data entry, often only discovered at a later stage of research, if at all, is the allocation of entries to incorrect or inappropriate categories. If the original record entry becomes 'lost' by the substitution of a code then it may prove impossible to ever discover such a mistake, let alone correct it.

9. See examples given in K Schurer, 'Historical Research in the Age of the Computer: an Assessment of the Present Situation', *Historical Social Research (Quantum)*, 36, 1985, pp. 43-54.

10. 1841 Census, *PP 1844, XXVII*, Abstract of the answers and returns made pursuant to Acts 3 and 4 Vic c.99, and 4 Vict c.7, for taking an account of the population of Great Britain; occupation abstract, 1841: Part 1, England and Wales and Islands in the British Seas.

11. A guide to the published census returns can be found in Office of Population Censuses and Surveys, *Guide to Census Reports, Great Britain, 1901-1986*, London, 1977.

12. The Chief Statistical Officer at the Census Office, William Farr, based his work on the seventeenth-century Italian physician Bernard Rainazzini, who believed that mortality and morbidity rates were determined by the materials people worked and came into contact with. In his 'zymotic' theory, Farr suggested that the blood was chemically poisoned by various materials that individuals had regular contact with. See E Higgs, 'The Construction of Statistics: the Struggle for the Occupational Census 1841-1901', in R MacLeod (ed.), *Government and Expertise in Britain*, Cambridge, 1988.

13. See W A Armstrong, 'The Use of Information about Occupation', in E A Wrigley (ed.), *Nineteenth-Century Society: Essays in the Use of Quantitative Methods for the Study of Social Data*, Cambridge, 1972, pp. 191-310; W A Armstrong, *Stability and Change in an English County Town: A Social Study of York 1801-1851*, Cambridge, 1974.

14. S R S Szreter, 'The Genesis of the Registrar General's Social Classification of Occupations', *British Journal of Sociology*, 5, 1984, pp. 522-46.

The Classification of Occupations in Past Time: Problems of Fission and Fusion

Occupational classification is one of the more difficult problems facing the computer-assisted historian who wishes to code and systematically record social data surviving in historical records. Unlike such other variables as age, place of birth, religious affiliation and recorded wealth, occupations are not self-defining, do not fall easily into interval or ordinal scales or categories, and present numerous exceptions, anomalies and downright mysteries, many of which appear to the historian only after he has decided upon his 'definitive' classification scheme. Some, alas, withhold themselves until after all the data have been collected, and the first stack of cross-tabulations or statistics present themselves for analysis. The most easily recognised of these problems are those of 'fusion' — that is, of combining into meaningful, coherent and appropriate categories the occupational labels that come down to us in censuses, directories, probate records and other historical documents. Equally important, but less well-known (certainly less widely admitted), are problems of 'fission' — of splitting into separate categories those people who are, but should not be, designated by identical occupational labels. As the latter are less likely to be anticipated or even recognised by historians who face the question of how best to organise occupational data, I shall deal with them first.

Consider a few examples of men whose occupations are described in nineteenth-century American city directories — contemporary publications that I and many others have used as standard sources for the classification and analysis of the industrialising American workforce. The New York City directory for 1850 uses the term 'cabinetmaker' to describe four men who happen to be mentioned also in the memoir of one Ernest Hagen, a German immigrant who worked in the furniture trade in New York during that year. Using only the city directory, the historian who wished to classify New York's workforce obviously would equate these four men, irrespective of the occupational classification scheme he employed. Yet, Hagen's memoir reveals that the differences between them could hardly have been greater or more fundamental. According to Hagen, Charles Baudouine was a wealthy manufacturer, importer and retailer of French and French-style furniture, who sold his wares from a large and fancy establishment on

Broadway. Henry Weil, who was also quite wealthy, owned a large factory along with retail outlets in New York and New Orleans. A Dohrmann, on the other hand, was the master of a very small shop that made cheap furniture for local retailers, and J Mathew Maier was a journeyman in Dohrmann's shop. Two wealthy capitalists, a small-shop artisan, and a wage-earning skilled worker, all 'cabinetmakers' in the New York City directory of 1850.[1]

Similarly, the very New York directories that listed J C Booth, H L Foster and Edward Fox as 'tailors' included advertisements on behalf of these men that clearly identified them as clothiers, non-manual businessmen who employed and supervised working tailors.[2] The anonymous journeymen who worked for Booth, Foster and Fox cannot be traced into the body of the directories, but in the absence of such specialised terms as 'cutter', 'sewer' or 'presser', it is more than probable that those journeymen who were included in the directories were also described as 'tailors'. Here too, therefore, 'white collar' bosses and 'blue collar' workers are identified by the same occupational label. Even more striking, finally, is the case of Cyrus Alger, who is listed in the Boston directory as a 'founder' — a skilled metal worker in everyone's occupational classification system. In fact, Alger was the principal owner of the South Boston Iron Foundry, and ran this large industrial enterprise from his office in downtown Boston. A very wealthy capitalist, who inherited his share of the business from his father, Alger appears never to have been a working 'founder'.[3]

The problem these examples point to is not that the city directories were peculiarly deficient, but that within the society as a whole the language of occupational differentiation was evolving more slowly than the differentiation of actual tasks and workplace relations. In the artisanal economies that prevailed in New York, Boston and other cities a generation or two before Henry Weil built his furniture factory or Edward Fox opened his elegant custom- and ready-made clothing store, terms such as 'cabinetmaker' and 'tailor' more accurately identified what men did for a living, and no doubt permitted more accurate estimates as to how substantial that living was. Even then, simple occupational labels camouflaged differences of fortune and workplace relations: few pre-industrial sources that I have seen systematically differentiate between masters and journeymen, for example, but the problem would grow particularly acute during the period in which work, ownership and employment were being radically transformed by industrialisation. Public officials, printers and others, who compiled what we now regard as the basic source materials of the early industrial era, simply lacked the vocabulary (and, apparently, the sense of a mandate for taxonomic invention) to describe the many new and fundamentally altered roles and relations within the industrialising economy. More or less successful efforts to generate more accurate occupational taxonomies are visible in American sources from around 1870, but we must not imagine that the problem has ever been fully resolved.[4] Before, during, and after the industrial revolution, in America and no doubt in most other countries as well, occupational data homogenise where they should differentiate, giving us atoms that badly need splitting (for peaceful purposes, of course, and without radioactive waste).

How, then, should these atoms be split? Memoirs such as Ernest Hagen's are lamentably rare, but data linkage of other sorts appears to be the only means of probing beneath occupational labels to more complex realities. A significant question, therefore, is the degree to which different historical sources can be combined to yield more precise information than either does standing alone. Manuscript census schedules, tax assessment rolls, probate records and membership lists of trade societies, are examples of sources that can help provide useful information about large numbers of individuals who appear on occupational lists. Linkage can also be made within a single source. Many of the city directories that list individuals and their occupations and addresses, contain supplemental lists of businesses and proprietors, arranged by business category. Clyde and Sally Griffen, in their excellent study of occupational mobility in the nineteenth-century American city of Poughkeepsie, New York, made good use of these business listings, comparing them to the body of the directory to differentiate between employers and employees in Poughkeepsie's trades.[5] The manuscript census schedules are also both an occupational list and a corresponding array of other variables, some of which can help illuminate the meaning of individual occupational labels. A few of the American census manuscripts list amounts of real and personal property, which can help differentiate a Cyrus Alger from his much less wealthy employees. All (since 1850) place individuals within their households, and list their ages, information from which employment status can sometimes be inferred.

The reliability of this kind of data linkage, either between sources or between variables of a single source, is, however, often suspect. The Griffens may have been able to separate owners from wage-earners in the small city of Poughkeepsie, but in larger American cities the directory listings of businesses and business proprietors seem to have been less complete; hence, it is less certain that those tradesmen listed in the body of the directory but not in the business list were employees. Where a residual method of this sort is used, the completeness of the secondary list is essential, but how many such lists exist? Is there a substantial city in which business listings identify *all* the city's businesses, or in which *all* the city's skilled wage earners appear on the surviving rolls of journeymen's trades' societies? Similar problems arise from the shortcomings of some of the most relevant census variables. Using reported property values to sort out large from small businessmen, or employers from employees, is a particularly risky business. While using the manuscript census schedules of 1860 to map the households of a Philadelphia neighbourhood, for example, I encountered two apparently propertyless cabinetmakers, neighbours on a street otherwise filled with merchants, lawyers and wealthy widows. I happened to know from a contemporary description of Philadelphia industries (not a complete description of course) that these two men were partners in a large manufacturing firm; like Charles Baudouine and Henry Weil of New York, they were industrialists, not artisans.[6] The absence of entries for real and personal property was an error, and, as it turns out, a quite characteristic one. In Philadelphia, more than 30 per cent of the men listed on this census as merchants, nearly 40 per cent listed as attorneys, and fully half of those listed as bankers, reported no property of any kind, real or personal, to the census enumerators. There is no reason to believe that the proportions of missing entries would be any lower for propertied master artisans, or for industrialists and other non-manual businessmen who happened to be identified on the census with artisanal occupational titles. How, then, can we tell which of the apparently propertyless were misrepresented businessmen, and which were workingmen?

In some settings, taxonomic problems of this sort may be less acute, and data for resolving them may be more readily available. The data describing the populations of highly specialised industrial towns and districts, for example, no doubt reflect their simpler occupational structures and less ambiguous class divisions, and I have already suggested that successful taxonomic 'fission' is more likely in small cities than in larger ones. Rural districts for which complete land ownership and tenancy records survive offer the possibility of accurately distinguishing between freehold farmers, tenant farmers and farm labourers (all of whom, in America census data, are often represented simply as 'farmers'). Whatever the setting, however, the lessons learned from questioning the meanings of historical occupational terminology are twofold. First, one must take the trouble to make those significant distinctions that are obscured by surviving occupational terms. And second, one must recognise, work within and be candid about the limits of terms that, owing to incomplete or faulty supplementary data, do not give way to closer analysis; those atoms that refuse to be split.

The problems of occupational 'fusion' derive in part from those of 'fission', for the obvious reason that meaningful categories require, at a minimum, meaningful units. However, even the fortunate researcher who possesses those meaningful units must address certain issues that are inherent in the very process of classification, and that are particularly nettlesome in the classification of occupational data. The first of these is the issue of equivalence. With respect to the issues being raised in the analysis itself, are the occupations placed within a single category sufficiently alike? Is anything gained from their combination? How much is lost? Do the gains outweigh the losses? Some occupations would appear to possess a natural categorical affinity; doctors and lawyers are both high-status and high-income professionals, in the contemporary world at least, while shoemakers and tailors, in pre-industrial and early industrial societies, were small-shop, consumer goods artisans. Labourers, cartmen, sailors and a variety of unskilled workers who earned low wages are usually grouped together with considerable confidence in the lowest occupational category. But were all professionals, or all artisans, or even all unskilled workers sufficiently alike to form categories that do not misrepresent social reality? This question becomes more pointed when one considers the many occupations that do not seem to fit so neatly with others: school teachers, surgeons, harbour pilots, jobbers and various specialised manual workers within industrialising trades are among those that present special difficulties of equivalence during long periods of history. Even fairly small and seemingly homogeneous populations are replete with these difficult occupations, which, depending on their numbers, can seriously confuse the meaning of the occupational categories to which the impatient historian assigns them.

The other side of the issue of equivalence is that of distinctiveness. With respect to the issues being raised, are the occupations placed within different categories sufficiently distinct? Historians may be tempted, for example, to apply contemporary distinctions between skilled, semi-skilled and unskilled workers to past societies. But were the economic and social distances between the occupations that form these categories great enough to justify the categories themselves? Both of these issues, equivalence and distinctiveness, may be understood with reference to the basic components of the statistical analysis of variance, which, as most readers of this essay will know, is based on the ratio between 'within variation' and 'between variation'. As in the analysis of variance, a good result is one that minimises the variation within each category, and maximises the variation between categories. In the language I have used, it is one that maximises the equivalence of occupations within each category, while maximising the distinctiveness of the categories from one another. My reference to the analysis of variance, incidentally, is not entirely analogical. If the principle of occupational classification is explicitly that of some interval-scale variable (average annual income, for example) this statistical measure is the appropriate test for various schemes of classification.

The dangers of resolving the issues of equivalence and distinctiveness by statistical means are obvious enough, and are compounded by a third issue, that of mutability. Most historical analyses extend over time, and the longer the span of time that is examined through a particular classification scheme, the greater is the danger that social reality will be distorted by the changing meanings of occupational labels. For occupations do change, often without corresponding changes in taxonomy (the complex evolution of modes of production and distribution, characterised by innovation, survival, and the co-existence of different modes at any one time, is, indeed, a major source of the 'fission' problem discussed earlier). 'Shoemaker' in the era of artisanal production meant one thing, the same term early in the age of highly subdivided and partly mechanised shoe production (when 'shoemaker' was still used to refer to those who worked on shoes in manufactories) meant quite another. 'Surgeon' has travelled from skilled trade to high-status, high-income professional over the course of two centuries. Many occupations, surely the majority of those that involve or once involved skilled manual work, have changed in significant ways that are not reflected, or that only gradually became reflected, in occupational taxonomy. It is obvious that an occupational classification scheme devised with reference to a particular workforce of the year 1800 cannot be applied without alteration to the workforce of the same country or city in 1900. What is less obvious, perhaps, is that the necessary alterations extend not only to the incorporation of new occupational terms, but also to the reconsideration of unchanging terms that no longer refer to the same kinds of work or rewards.

A final issue is the appropriateness of the classification scheme to the analysis it is intended to serve; or, the comprehensiveness of the scheme if it is meant to be a more general tool, serving more than one type of analysis. Occupations can be classified in different ways: by functional economic sectors, by different types of manual and non-manual work, by measures of differing economic rewards, by levels of prestige as reported by questionnaire respondents, to name some of the most prominent. These different methods can produce very different results; poorly paid clerks, for example, who might be placed in the second highest category of a four- or five-category scheme based on types of manual and non-manual work, would be placed in a significantly lower category of a scheme based on income or wealth. As in all types of research, the questions being asked should shape the tools being forged to provide the answers. But how can this tool be made to perform quite different tasks? This question leads me at last to a concrete suggestion concerning the problem of occupational 'fusion'. Historians who classify occupations for different kinds of analysis should maintain flexibility in their classification systems, so that the system can be altered, even after all the data have been collected, to suit the analysis. Once recognised as a strategy, this becomes a technical matter of multi-digit occupational coding, wherein each occupational label is assigned a unique code, to which is added additional digits representing variant classification strategies. The latter typically are introduced at the outset, as data are collected, but they can be added later as well, and ought to be, as the researcher learns more about the occupations themselves.

Others have discussed these technical strategies in greater detail than I wish to here.[7] I will conclude instead by reiterating the more fundamental observation that occupational data, from most times and places, come down to us in a less perfect form than we would prefer, or than we generally recognise in our haste to get on with the job. Yet, we must remind ourselves that part of the job of serious and responsible historical research consists of just this recognition of the difficulties and limits of historical evidence. And if much of the rest of it consists of wringing meaning out of evidence despite its imperfections, then the classification of occupations must be seen not as technical preparation for research, but as part of the substance of our ongoing historical inquiry.

Notes

1. Elizabeth A Ingerman, (ed.), 'Personal Experiences of an Old New York Cabinetmaker,' *Antiques*, 84, 1963, pp. 576-80; *Doggett's The New York City Directory for 1850-51*, New York, 1850.
2. *Doggett's The New York Directory for 1851-52*, New York, 1851.
3. *The Directory of the City of Boston*, Boston, 1850; Thomas C Simonds, *History of South Boston*, Boston, 1857, pp. 251-60.
4. Margo Anderson Conk, *The United States Census and Labor Force Change: A History of Occupation Statistics, 1870-1940*, Ann Arbor, 1978.
5. Clyde and Sally Griffen, *Natives and Newcomers: The Ordering of Opportunity in Mid-Nineteenth-Century Poughkeepsie*, Cambridge, Mass., 1978.
6. Edwin T Freedley, *Philadelphia and its Manufacturers...*, Philadelphia, 1858, p. 274.
7. Perhaps the most elaborate application of this strategy is described in Theodore Hershberg and Robert Dockhorn, 'Occupational Classification', *Historical Methods Newsletter*, 9, 1976, pp. 59-98.

IV.
Teaching

13. *Frances Blow*

Seeking Patterns, Making Meanings: Using Computerised Sources in Teaching History in Secondary Schools

Primary source material is more widely used in secondary school classrooms now than it has ever been. The 'New History', a movement to promote the use of such source material which began in the 1970s, was fostered by the Schools History 13-16 Project[1] and many publishers of history text books, and became part of the establishment with the definition of the national criteria for history in GCSE.[2] The national criteria for history which apply to all the examining boards and all the syllabuses offered for examination at sixteen-plus include the following: 'All candidates will be expected to show the skills necessary to study a wide variety of historical evidence which should include both primary and secondary written sources, statistical and visual material, artefacts, text books and orally transmitted information.'[3]

This new status for primary source material in schools was not a permeation down of the gobbet[4] tradition from undergraduate courses. The gobbet functioned as a prompt to an exposition on the context of the extract — the period, the events, the people and ideas referred to in the gobbet. By contrast, the source movement in school teaching of history was intended to develop pupils' knowledge of how historians work and the processes they employ in order to make sense of raw historical material. It was also seen as a means by which children could discover the nature of history, how it is constructed — indeed perceive history as a construct, not as a set of given and unquestionable truths. Since this sort of activity had previously been restricted to undergraduates or even to postgraduates, such a venture was criticised as ambitious and as being too difficult for school children. However, it was also welcomed as enabling teachers and pupils to make sense of differing accounts of the past and to distinguish history with its particular methodology from English literature which also often contains stories set in the past. That children could cope with this approach to history teaching was proved by the consistently growing numbers taking the Schools History Project exam at sixteen-plus and the acceptance of this methodology by the GCSE exam boards.[5]

When micros moved into schools in the UK in the 1970s the possibilities of putting source material into computers were quickly recognised. In particular, teachers readily identified the advantages of entering into computers information that came in the form of lists. This data was tedious to read and difficult to assimilate in its original form. The computer's ability to sort and count could justify its use. Many, however, had major reservations about putting passages of *text* on the micro screen. It was felt to be easier to read print on a still page of paper than on a flickering monitor that might also be coloured. What advantage could be gained from putting a book of source material into a micro? Certainly simulations contained text, but usually text that was minimal and was the basis for immediate action — decision making. Computerising text in this way significantly altered its length, appearance and quality and did not involve the reading of extensive and continuous prose.

However, an alternative type of program has emerged recently that contains a variety of source materials — including passages from documents and descriptions of non-documentary sources. These sources are embedded in a program structure that enables pupils to access them in a variety of sequences. That sequence is determined by the pupils' own lines of inquiry. The order, therefore, in which the information is acquired is not predetermined and will not necessarily in itself constitute a narrative. Such a program enables students to simulate an historian's investigation and so can assist students in making the transition from perceiving a source as information to using it as evidence. In this transition two major elements are combined: first, the student has to master certain skills of source interpretation which will include evaluation for reliability and consistency and the ability to infer and to cross refer; second, the student has to develop an understanding of causal connections and the techniques of constructing an explanation.

The order in which information is presented influences perceptions of its meaning and significance. Helping pupils to perceive this is not easy. They have to learn that it is possible to construct differing accounts of events depending on which sources they select as relevant, reliable and important. The ways in which a source is interpreted, the connections they make within a source and between sources, all determine the outcome. Shuffling the sources into different orders requires pupils to examine more closely the internal detail and to evaluate critically the information for connections and patterns.

In this context the computer can assist students directly to develop their conceptual thinking in history in at least four ways.

i) When the information is 'hidden' in the computer program, pupils cannot be certain in advance of what they will find in an investigation. They cannot know what they may discover in terms either of content or kind. The source might be a description of an artefact, an extract from a letter, a quotation from a Royal Commission, a statement made in court, reported gossip or hearsay. Thus this type of source-based program differs from the more common data retrieval programs which contain information given in standardised lists such as census returns where particular *details* may be unknown in advance of a search but the *format* is likely to be familiar.

ii) The sequence of the revelation of sources will not be known in advance. The arrangement of the sources within the program cannot be seen by the students in the way they can obtain an overview in a textbook with its chapter headings, side headings, indexes and contents pages.

iii) In playing such a program, pupils can shuffle the material they acquire, juxtapose texts, create patterns, turn back and review sources in the light of subsequent discoveries and new possibilities, and identify gaps in the patterns and information. This process in itself can generate new hypotheses and views of what pupils have found.

iv) The teaching strategy is essentially one of drip feed, in contrast to the total immersion strategy which can obscure and impede comprehension even at postgraduate level. Piecemeal access to data can aid assimilation, encouraging repeated reflection as each new piece of information is discovered. Does this fit with what we already know, with what we currently believe? Does this information require us to revise completely our view of events? What should we do with the information if it doesn't fit at all? This strategy can promote a range of cross-referencing skills. At the simplest level the student may regard the new source as something simply to be 'added on' and merely check for contradiction with what is already known. At a higher level the student considers the possibilities of revising previously held theories even to the point of acknowledging that earlier ideas might have been completely wrong.

This approach to software design can be illustrated by a brief description of two programs produced by the combined Computers in the Curriculum — Schools History 13-16 Project.[6] They contain different approaches to the use of source material: Godfrey is based on documentary sources of the seventeenth century; Shallow Hill is based on sources of a non-documentary kind which are accessed in the form of descriptions of archaeological finds. Both programs were designed by practising history teachers and have been used extensively in secondary schools with pupils across the ability range, aged 11-19, both during development and after publication.

Godfrey is based on the mystery surrounding the death of Sir Edmund Berry Godfrey whose body was found in London in October 1678. He had been strangled and then run through with his own sword. Three men were then charged with his murder and subsequently hanged. Six months later they were exonerated of any responsibility for Godfrey's death. Since the seventeenth century historians have attempted to explain Godfrey's death, but no single explanation has been accepted as fully satisfactory. Godfrey was a Protestant magistrate; it was to him that Titus Oates made his deposition concerning a Catholic plot to kill the king, Charles II. This context of religious and political intrigue, combined with the personal and financial circumstances of Godfrey, suggests several possible motives and explanations for his death. The topic thus lends itself to a consideration of the ambiguity of sources.

The computer program offers four initial motives for Godfrey's death for student investigation: murder for revenge, murder for political reasons, murder for profit, and suicide disguised as murder. These provide a basis for an initial response, but progress through the program encourages pupils to consider additional possibilities and to advance alternative theories.

To embark on an investigation of Godfrey's death the students must enter a maze. As they explore the maze they discover clues or sources that they must interpret either as evidence to support their theory or as simple information. The maze is used as an analogy for historians' lines of enquiry or research. They frequently will not know whether a line of enquiry will produce the information that will enable the initial thesis to be tested. Historians may find information unexpectedly, causing a radical reassessment of the line of enquiry. The exact location of the information may not be known and the order in which relevant data will be found can rarely be predetermined. Research can also lead to dead ends if the evidence desired does not exist, cannot be found, or is not available. In all these different ways historical research can often feel like floundering about in a maze!

The point at which the students will enter the maze is determined by their selection from the given range of motives. While the sources located in each part of the maze are loosely linked to the selected motive, what the students actually find will be determined by the route they choose through the maze. Many routes are possible. The sources hidden in the maze are of varying kinds and derived from primary and secondary sources. They include extracts from House of Lords records, constables' reports, historians' accounts, medical evidence from the seventeenth century, and twentieth-century doctors' analysis. (The latter concludes from the detailed medical evidence of the seventeenth century that Godfrey could not have committed suicide; the marks on his throat were too low for him to have hanged himself.) The longest source contains 34 words; most are shorter.

Information once found is pulled out into the student's information bank in the computer, which can be reviewed at any time.

Observations of pupils and teachers working with Godfrey testify to the capacity of the evidence arranged in this program to promote heated discussion among the groups at the keyboard over differing versions of events. The program does not confirm one explanation as being the truth; instead it offers reasons which make it difficult to accept any explanation as the conclusive one. A key aspect of Godfrey therefore lies in the class session following the lesson with the computers. Pupils should be urged to choose the solution that seems to them the most probable in the circumstances. Otherwise they might conclude that 'you cannot decide' and that historians are fence sitters, rather than scholars and students attempting to provide an answer even if it is only an approximation of the truth.

One of the difficulties of Godfrey is actually reconstructing the sequence of events as well as deciding who killed the magistrate and why. A different type of problem is posed by Shallow Hill, which uses the device of retrieval and ordering of data in another way as an aid to determining meaning. This program is a simulation of an archaeological excavation of a fictitious site which is loosely based on the Iron Age hill fort of Maiden Castle. A fictitious site was chosen so that it was possible to include a range of 'typical' finds and problems for teaching points. The aim of the program was to introduce pupils to the types of non-documentary sources used by historians and their methods of interpretation of relics, not to teach pupils about archaeologists' specialised techniques. Students are told that Shallow Hill is a valuable historic site about to be destroyed in the construction of a new motorway, and that they have only 30 days to find out as much as they can about the site. Their days are used up as they dig trenches; the number of days spent is determined by the depth of the trench they choose to make. The program is so constructed that it is not possible to uncover the whole site within the time available. Pupils are required to tackle the problems of handling two kinds of incomplete information: sources that are incomplete because they have been partially destroyed over time and sources that will only represent a sample of the total available.

The relics they will find as they excavate the site are of various kinds, including remnants of animal and human bone, pieces of pottery, shells, jets of iron, burnt fragments of wood, shaped stone, carved objects and discolourations of the soil. In the program that was sent for trials some of the soil markings were described in the program as post holes. Some teachers wrote in to say pupils were puzzled as to how they could dig up a 'hole', so the description of a post hole rapidly became 'marks containing fragments of wood arranged in a circle of ten meters diameter'. These finds are located at different levels corresponding to different periods: Bronze Age, Iron Age, Roman period. Some of the finds are displaced so that pupils will be faced with some problems of dating their finds. They classify their finds in terms both of kind — for example as evidence of a furnace, a refuse pit, housing or defensive structure — and of date. The pupils' classification is then recorded on the plan of the site on the computer screen. The computer does not respond to their interpretation; it simply records their analysis as it is made.

Current classroom research is yielding detailed information on the nature of pupils' response to source handling in Shallow Hill.[7] Most pupils choose to explore a section of the site down to bedrock rather than to excavate one level across a number of sections of the site. They thus encounter cross sections through time and a *portion* of a set of evidence. Indeed the program is a valuable aid in helping pupils to learn the significance of *sets* of evidence. A program that might appear to encourage pupils to see the historian as a treasure hunter in fact obliges them to realise the limited amount of information that can be gleaned from the isolated clue. Pupils begin to perceive the importance of the *context* of a find for determining its meaning. That context could be the level or location of a find, or it could be the other finds that are adjacent to it.

Pupils also have to tackle problems of ambiguity of a source. Is this discolouration of the soil evidence of a domestic hearth, a furnace, a refuse pit, a cemetery? Cross-referencing to comparable discoveries in other parts of the site and to accounts of excavations on comparable sites (provided on students' leaflets) supplies a basis for making a judgment.

Depending in part on ability, in part on previous teaching, pupils begin to form and test hypotheses about the site. Selection of areas of the site for investigation becomes coordinated rather than random as pupils attempt to confirm or reject a theory. An integral part of the learning process in source interpretation is the review and revision of ideas as new information is acquired. The program facilitates this by allowing pupils at any time to call up the screen that displays their analysis to date, and to change that analysis at the press of a key.

Shallow Hill highlights in a very simple way to pupils and teachers the importance of the ordering of sources to create patterns and how the order depends on the attribution of meaning to any single source. As the interpretation of individual finds mounts up on the screen, any inconsistencies and irregularities in the pattern begin to emerge. Is a Bronze Age gateway in the middle of an Iron Age village likely? Does something that appears to cross two squares on the site plan and which is classified as a Roman house in one square and a Roman temple in the adjacent square merit a review? The whole exercise prompts pupils to consider the meaning of the total picture as well as of the individual parts, and to root their speculation about elements within a contextual framework.

Professional historians have a vast knowledge base that enables them to attribute significance to any new data they acquire. Pupils aged between 11 and 19 have very incomplete and partial pictures of the past as well as of human nature, social organisations and political and economic systems. Equipping them — by means of programs such as Godfrey and Shallow Hill — with the skills of source handling while they learn about particular periods in the past can promote mature conceptual understanding and discourage the acceptance of simplistic views of how and why things happen in human affairs. The aim of history teaching must be to convey to pupils the meaning of the past, not merely a narrative. They need to consider not simply what happened but why, and how do we know, and what basis have we for saying so. Therefore our teaching strategies must encourage pupils to seek patterns and not provide them with ready-made accounts. They must enable pupils to see that meanings are the products of patterns and that there is a major distinction between a chronicle and an explanatory account. Of course, it is possible to teach in this way without a computer. Nonetheless, appropriate software can facilitate pupils' discovery of these distinctions.

Notes

1. See, for example, D Shemilt, *History 13 — 16 Evaluation Study*, London, 1980.
2. GCSE stands for General Certificate of Secondary Education. It is the main state examination for pupils at age 16.
3. Department of Education and Science, *The General Certificate of Secondary Education: The National Criteria: History*, London, 1985.
4. A gobbet in this context is a short extract of text, often from primary historical sources. A selection of gobbets from set texts are frequently included in honours degree exam papers, and students are required to demonstrate their knowledge and understanding of such texts.
5. All the English examination boards for GCSE include examinations for the Schools 13-16 Project.
6. Both Godfrey and Shallow Hill were published by Longman Micro Software, London in 1986. The Computers in the Curriculum Project is based at King's College, University of London and has produced educational software for teaching languages, maths, sciences and the humanities since 1973.
7. These classroom investigations were undertaken in preparation for the INSET Guide, S Bennett, A Tapsfield and F Blow (eds.), *Using Computer Simulations in History*, London, 1989. See also: Blow, 'Evaluation of CAL in the Humanities', in *The Proceedings of the European Conference on Information Technology*, Oxford, 1986 and Blow, 'Evaluation of Computer Assisted Learning in History', in W A Kent and R Lewis (eds.), *Computer Assisted Learning in the Humanities and Social Sciences*, Oxford, 1987.

The Microcomputer in the History Classroom: Opportunities and Challenges for Pupils and Teachers

The availability of the microcomputer presents opportunities and challenges for both pupil and teacher in the history classroom. In this article these dual themes will be developed by drawing on the experience of history teachers in Glasgow Division of Strathclyde Region.[1] All the examples cited draw on classroom practice in history departments in schools in Glasgow.[2]

It seems most appropriate to start with the pupils and to illustrate some of the opportunities and challenges which the availability of the microcomputer in the history classroom presents to them — although they may not see it in these terms, of course. One effect of recent curricular developments is to increase pupils' responsibility for their own learning. This applies in history as much as in other areas of the curriculum. This new emphasis does not mean that the teacher ceases to have an important and active role to play in the classroom, but it does encourage pupils to be more actively involved in their own learning. The microcomputer has an obvious relevance here.

Imagine a school in one of the large peripheral council estates of Glasgow, a school where attendance, motivation and academic performance are perhaps below average. A small group of S2[3] pupils leaves the history classroom and moves to an adjacent room where they load and run Into The Unknown,[4] a simulation based on sixteenth-century voyages of discovery. They refer to information on screen, on a wall chart, and on information sheets. They discuss the situation or problem, reach some agreement and key in the appropriate move or answer. This continues for 10 or 15 minutes. This part of the work complete, the group returns to the classroom and another takes its place.

Although many teachers will have some reservations about the use of such historical simulations in the teaching of history, from the pupils' point of view they provide fascinating opportunities and challenges.[5] Simulations such as Into The Unknown and similar programs provide opportunities for purposeful classroom discussion and decision making. The pupils are often in control of the pace of their learning. In addition, the pupils are gaining an insight into the fact that in the past, as in the present, things happened because of decisions taken by individuals and groups.

Of course it is not only the use of simulations which presents opportunities and challenges for pupils while helping them to take greater responsibility for their own learning. A few schools have used word-rocessing packages with pupils. For one small group of pupils there seem to be particular advantages in this — the pupils who have great difficulty writing and for whom the task of holding a pen or pencil and forming letters is a very demanding one with results not commensurate with the effort. A simple word-processing package can change all this. Of course effort is still needed; the pupils do not have keyboard skills. That's the challenge. But mistakes are easily rectified, and the end result on paper is perfectly legible, an enormous incentive to the pupils. Self esteem is increased and motivation for learning is maintained or perhaps increased. That's the opportunity.

Closely allied to the new emphasis on increased responsibility to the pupils for their own learning is an increasing awareness of the importance of resource-based learning — the provision of a range of resources with which the pupils can work, perhaps independently, perhaps in groups, in the history classroom. Imagine another school in another peripheral estate. In the history classroom pupils are engaged in a variety of activities — some are using the class resource centre to find books relevant to the examination course which they are following, some are working on the microcomputer, perhaps on a database, perhaps on a simulation, perhaps typing in some notes or a report on a piece of work they are undertaking. Let's take a closer look at the pupils working at the microcomputer. The pupils are becoming familiar with the scope of an 1851 census datafile using the Quest[6] data handling package. They have in front of them a simple exercise to help introduce them to the fields and the nature of the material in each record. They are being asked to imagine that they are living in 1851 in a street included in the census; they have to write a letter to a friend in which they say something about their neighbours and their families. The pupils work on this as a group: they select appropriate relevant information; they communicate it in writing to others; they become familiar with the datafile and with the census.

It is now appropriate to emphasise the challenges that the pupils face. This time the example is drawn from a small school in the West End of the city. It is a school which appeals to parents, for some choose to send their children there, rather than to their own neighbourhood school. It is however a comprehensive school and in general its intake is fairly mixed socially and academically. An S4[7]examination class is being introduced to databases and in particular to the census datafile for 1851 for the Gorbals area of Glasgow, a socially mixed district which had not yet descended into its notorious early twentieth-century decay. The pupils are studying the topic 'Britain from Waterloo to the Great Exhibition' for the Scottish 'O'

Grade examination in the Scottish Certificate of Education,[8] so they have important contextual background about urban conditions, life expectancy, employment and migration. They have also been given some information about the census and about the Gorbals area of Glasgow.

The task which they have been set is to test some simple hypotheses against the evidence of the datafile. Some prompts are given, but the pupils are encouraged to come up with their own ideas to try out — about the size of families, the number of old people, the number of young people working, the proportion of the population coming from Ireland and so on. Working in pairs, they carry out the searches. They note the results and run other searches. At the end of the work they are given the opportunity to present their findings to the rest of the class. A simple questionnaire at the end of the short series of lessons clearly revealed that the pupils had enjoyed the work; some of this enjoyment came from the novelty of the experience. But the replies to the questions revealed more: pupils had been given a new insight into history, their own knowledge had been challenged, they had been made to think of history in a different way, they had been engaged in a new type of activity. They were being given the challenge of thinking more directly about the nature of historical knowledge. Some pupils were beginning to ask important evaluative questions about the reliability of the census and about the reliability of the textbooks.

Other examples could be given concerning work in relation to the Certificate of Sixth Year Studies[9] in secondary school or to the historical input into environmental studies in primary school. What then, of the opportunities and challenges which the microcomputer presents for the history teacher? The first challenge is easy to describe — find a microcomputer! Some history departments in Glasgow secondary schools — just a few — have their own microcomputer or share a system with the other social subjects. Others have to borrow or beg a machine. Indeed it seems to be increasingly difficult to borrow a computer from colleagues in school, partly because of the growing uptake of computer studies, partly because head teachers prefer the microcomputers to be in a secure lab or suite. This arrangement may be ideal for reasons of security, but is not necessarily the most appropriate one for the history teacher. Problems of access to microcomputers present a Catch 22 situation; history departments can only make the case for increased use of the microcomputer if they can gain some classroom experience in the first place. Experience suggests that embarking on the use of the microcomputer in history in the computer lab is not the best approach.

The second challenge for the history teacher might be just as great — or even greater — than the first. More than any other educational innovation the microcomputer requires the teacher to become a learner. This can be a useful if frightening change of role. The teacher who has never used a microcomputer usually comes to it with a number of fears, the greatest being that of damaging the microcomputer beyond repair. Once that fear is overcome - which it can be quite quickly — the teacher has to learn quite a number of new skills. Running simulations is technically one of the easiest applications and therefore a good starting point. Mastering a data handling system or word processing package can be quite demanding. There have to be support services and training available to help the teachers overcome these hurdles. For those providing such support and training, one satisfaction is that the teachers usually genuinely feel that they have learned some new skills.

A third challenge is that use of the microcomputer might, as the examples used earlier suggest, necessitate changes in classroom methodology and organisation. For the teacher used to a teacher-centered approach the move to an approach which involves group work, resource-based learning, or increased responsibility by pupils, can be unsettling. Conversely there is some evidence from the experience of history departments in the Glasgow Division of Strathclyde Region's Education Department that the use of the microcomputer can facilitate the introduction of such approaches. Obviously the use of a single microcomputer in a classroom or an adjacent room presents fewer problems than a bank of a dozen computers in a lab. It is for that reason that most of the departments which have ventured into the use of microcomputers have done so with single machines.

A further challenge is to integrate the microcomputer-based work into the history course. All the advice — and all the local experience — indicate that the use of the microcomputer in the history classroom is most successful when its use is integrated into the course work. The earlier example about the use of the census datafile with the examination class is a good illustration of this, for the success of the microcomputer-based work was dependent on the course work which had preceded it. The pupils needed to have some background knowledge of the period to be able to pose relevant questions and to make full use of the information obtained from the datafile.

One further challenge is worth highlighting. In time, the history teacher will need to confront the issues of progression and continuity in the use of microcomputers in the history classroom. There are several aspects to this. One relates to liaison between the primary and secondary sectors of education. Already many primary schools are using microcomputers in the environmental studies area of the curriculum. Primary school pupils are using simulations and databases; some, even very young, primary children are being introduced to elementary word processing. These pupils will transfer to the secondary school with certain expectations; they will expect to be able to continue and to develop their use of the microcomputer not just in computing classes but across the curriculum, including history. Likewise within the school history department thought will need to be given to progression in the use of the microcomputer.

There will be questions about the size of datafiles, the complexity of individual records, and the stage at which pupils should start creating datafiles rather than merely interrogating them.

What then of the opportunities which the microcomputer presents for the history teacher? Obviously these are many, some of which can be deduced from the examples of classroom practice already quoted. The greatest opportunity arises from the fact that the use of the microcomputer in the history classroom seems to be in accord with some of the more general changes which are taking place in history courses.

The major current development in Scotland is the introduction of the new Standard Grade course to replace the Ordinary Grade course.[10] This new course is being phased in from August 1988 with the first examination in 1990. An important feature of the new course is that all pupils following the course need to carry out an 'historical investigation'. Briefly, each pupil is required to work on a topic — probably quite limited in its scope — which relates to the history of Scotland or an area or community within Scotland. Work for this involves pupils planning the investigation by, for example, defining the purposes of the investigation; locating appropriate resources and recording relevant information; and finally presenting the findings of the investigation. The historical investigation presents a golden opportunity for teachers and pupils alike to use the microcomputer in the history classroom. Of particular relevance for the historical investigation will be datafiles. These can contain a large amount of information from which a variety of different questions and issues can arise. Combined with other material the datafile offers great opportunities. The potential of datafiles for the historical investigation in Standard Grade has encouraged the education officer at Strathclyde Regional Archives and myself to work on the creation of a number of different datafiles.[11] The biggest project is the census database. This involves the creation of datafiles for 1851 and 1881 for a sample of communities throughout Strathclyde Region. Other projects include the creation of a datafile on the trade in and out of one of the Clyde docks early this century and a datafile on those applying for poor relief in one of the local parishes in 1867. In every case the datafile has been accompanied by a collection of documentary evidence and background historical notes and in some instances audio-visual material.

It is impossible to tackle the theme of the challenges and opportunities presented for the pupil and the teacher in the history classroom without taking a look into the future. Obviously better hardware and software would be a great advantage. For history and the social subjects in general the case needs to be argued for systems with better graphics and larger capacities than the BBC or the BBC Master. 'Content free' software[12] needs to be investigated to assess its potential for use in the history classroom. The whole area of centralised datafiles accessed by telephone link is an exciting one, but at present there appear to be few developments which are directly relevant to school history. The areas of interactive video and CD-ROM are also alluring but largely untapped. Clearly there is considerable potential for schools in these technologies in conjunction with photographs, film, industrial archaeology, historic buildings and archives.

There is absolutely no doubt that the microcomputer offers tremendous opportunities for history pupils and teachers. Perhaps the biggest challenge will be to maintain and expand current initiatives in the use of the microcomputer in history teaching in order to make the case to those in authority for better provision of software and hardware in the future.

Notes

1. Without the pioneering work of these teachers this article could not have been written.
2. All the examples are based on the use of the BBC microcomputer.
3. In Scotland pupils transfer from primary school to secondary school around the age of 12. The first year of secondary education is designated S1, the second S2 and so on.
4. Into The Unknown is produced by Tressell Publications.
5. See the essay by Frances Blow in this volume and the works cited here.
6. Quest is produced by Hertfordshire Education Authority's Advisory Unit for Microtechnology in Education.
7. See note 3 above.
8. In S1 and S2 pupils generally follow a common course. At the end of S2 they are offered a choice of the subjects which they will study in S3 and S4. For each subject the courses are based on a syllabus prescribed by the Scottish Examination Board. Until the mid 1980s the courses led to the examination on the Ordinary Grade of the Scottish Certificate of Education, broadly comparable to the 'O' Level of the General Certificate of Education in England. From the mid 1980s the 'O' grade courses and examinations are being replaced in a phased development by Standard Grade courses and examinations of the Scottish Certificate of Education, broadly comparable to the General Certificate of Secondary Education in England. Both the 'O' Grade and 'S' grade examinations are taken towards the end of S4 when pupils are around 16 years of age.
9. In Scottish schools in S5 pupils can follow one-year courses leading to examinations on the Higher Grade of the Scottish Certificate of Education. Awards in Higher Grade examinations are the normal qualification for entry to higher education. In S6 pupils can follow courses leading to the award of the Certificate of Sixth Year Studies.
10. See note 8 above.
11. The creation of these datasets has been described by Alison Gray in 'The Creation and Documentation of Teaching Datasets', *Computing and History Today*, 4, 1988, which is based on another paper given at the March 1988 Glasgow conference.
12. I have in mind the potential of a range of software such as Archaeology (Cambridgeshire Software House), Microtext (Acornsoft), applications of HyperCard on Apple Macintosh microcomputers and even the programming language Prolog.

15 *Robert K Munro*

The Future of the Past: The Use of the Multisource Visual Database to Aid Historical Understanding

The computer has been available as an educational resource for only a relatively short time, but already it has exerted a significant impact on the teaching and learning of many subjects. Historians have responded very positively to the educational challenges posed by the computer, developing and deploying historical simulations and data-handling software in a variety of contexts. As the skills associated with the collection, organisation, interpretation, analysis, presentation and communication of information are so vital to historical understanding, it is hardly surprising that data-handling software, enabling users to create and interrogate datafiles, has been widely used at all levels of education from the primary school to the university.[1]

The type of data which has been most enthusiastically quarried by historians has been the population census, especially the British censuses of 1851 and 1881. Availability of the sophisticated data-handling package Microquery/Quest together with sample datafiles undoubtedly stimulated teachers to integrate computer analysis of population census data into history curriculum work. Many other data-handling packages such as Find, Grass, Inform and Key have been developed in response to particular pedagogical problems perceived when Microquery/Quest has been used with younger children. However, all of these packages analyse their data in a way similar to Microquery/Quest, and most have been used predominantly for population census analysis.[2]

There are powerful learning advantages to be gained from the use of such packages. Their use has developed the information skills mentioned above, has stimulated the investigation of localities and has helped many students appreciate the concept of change. As it is possible to compare and contrast demographic and socio-economic characteristics over time or in different locations, the identification of activities and trends which merit further investigation is encouraged. The use of data-handling software also encourages students to hypothesise, to test these hypotheses and to refine them as a result of this testing. Thanks to the computer, these complex skills can now be developed from an early age.[3]

While many advantages may be discerned, enthusiasm for the use of data-handling software in history must be tempered by an appreciation that the datafiles which are commonly used are very localised in content, are relatively small and are frequently analysed without reference to either censuses from other periods or other resource materials.

Hardware constraints imposed by many of the microcomputers used in schools limit the size of datafiles, for the larger the file the slower the search procedure. While a file of 400 records may permit investigation of the total population of a small village, it does not allow for the analysis of trends and patterns within the wider parish or community in which the village lies or with which close interdependent ties existed. Furthermore, in the case of urban areas, such a small file permits investigation only of a street or a couple of tenement blocks. Obviously, many conclusions which may be derived from the data in a small localised file cannot be extrapolated to larger areas. In most cities and towns marked internal socio-economic disparities demand extremely judicious selection of data if students are to avoid misconceptions. The difficulties of extrapolating to an entire country are of course even greater. Yet truly representative datafiles have been difficult to develop given constraints on time and money, while shuttling through many separate files to explore specific questions is very time consuming.

Similar problems exist regarding the time period covered. Frequently the sheer effort expended by the individual teacher in obtaining data for a specific location inhibits the analysis of more than a single point in time. While a snapshot of a community may be fascinating, it is the change in that community over time which is of prime importance. Students will gain a much fuller appreciation of their study area from the analysis of similarly constructed datasets drawn from a selection of time periods than they will from an investigation of an isolated time period. They will be able to develop the concept of change over time and to compare their observed trends with those exhibited by larger areas such as the country as a whole. The value of having a range of time periods to support investigation is especially important for evaluating hypotheses; those which hold in 1851 may be quite spurious when 1881 is considered.[4] Identifying the reasons for such inapplicability develops additional critical thinking skills.

Pedagogical difficulties also flow from the practice of undertaking data analysis in the absence of associated or related data.[5] Students are denied the opportunity to develop a more rounded appreciation of life in past society. The study of simple census data in isolation from birth, marriage and death registers, gravestone inscriptions, estate farming records and information on buildings, industries and communications means that only one-dimensional conclusions are reached.

Related to this difficulty is the neglect of spatial information. Population census data, like most data subjected to computer analysis, is textual and numeric; the results are displayed as lists or as tables of text and numbers. Conclusions based on the number of people in particular industries, the average size of families, the number of people who have migrated into an area, bar graphs of different surnames and occupations, and correlation graphs tell only part of the story of the past. Such an approach ignores the spatial distribution of the population within the village or urban area, obscuring for example the distribution of immigrants (where they came from and where they settled), the association of employment type with housing type (clusters of miners in miners' rows or steelworkers close to a foundry), the physical distribution of farmers owning over 100 acres and the distribution of houses with more than six rooms. Thus spatial representation of data is of great importance to analysis, illustrating relationships which lists and tables cannot. Without this spatial dimension historians explore blindly, aware only of the general location of the place from which their data derive. An awareness of the internal structure and the spatial distribution of features within the environment under study is essential to the identification and understanding of key features of past society.

Admittedly many of these criticisms reflect the inability, until recently, of computers and their associated software to handle large quantities of data in anything but a textual or numeric way. Since the mid-1980s there has been a quantum leap in the development of both hardware and software; historians now have very sophisticated resources at their disposal to assist their investigation of the past. Microcomputers with a megabyte or more of memory which can be linked to hard disc storage of up to 80 megabytes, to videodisc or to compact disc, have swept aside earlier information storage constraints.[6] Development of cheap scanners and advances in screen resolution mean that the potential for the display of graphs or pictures on screen is considerably enhanced. Links can be established with a range of external devices allowing multimedia storage and presentation of information. New, extremely sophisticated, user-friendly software permits information to be stored in a totally different way — essentially as objects to which comprehensive data can be attached — and to be explored in different ways.[7] These hardware advances and the development of visually-oriented database software release educators from the straitjacket which has constrained teaching and learning development over the past ten years. Now huge amounts of information, stored electronically in many diverse forms, can be quickly accessed and processed, and the results of the analysis can be displayed in a wider range of display formats.

As far as population census data is concerned, these advances mean much larger, more representative datafiles can be created for exploration, and it becomes possible to flip through multiple files of data illustrating different time periods. In addition, a comprehensive range of diverse support material can be integrated with the population census data. Most importantly, the environment to which the data pertains can be observed, and the results of data searches can be displayed spatially.

The educational potential of these new approaches can be illustrated by reference to a hypothetical visual database framed around the history of the Scottish village of Blair Atholl. Located in Perthshire about seven miles north of Pitlochry, Blair Atholl is for much of the year a quiet rural backwater. In summer it comes alive as car- and coach-borne visitors flock to see the world-renowned castle. If they were to explore the rest of the village they would find a working meal mill, a railway station with a disproportionate number of sidings and sheds, some small shops, two hotels, two churches with associated graveyards, a golf course, a primary school, a garage, a bowling green, a craft shop and a museum as well as a great variety of housing. The historian, therefore, has available for exploration many rich environmental features and a multiplicity of information sources both within the village (such as tombstone inscriptions, estate records and various artefacts) and outwith (maps, documents, poor law records and population census data). If all of this information could be drawn together and assembled on a computer, the historian could analyse it, identify certain features about life in the village in the past and suggest reasons for features and trends. The more comprehensive this information resource, the more likely that historians will be able to understand the relationships, trends and processes of the past.

A large number of different 'environments' can be created. The first might be of the village set within its regional context. Either a map can be scanned to provide a background on which features of the locality could be added, or each item can be drawn from scratch. The visual environment created will be an agglomeration of objects of different types, each with an associated record of information which can be as brief or as complex as the designer of the environment wishes. The record of information for any object in the environment can contain text, numbers, sounds or pictures. Very complex environments can therefore be created, but criteria can be set for searching the information, with objects matching the criteria displayed in highlighted form.

Another potential useful 'environment' would be a more detailed picture of the village today. This can include as objects all of the features of the village listed above: for example, the mill, museum, houses and castle could all be recorded as 'buildings'. Detailed records for each of the objects can be built up using information drawn from a variety of sources. Once created, this environment can be linked to the village area on the first environment, making a start in the creation of an interconnected web of information. The new village environment can either be browsed through or specifically explored, for example to identify all of the buildings made of local stone and constructed before 1900.

Certain local features may be considered worthy of deeper study, notably the castle, the graveyards and the meal mill. From the castle in the village environment, a link can be set up to a detailed view of the castle from the front drive. This can in turn be linked to ground floor and upper floor plans, and from these there may be further links to very detailed drawings of particular rooms, the works of art hanging on one wall or to a bookcase showing estate documents and books. From this bookcase links can be set up to specific estate records. The graveyard on the village map can be linked to a detailed graveyard map showing all the tombstones, and every tombstone will have a detailed record or transcription. Some, erected in memory of the nobility or recording an unusual inscription, can link to short histories of the dead person or to a detailed picture of the tombstone. From the mill, links can extend enquiry down through detailed floor plans to drawings and descriptions of particular aspects of the process involved in making meal to mill accounts and to maps showing the former catchment area of the mill with customer information.

Many of the suggested environments reflect the dimension of time. This dimension can be specifically catered for if a set of environments illustrating the village at particular time periods is created. These can focus on population census years or on periods when interesting historical events took place. Such environments will show the buildings which existed at the time, and the buildings can contain objects representing the people who inhabited them. Thus the environment for 1841 or 1881 will include the actual population census data, and this 'particular object dataset' can be subjected to normal census analysis, with the results highlighted on the environment to illustrate their spatial distribution. Environments for those years can also be created to illustrate major changes in transport: for the 1840s bills, stabling details and coaching timetables will form the raw material, whereas 40 years later railway-oriented data will be critical. Finally, an environment can be created taking advantage of the Duke of Atholl's unique privilege of heading a private army which, as the Atholl Brigade, fought in 1745 at Culloden. This environment can use the well documented membership of the army and information on its campaigns of the Jacobite period.[8]

The village, therefore, can support the development of a very comprehensive database (Figure 1) which provides a complex courseware resource. The resultant database integrates many datafiles or environments which in various ways reflect aspects of life in Blair Atholl now and in the past. Indeed scenarios for the village in the year 2000, focusing on planned ski developments and the impact of general socio-economic changes, could be incorporated.

Thus the visual database encompasses environments which can range from the simple to the extremely complex. These environments contain information culled from a variety of sources and, stored in a variety of ways, linked together to provide pathways of exploration and subsume issues, events and relationships of historical significance. If the computer is then linked to external devices such as videodisc and CD-ROM, multimedia hypertext applications may be created. Such materials will stimulate student investigation, promote enquiry and critical thinking skills and encourage students to hypothesise, test and redefine these hypotheses.

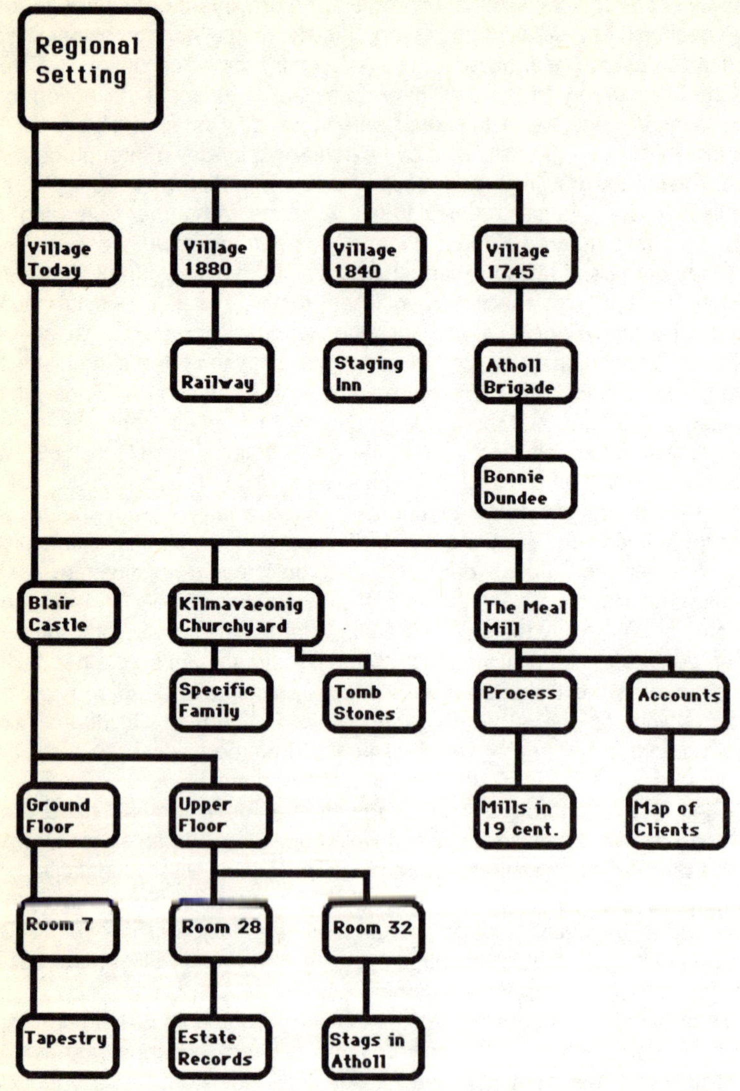

Figure 1: Example Visual Database Framework

This sophisticated and powerful resource offers historians tremendous potential to promote fuller understanding of historical events and processes and to aid the development and reinforcement of historical concepts and skills. Historians must exploit this resource as vigorously and effectively as they have exploited the more limited data-handling resources of the past decade.

Notes

1. In this regard the extremely successful educational courseware package The Desperate Journey used in many primary schools with pupils aged 10-12, contains nineteenth-century census datafiles for Golspie Village, Bell Street, Glasgow, and Kildonan, Winnipeg, Canada. Strathclyde Regional Council has produced a number of secondary school-oriented courseware packs built around nineteenth-century census datafiles of selected areas within Glasgow and small towns and villages in west central Scotland (see article by McArthur in this volume). At the tertiary level significant developments have been instigated by the DISH Project of the history and archive departments of the University of Glasgow (see essays by Moss, Munck, Mawdsley and Whitelaw, and Trainor in this volume).

2. Microquery is produced by the Advisory Unit for Microtechnology in Education, Endymion Road, Hatfield; they also market Quest. Find is produced by Resource, Exeter Road, Doncaster; Grass by Newman College in Birmingham; Inform by Nottinghamshire County Council; and Key by the Independent Television Companies Association, 6 Paul Street, London. For analyses of the use of these packages see: D Freeman and W Tagg, 'Databases in the Classroom', *Journal of Computer Assisted Learning*, 1, 1985; R K Munro, 'Using Historical Databases in Schools' and 'Evaluation of Some Common Datafile Packages', in J M McArthur (ed.), *Databases in History Teaching*, Glasgow, 1986.

3. Freeman and Tagg, *op.cit.*; A Ross (for MEP/CET), *Making Connections*, London, 1984; D Marshall, 'Facts from the Animals', *Educational Computing*, 9, 1988.

4. The best example of continuous time series data is supplied by the Advisory Unit at Hatfield in their files on the village of Datchworth. Discovering Datchworth includes population census datafiles for 1851, 1861, 1871 and 1881 together with datafiles of church registers, births, marriages and deaths. Some of the courseware produced by Strathclyde Regional Council (see note 1) incorporates datafiles for 1851 and 1881, e.g. Sanydford and Gorbals.

5. The Strathclyde Regional Council courseware must be noted as an exception. Created as a result of co-operation between the Education Department and the Regional Archives, it contains a wealth of associated textual materials.

6. CD-ROM offers storage capacity of 656 megabytes of information, equivalent to approximately 270,000 pages of text.

7. For example, a screen display of a graveyard may illustrate 20 gravestones and part of a church. Each of the gravestones, may be considered as a separate object within a set of gravestones and a comprehensive file of data can be associated with *each* of the gravestones. The church also can be considered an object but of a totally different type and with a totally different set of data. Software of this types includes: Business Filevision (Tele Software), HyperCard (Apple Computer UK), Linkway (IBM UK Ltd).

8. A Livingston, C W H Aikman and B S Hart, *Muster Roll of Prince Charles Edward Stuart's Army 1745-46*, Aberdeen, 1984.

Taking the Plunge: Planning a Course on Computing for Historians

History is about the past: this paper is about the planning of a course outlining the uses of the computer to historians which has yet to be given.[1] It is primarily a discussion, inevitably tentative, of aims and anticipated obstacles in the introduction of such a course at Manchester University. The paper might have two uses beyond the benefits to the author of a discussion of his problems. First, there are departments of history which do not involve computers in their teaching. To them the struggles to give birth to a computing course in one history department might be a help, even an encouragement, at worst an amusement! Second, the proposed course has no special grants or funds made available; it draws from the existing manpower resources of the history department and the University's computer centre, and depends on centrally provided hardware and software. The circumstances therefore differ from those introductory teaching projects which have grants to fund their own hardware, software and staff. The Manchester experience might become more common now that funds for introductory computer teaching projects within individual British universities are no longer available.

Most arts honours degree programmes at Manchester University require one examined course of roughly 60 contact hours outside the specialist discipline. Since the early 1970s the history department has preferred as subsidiary courses those providing auxiliary skills for historians: for example palaeography, statistics and modern and ancient languages. Then in 1984 along came students asking to be allowed to offer a computer course. There seems to have been no doubt that computing was appropriate, but there was no acceptable course. The departmental board discussed whether or not to mount such a course. In favour was student demand and a progressive image associated with computing. Against, were doubts about what such a course should do (should it teach programming or just the use of packages?), the competence of historians to teach it, and the willingness of computer specialists to use historical problems in their teaching. The proposal fell, but two years later, after the first conference of the Association for History and Computing, and as news spread of computing in other history departments, it was successfully revived.

We began with three seminars at Manchester about computing for historians at other universities: about Dr Ron Weir's long-running course at York, about a new course at Durham under Dr Peter Wardley,[2] and about Glasgow's DISH Project from Dr Nicholas Morgan. These speakers attracted, overall, a third of the history department's staff, most of whom were computer illiterate. Four basic questions came out of their talks.

The first of these was: why teach with computers? We came up with four answers. Firstly (and most importantly), computers can sort large amounts of data very quickly and calculate on that data. Four areas of history being taught in the department in 1986 could benefit from such abilities: social structure, demography, psephology, and econometrics and statistics. Research work with computers already existed in one of these areas, and work was about to start in a second, so that the long-established and beneficial relationship between teaching and research could continue. Secondly, it had been argued convincingly by one of our three mentors that students could only have a second-hand appreciation of some of the work in, for example, demography or econometric history, and no chance to evaluate that work at first hand, unless they had knowledge of computing. Thirdly, in 1986 Manchester's history department comprised 38 members of staff. Such a large department must be capable of teaching a wide range of methods and approaches to undergraduates.[3] If computers are being used in history then they should be available to students. It could be a legitimate criticism of a department as big as ours that computing had passed it by. Lastly, student demand for computing, based on previously acquired experience, seemed to be developing. Although applications to read history at Manchester continued to rise, to restrict the student experience by not offering computer work might damage our admissions position. The counter point was that a computer course might put off applicants. An informal survey suggested that half of one first-year intake would welcome such a course on a compulsory basis; some would seek to avoid it; and others did not mind provided they did not have to do the course.

The second major issue was: how would the students gain? We felt they would enjoy a triple benefit, firstly for the academic reasons outlined in the preceding paragraph. Secondly, word-processing would assist the presentation of their major piece of assessed work in each of their second and third years, and computing could extend the range of third-year BA thesis topics. Lastly, it was argued that some experience of computers would be good for students in the job market. Students would not become more readily employable because of an elementary computer course, but they would have some self-confidence where computers were concerned.

The third major issue concerned the type of course to be taught. There was an opportunity to achieve a high level of integration between history and computing skills by using computer work in an existing history course covering a set time period or problem. But in the existing degree structure the first two years comprise compulsory collaboratively taught courses, in which many of the contributing staff had neither computer expertise nor interest in using computers for teaching. The specialist courses into which a large component of computing might be conveniently fitted come in the final year of the degree course. We had previously decided that third-year students should already have computing skills. Furthermore third-year courses have tight limits on student numbers, and, in practice in 1986, it was likely that only one member of staff could, using his own research material, mount such a course. As a consequence computing would become an adjunct available to a few specialists rather than something generally available.

The alternative was the proven concept of an auxiliary skill, already recognised in the department's regulations. Its coherence would lie in introducing a range of skills and techniques, thereby offering flexibility in both course content and resource allocation, especially staff time. Against, was the danger of history lecturers masquerading as teachers of computer science. A more serious problem was whether there were enough history staff to teach a variety of skills and techniques amounting to a 60 contact-hour course. Finally, there were the questions of how a subsidiary-subject type course would be examined, and whether we might fail good historians in a computing examination. But there was hope of overcoming the practical problems, and in the end the auxiliary-skill approach seemed to offer the best value to the students.

The final principal issue was whether the course should be compulsory or voluntary. The visiting speakers from other universities had tried both approaches. They reported that students thought a voluntary course to be, by definition, not worth the effort. On the other hand, we worried lest a compulsory computer course might put students off history. We rapidly concluded that the input of staff time could not possibly justify a voluntary course. We also feared that a voluntary course would be accorded a lower-priority access to hardware facilities, which in the autumn of 1986 were fairly limited. The decision to make the course compulsory was a relatively easy one to take. On the basis of these discussions the history departmental board decided to introduce a course called 'Computing for Historians'.[4]

At this point in our thinking we had a compulsory course of 60 hours contact time, which would be examined, and which the students could thus fail. Two questions immediately arose: did we want to erect such an examination hurdle; and could we find the staff time to teach such a course for a year's intake of 90 or so history specialists?[5] The answer to both questions was no, and thus we broke away from the subsidiary course concept. We were concerned to help historians to use computers, not to prevent them from becoming historians by failing a computer examination. We decided to abandon examinations and substitute instead a requirement that students complete the course satisfactorily.[6] It was clear that we could not find the staff time to mount a course for 90 students when the largest computer cluster available was 20 strong, so that even with an unsatisfactory two students per station we would have to teach the course three times, involving 180 hours of staff contact time. This problem was solved by opting for a one-term course of three hours per week, with a further optional two hours per week of hands-on time for the students to work up their material, taught only to the honours school of Modern History with Economics, which has an intake of about 20 students. Thus the course would not be available to the majority of history students. The inter-relation of compulsion, staff time and student numbers will clearly be one of the prime issues when we evaluate the outcome of the first course.

The decision to opt for a short course reinforced our inclination not to teach programming. All teaching would be done using off-the-shelf packages, although some of these might have to be tailored to our purpose. This avoided a heavy call on the time of the computer professionals. The initial course[7] would comprise: word-processing, a practical tool with many uses; some elementary text analysis; and database work. The latter would use pre-inputted data on: seventeenth-century urban social structure; capital formation in the nineteenth-century gas industry in north-west England; an edition of the *Taxatio* (a statement, for tax purposes, of the wealth of the medieval English church); and statistics from a comparative study of trade unions in Britain and Germany between the world wars. Each exercise would have four parts. The first would provide historical background, indicating why the issue is worth studying by historians and making the case for the computer as a useful tool. The second part would concern data preparation, discussing any problems arising from preparing the raw source for the computer and the effect of data preparation and input on the outcome of the exercise.[8] The third part would consist of exercises on the data, while the fourth would help the students to produce a printed report. Finally, there might be a project for each student, or perhaps pairs of students, to attempt on their own.

Thus the teaching would be done by history staff, using research work experience in part, though one contributor would be getting up computer skills purely for the course. One member of staff, initially the author of this paper, would act as course coordinator, teaching the general background, word-processing, the first database sessions, and being present at all ten sessions of the course; a second colleague would also be present at all sessions in order to alternate as coordinator in subsequent years. We calculated that these arrangements would increase the course coordinator's workload by about 15 per cent, but for those teaching the individual segments of the course the increase in load is obviously less. For the students, formal contact time would increase by 12 per cent.

Once we had decided what we wanted to teach, we had to find the necessary hardware and software. Fortunately, a major change in computing policy in Manchester University increased the number of computing clusters, and 20 PCs (initially stand-alone) were placed in the history department for use by students and staff. These machines are 30 megabyte hard disc Opus computers with one floppy disc drive; three printers are each linked to a group of computers. The hardware was thus provided for us. A networked cluster, and/or mainframe links might have had advantages. But, whether we would have chosen anything significantly different, had we been funded say by a grant under the Computers in Teaching Initiative, is now a hypothetical question. In arts faculties with limited equipment grants, hardware is difficult to acquire, more so if Computer Board-funded hardware is centrally available in the university. If computer teaching moves away from the central government grant-aided phase for hardware provision, to provision and up-dating of hardware from the individual university, then our experience will become more common. Indeed, it may already be the norm for most.

For software the presumption appears to be that users will find the available centrally-funded packages to be appropriate. One has to be able to make a good case for each piece of additional software, and packages which can be made to suit more than one user become the most attractive. An element of compromise on specifications might be involved. The co-ordinator of the course needs to know early in the project what will be taught so that appropriate software can be found. Here expert advice from our contact in the university computer centre has proved invaluable. Our preferred database software would not, it transpired, cope with the complexities of the shared printer environment of the cluster, another of the pressures of using centrally provided equipment. We rejected SIR (PC) as too complex, and dBaseIII as too expensive, for our purposes. Not all software houses will make inspection copies available, and what is accessible tends to be on hand for fairly short periods of time. We anticipate using Minitab for statistics and Microsoft Works for word-processing and database functions. The latter package appeals to another university department, though none of the history course teachers are using it for their own research, and material is thus having to be specially prepared, and new systems learnt, for teaching purposes.

Inevitably the first running of the course (after some dummy sessions to familiarise us with a new mode of teaching) would raise a series of important questions. For example, how would the students react to teachers who are historians rather than computer scientists, and what would go wrong on some student's computer that we would not be able to understand and rectify ourselves?[10] Yet whatever the problems that lie ahead, it seems clear that the elaborate planning process described in this article, including the resolution of a large number of curricular, pedagogical and resource questions, has been prerequisite to the course's being run in a way that gives it a reasonable chance of success.

Epilogue

A few comments can be made[11] on the first running of the course during the academic year 1988-1989. Problems peculiar to Manchester aside, most students lacked keyboard skills and therefore found work painfully slow. The database work needed to be more integrated into aspects of history courses studied concurrently. We have taken steps to improve the course with these points in mind. The ratio of three staff demonstrating to one lecturing was just about right. The amount of staff preparation time was horrendous, though of course it will be less next time, we hope! Microsoft Works and the hardware performed well. The course will be taught a second time during 1989-1990.

Notes

1. Still at the planning stage at the time (March 1988) that the paper on which this article is based was delivered, the course was given for the first time in Lent Term 1989. See Epilogue.

2. Now at Bristol Polytechnic.

3. Equally, it might have concentrations of expertise in particular fields.

4. This proposal was of course scrutinised by the Board of the Faculty of Arts before approval by the Senate of the University.

5. The total intake of all the main history schools is about 170.

6. This will be interpreted to require good attendance, and require written or printed evidence of a reasonable attempt at all exercises.

7. We anticipate that the group of staff teaching the course may change from year to year. Work on the psephology of nineteenth-century England is under preparation for a second course.

8. Although the students will do any exercises on pre-inputted data, they will be required to format and input some data of their own.

9. An integrated package providing also spreadsheet and communications applications.

10. One of the staff of the University's computer centre would help us on the first course, a great reassurance. I owe a great debt to Mrs S A Davnall of the University of Manchester Regional Computer Centre for help with this course; others of her colleagues have helped more than they probably realise.

11. These were written in September 1989.

17 *Jeffrey L Newton*

Computers, Education and the Transmission of Historical Knowledge: Project Clio[1]

Historians have been using computers to support their basic research for nearly a generation. In some branches of historical inquiry, such as economic or demographic history, the use of computers has made possible the analysis of important historical evidence which would have been unmanageable without the computing power of these machines.[2] Not only has the use of computers helped historians to develop new interpretations of the past, but the preparation of research materials in machine-readable form has ensured that a great amount of historical data will be preserved for future generations of historians. In both the preservation and interpretation of the past, computers have served as powerful allies to the historical profession. In the area of teaching, however, the situation is slightly different.

The use of computers in the teaching of history is a relatively recent development; we are only beginning to acquire the experience necessary to evaluate the role which computers might have in the transmission of historical knowledge.[3] Although some attempts were made in the late 1970s to explore the potential of computers to enhance the teaching of history,[4] it was only in the 1980s that widespread, sustained programmes were established to develop and disseminate educational software targeted specifically for adoption by college and university history teachers.

Several factors help to explain this proliferation of interest in educational computing: the familiarity of younger academics with computers, the need to address the real or perceived decline in student enrolments with innovative teaching methods, and the successful efforts on the part of energetic administrators to involve teaching staff in the activities of their computing centres. But perhaps the most important factor which helps to explain the growth of interest and commitment on the part of historians in educational computing is the availability of funds. In the mid-1980s every major computer manufacturer invested large sums of money in the development of university-level educational software and helped to establish distribution centres intended to disseminate this software throughout the academic community.[5] The timely donation of expensive computer equipment by manufacturers meant that university budgets could be shifted to support software development if the administration felt this to be a worthwhile activity.

Academic courseware developed by historians over the last several years can be sorted into several categories: database packages, simulations, inter- or hyper-media applications and tutorials. As early as 1974 efforts were made to produce educational packages based upon historical databases;[6] recent projects such as the Great American History Machine at Carnegie Mellon University and the DISH Project at the University of Glasgow have experimented with visual representation and the presentation of original sources as aids to the student manipulation of datasets especially adapted for teaching.[7] Meanwhile, with the active encouragement of the computer industry,[8] simulations have taken pedagogical advantage of the multi-dimensional functions of the computer, notably in programs such as The Would-be Gentleman developed at Stanford University.[9] Inter- or hyper-media software, pioneered in Project IRIS at Brown University and in Project Perseus at Harvard and Boston Universities, allows students to jump from one piece of information to related information of a different nature in a continuing search for meaning or 'links' in the general body of knowledge available on the computer system. Finally, tutorial software relies upon the ability of the computer to pose questions and respond in a meaningful way to student answers.

An innovative but technically rather simple version of an interactive tutorial program, intended for use in the introductory history course, began to attract modest investment from the administration of Rhode Island College in 1982. By September 1983 most of the work was completed on the tutorials which covered material from ancient Mesopotamian society to the Second World War.[10] The enthusiastic support which this early work received from both the Chair of the History Department and the Dean of Arts and Sciences led to collaboration on the enhancement of the tutorials which were adopted for use by several members of the department.[11] In June 1985 Digital Equipment Corporation awarded Rhode Island College a Special Investment Grant to develop a new version of the tutorial programs for use on Digital's Vax computers, and Project Clio was launched.

From 1985 until 1988 the administration of Rhode Island College provided substantial financial support to the Project, permitting various faculty members and student assistants to work on the development of the software as well as on the pedagogical structure of the programs.[12] From the outset, the goal of Project Clio was not simply to produce a series of software programs, but to conceptualise a way in which the existing introductory history course could be altered to allow for more classroom discussion of original historical material. We believed that much of the contextual information being presented in classroom lectures could be delivered to students in an interactive, computer-based format which they could complete outside of the classroom as part of their preparation for discussions. We also wished to increase the amount of individual attention which could be given to students in classrooms which typically numbered 30 or more students per session.

Our goal in the first phase of the Project was exciting but unrealistic: the creation of an 'electronic textbook' which would serve as a guide for students as they learned to read difficult historical sources on their own. This initial phase was known as Cliotext, and a prototype was completed on the theme of Renaissance Humanism. The prototype included an interactive lesson which presented historical material relevant to the rise of Renaissance Humanism, a 'quiz' which students used to judge their mastery of this material, and a series of close textual readings of selected portions of humanist writings from Petrarch to Machiavelli designed to develop a student's critical reading of these sources by concentrating on the meaning of particular phrases and words. Eventually students were asked to read, in printed form, a long extract from Cellini's *Autobiography* and then return to the computer for a final session. This last exercise was intended to help students transfer the critical reading skills developed on the computer to their own private reading of printed material. Students were then to be assigned a complete humanist text (such as Machiavelli's *Prince*) to be read in preparation for a series of classroom meetings that would begin immediately with an analysis of Machiavelli within the context of the humanist tradition.

There are at least three important reasons why the entire series of Cliotext lessons was never completed: technically, the production of the lessons required enormous amounts of time to program; administratively, the proper implementation of the lessons would have required a radical restructuring of the entire introductory history course; and professionally, given the interpretative nature of the original exercises, the lessons tended to reflect views of Renaissance Humanism which were defensible but open to criticism. In various ways each of these problems also limited the likelihood that this type of software would be adopted by other departments, instructors or institutions.

After several months of work on Cliotext the project staff decided to shift the focus of development toward a modified series of software programs based upon the work which had been completed between 1982 and 1985. It was agreed that a version of these programs enhanced with colour graphics, illustrations, maps and additional material was not only a realistic but a desirable goal. Since the programming and writing skills of project members had been honed by their experience on Cliotext, work on what became known as Cliotutor proceeded with efficiency and speed.

In 1986 we began demonstrating Cliotutor at various professional meetings and establishing contact with colleagues at other colleges and universities who shared our interest in the potential of computer-based educational material to enhance the introductory history course. These informal contacts eventually led to the establishment of the Clio Consortium which consisted of individual academics willing to use the

Cliotutor material in their own courses and, by their criticisms, to help the Project staff improve the final series of tutorials.[13] A year later the first version of Cliotutor on the Vax was completed and released for general distribution.[14] In October 1988, Apple Computer Incorporated donated equipment and funds to Project Clio to begin work on a Macintosh version of the software. The first lessons of this new version were released for review in early 1989.[15]

How does a Cliotutor lesson work? In contrast to many tutorial programs (notably the drill-and-practice CAL of the early 1970s), in Cliotutor the dialogue which takes place between the student and the computer is not intended to serve as a judge of the student's knowledge but rather as a coach or a guide as the student works through a limited and defined body of information. In the Macintosh version of Cliotutor (which is greatly enhanced over the Vax version) students are provided with numerous original sources which relate to the topic under examination. The sources can be read on their own, or the student can access a textual 'gloss' which focuses attention on key words, phrases, passages and the like, much as an instructor might do in a tutorial or seminar environment. A text-specific dictionary and an historical vocabulary can also be accessed while reading the sources. An atlas with relevant maps is always available, as are various other educational supports. Unlike the hyper-media environments, the extent of the information available to students is strictly limited to that which the authors consider relevant or important to the topic under investigation. The central activity of the lessons is a series of tutorial lessons which are in effect a discussion of the historical topic in an interactive mode: that is, students are constantly asked questions as the program presents the discussion. They are notified at various points in the discussion when they should read relevant original sources; it is suggested that they take the lessons in a predetermined order, although at all times students can freely choose any activity. They are never locked out of any resource. Finally, a quiz is included in the software which randomly selects a number of questions from a question bank (the number is determined by the student) and presents these questions for the student to answer. Following the quiz, an evaluation informs the students of their performance and suggests areas which may need further study.

The evaluation, like all of the material included in the Cliotutor lessons, is intended for student use: ultimately it is up to the students to control the logic of the lesson and to assess their level of knowledge. Students also have access to whatever additional information is available on their computer system, including hyper-media environments which they may choose to explore, returning to the Cliotutor lesson if they wish additional information or become lost or confused.

How has Cliotutor been received? The reaction of members of Rhode Island College's history department to the use of the package on the Vax has been strikingly similar to the responses of their counterparts at Notre

Dame to the introduction of computers a decade earlier.[16] Without exception, those critical or even hostile to the use of Cliotutor were individuals with little or no experience with computers: for many academics and students, the use of Cliotutor was their first exposure to the use of computing facilities for any purpose other than word-processing. In general, younger academics and those more comfortable with conducting their classes as discussions rather than lectures found Cliotutor valuable. Informal student reaction had almost always been favourable to Cliotutor except for occasional complaints that it increased the amount of work required of students or, in one case, caused panic due to computer phobia.[17]

Since the introductory history survey at Rhode Island College is required of all students, more than 1,000 are enrolled in the course every year. Just under half are currently enrolled in sections using the Cliotutor lessons as part of their course assignments. In addition, members of the Clio Consortium have been using the lessons in a variety of ways in their own courses; it was only logical, once the tutorial lessons were completed and being used in a variety of settings, to begin to ask ourselves how the use of these tutorials changed the way in which we teach and students learn. In other words: what happens when computers are used to help transmit historical knowledge? To help us address these important questions, Project Clio and the Clio Consortium were awarded a two-year grant from the United States Department of Education's Fund for the Improvement of Post Secondary Education (FIPSE). Our evaluation of the impact of computers on the teaching and learning of history began in October 1988 and will be completed in 1990.[18]

In the context of this ongoing evaluation, firm judgements about the pedagogical value either of Cliotutor in particular or of tutorial software in general would be premature. But the verdict which emerges is likely to be mixed, to judge from experience throughout the profession with the other major types of historical software: databases are easily exportable but need not involve much interaction between student and computer; simulations excite student interest in a very immediate fashion yet have difficulty in approximating the complexity of historical events; inter-media applications allow students to deal with a vast amount of disparate information but run the risk of bewildering them in the process.[19] Preliminary experience with Cliotutor also suggests problems, notably with regard to agreement on the historical judgements incorporated in the lessons. Yet, Cliotutor also suggests that carefully designed tutorial software is well adapted to a multi-dimensional enrichment of student learning in conjunction with more conventional teaching formats. Moreover, tutorial lessons such as Cliotutor evidently can serve as valuable 'front ends' to statistical or hyper-media databases, providing the context and guidance needed to help students organise and digest the historical information available. Thus Cliotutor, and a new generation of tutorial software more generally, seem well placed to establish themselves among a number of viable approaches to computer-based history teaching.

Whatever the specific approaches adopted in future historical teaching software, it is important to note that the various existing models for educational packages in history have been developed for the most part within history departments. The active participation of historians in the development of the next generation of educational software, however, cannot be assured unless that participation is seen as beneficial to their professional advancement and career. To address this concern a committee within the Educom Software Initiative has been formed and is currently investigating the possibility of generating scholarly reviews of academic software which may prove useful for promotion decisions within academic departments.[20] If the development of educational software does not gain wide acceptance as a professionally creditable activity for historians, the direction of future software developments may well pass into the hands of other individuals, such as members of education departments or private business. Not only would this lead to the pyrotechnics so commonly associated with advocates of 'motivation' theory[21] (which can have more in common with the advertising world than with the world of higher education), but history departments would lose a significant source of funding from both private and public entities. The historical profession can be well served by supporting the exploration of knowledge not only for the tangible benefits to be derived from such activity but from the theoretical implications which these new avenues of communication have for the construction of historical arguments in a truly multi-causal, multi-dimensional form of discourse.

Notes

1. I am grateful to the Office of the Dean of Arts and Sciences of Rhode Island College and to the Computers in Teaching Initiative Support Service (CTISS), University of Bath, for financial support, and to the Design and Implementation of Software in History (DISH) Project, University of Glasgow for its hospitality.

2. An excellent example is the analysis of the Florentine Catasto of 1427 in D Herlihy and C Klapish-Zuber, *Tuscans and Their Families*, New Haven, 1985.

3. Although the examples which follow are mainly drawn from North America, the arguments which they illustrate are, *mutatis mutandis*, often applicable in Britain and Western Europe as well.

4. Members of the history department of the University of Notre Dame were among the first to develop computer-based educational materials for introductory history courses. Their collective experiences, both professionally and personally, anticipated many similar experiences a decade later. See R E Burns, 'Computer-Assisted Instruction in History: The Tutorial Approach', in S Olsen (ed.), *Computer-Aided Instruction in the Humanities*, New York, 1985, pp. 3-12.

5. Digital Equipment Corporation helped establish the Clearinghouse for Academic Software at Iowa State University; IBM supported Wisc-Ware at the University of Wisconsin. Kinko's Academic Courseware Exchange, though independent, features software written for the Apple Macintosh. See P Seiden (ed.), *Peterson's Directory of Software Sources for Higher Education*, Princeton, 1987, pp. 41-5.

6. M B Baer, 'The Pre-Industrial City: Population and Society in Renaissance Florence', The Laboratory for Political Research, University of Iowa, 1982 (originally developed in 1974).

7. For information on the Great American History Machine, contact Professor David Miller, Department of History, Carnegie Mellon University, Pittsburg PA 15213-3809, USA. For the DISH Project, contact Michael Moss, History Computing Laboratory, University of Glasgow, Glasgow G12 8QQ.

8. In announcing the formation of his new computer company, Next Inc., Steve Jobs, the co-founder of Apple Computer Inc., singled out historical simulations as one of the most desirable developments in educational computing (S P Jobs, 'The Future of Computing in Higher Education', *Educom Bulletin*, 22, 1987, pp. 6-8).

9. Developed by Carolyn Lougee and winner of the 1987 Educom/Ncriptal Award for best Humanities Software, The Would-be Gentleman is available from Kinko's Academic Courseware Exchange, Ventura, California.

10. Anyone unfamiliar (or even familiar) with the typical American introductory survey course will no doubt find the sheer scope of these tutorials audacious. It is. The tutorials were originally intended to be used with a popular textbook.

11. A complete description of these early tutorials can be found in J L Newton and D S Thomas, 'The Clio Project: A Program of Computer-Based Instruction in the Western History Survey', *The History Teacher*, 19, 1986, pp. 181-99.

12. Project Clio, at the height of development, included two principal authors/directors, a reading specialist from the Department of Education, several academics who helped to revise the material, and student programmers who assembled most of the code.

13. In addition to Rhode Island College, members of the Clio Consortium include Ball State University (Indiana), Duquesne University (Pennsylvania), Hollins College (Virginia), Western Michigan University and the University of New Orleans.

14. Cliotutor is available through the Clearinghouse for Academic Software, The Computation Center, 104 Computer Science Building, Iowa State University, Ames, Iowa 50011, USA. A new version was completed in January, and released in June, 1989.

15. Information on the Macintosh version of Cliotutor is available from Jeffrey L Newton, 207 Garland Hall, The Johns Hopkins University, Charles and 34th Sts, Baltimore, MD 21218, USA.

16. Burns, *op.cit.*, pp.10-2.

17. In a survey conducted of 287 students who used Cliotutor for a semester, 81 per cent described their experience as positive or 'very' positive, and looked forward to using the tutorials again. 70 per cent spent two hours or more per week using the tutorials.

18. Details of the evaluation can be obtained from Dr Robert Carey, CERRIC, Rhode Island College, Providence, RI 02908, USA.

19. On the latter, see for example, Patrick J McQuillan, 'Computers and Pedagogy: The Invisible Presence', Institute for Research in Information and Scholarship (IRIS), Brown University, Providence RI 02912, USA.

20. The chairman of this committee is Dr Jack Chambers, Loyola College, Charles St and Cold Spring Lane, Baltimore MD, USA. Reports from the committee indicate that it will abandon the search for 'scholarly' reviews in favour of more popular evaluations. See J A Turner, 'Panel Fails to Devise a System of Scholarly Reviews for Academic Software', *Chronicle of Higher Education*, 16 August 1989, p.13.

21. Motivation theory appears to be distinctively American, rooted in a situation where higher education is widely available to a student body frequently perceived as unwilling participants. For an example of the increased interest in such motivational aspects of educational software see G V Davidson, 'The Role of Educational Theory in Computer Mediated Instruction', *The CTISS File*, 7, 1988, pp. 33-38, esp. p. 36.

Computing for History Undergraduates: A First Year Foundation Course

In the autumn of 1987 the History Department at the University of Hull embarked upon an ambitious new teaching programme aimed at achieving a thorough integration of computation into the undergraduate history syllabus. Computer-assisted teaching has been a feature of the Hull degree course since 1980, but serious work (that is, not including word-processing classes) has been restricted to two third year special subject courses, 'Domesday England' and 'The Age of Walpole'. The award of a UGC/Computer Board grant as part of the Computers in Teaching Initiative (CTI) provided the means for a dramatic increase in the department's commitment to computer assisted teaching.[1] At the heart of this new initiative, and crucial to its success, is a foundation course, taken by all first year single honours history undergraduates. This course, representing about a quarter of a first year student's overall workload, provides a broad introduction to the computing facilities which may usefully be exploited by the historian. Although involving a serious history element in itself, the primary aims of the foundation course are to demonstrate to students the potential of historical computation and to provide them with a sound grasp of both the software and underlying methodologies, enabling them to take full advantage of databases integrated into courses in their second and third years.

Our students begin by becoming competent users of a word-processing package, but the bulk of the foundation course focuses on the design, construction and interrogation of databases. A central place in this course is occupied by conventional flatfile databases on the microcomputer, for it is this type of database which students are most likely to encounter in their other courses; but they are also introduced to more sophisticated database structures — such as textbases — and to the possibilities offered by mapping software. In addition, they gain an insight into the world of communications: interrogation of distant databases serves to demonstrate how their work need not be confined to the resources of the departmental microlab, or even to those of the campus mainframe.

The main element of the foundation course — the bulk of the classes in terms one and two, and three of the four essays undertaken by students — involves the use of relatively simple 'flat-file' databases on the micro. The software used is Borland's Reflex, an extremely friendly package with a good range of analytical tools.[2] Students are shown the essentials of the software in microlab sessions; this instruction is backed up and amplified both by exercises which they work through in their own time and by the work for their own database projects.[3] Students are, of course, learning far more than simply the mechanics of a single piece of software: they are learning how to formulate systematic strategies of analysis, acquiring methodological skills which can be put to good use whatever software they happen to be using. They also become familiar with the problems and intricacies of a range of different source materials.

What kinds of data do we use during this crucial learning stage of the course? The History Department at Hull has a varied and expanding stock of both mainframe and micro databases. Some were developed for research and then adapted for teaching purposes, whilst the majority have been set up primarily for integration into undergraduate courses.[4] Not all, however, would be appropriate for use with the foundation course. Apart from a desire to provide something which students will find interesting and stimulating, and which has a solid and worthwhile historical content, the selection of databases for foundation course teaching has been determined by several practical criteria. In the first place, the database should be composed of a suitable combination of data types (nominal, ordinal and interval data) and have a structure enabling the demonstration and exploration of a range of important database principles and analytical techniques. Secondly, it should be disaggregated, to allow direct comparison with the documentary sources from which it has been derived. Lastly, it should not be too large or unwieldy, or software response times will become prohibitively extended.

Within these limitations, there are obvious advantages in employing databases linked to, and arising from, the research interest of the lecturers. Both the foundation course tutors are medievalists, and so whilst we use Victorian census materials (enumerators' returns for villages around Hull, as well as the tables from the published census reports), a distinctive feature of our course is the prominence given to databases derived from medieval documents. There is, we believe, a particular educational value in our emphasis on medieval databases. Students, whose primary and secondary school history concentrates almost entirely upon the recent past, are not surprised to find that Victorian Britain left a vast legacy of records suitable for computerisation. Far less expected, however, is the huge corpus of often highly detailed records surviving from the medieval centuries. England's greatest public record, *Domesday Book*, is eminently suitable for our purposes: a unique repository of information on eleventh-century social and economic structures, Domesday can be handled very comfortably by database software in county-sized portions. We also use a database derived from the detailed financial records of English royal armies involved in the early stages of the Hundred Years War. Having, like Domesday, a fine structural regularity, these mid fourteenth-century military records have transferred very naturally into database form; also like Domesday, they provide much scope for students learning the simple yet powerful analytical tools offered by the database software.

Students are required to undertake three database projects for the foundation course, each involving the analysis of a database and the writing up of findings in the form of a word-processed essay. For their first project, the students use an established database of census data: the enumerators' returns from the parish of North Ferriby in the East Riding of Yorkshire for four consecutive censuses, 1851-81. The second and third database projects are intended to stretch the students a little farther, for one involves the input of data into an existing database, whilst the other requires the creation of a database from scratch by each student. The former forces the students to come to grips with the text of Domesday Book; the latter obliges them to find (under guidance, if necessary) a suitable data source, design a database for it and input the data. We encourage students to look for a subject which interests them, as this is likely to lead to greater effort, better informed analysis and an inclination to experiment.

The third database project represents perhaps the most important component of the foundation course; it is at once a demanding and an extremely valuable exercise for the student. Although creating a database can be a time consuming and laborious task, it can also be an extremely beneficial one; the benefits gained, we believe, are far less likely to come from simply using established databases. By necessity, database creation thrusts the students into a very healthy close proximity to the source material; it requires them to think very carefully about the structure of the data, identifying any eccentric or ambiguous elements. In short, it is necessary for them to *understand* their sources before deciding upon a structure of records and fields, and systems of data classification, for their databases. Designing databases is a technical skill which is acquired only gradually, and with experience; it requires logical and well-ordered thinking and depends upon a knowledge of database and analytical principles in general, and of software limitations in particular. By the end of their first year as undergraduates, our students should be well on the way to developing a new technical skill of value to them as historians and as graduates.

The range of periods and subject matter tackled by students for their third database projects has been refreshingly varied, including studies of national election results, trade statistics, various blocks of data from the census reports, and the structures of armies and navies. Many of the projects used conveniently assembled collections of data, a colourful example being a simple prosopographical database of Pizarro's *conquistadores* in Peru.[5] Some of the projects were, however, rather more enterprising, requiring a substantial amount of data collection by the student. A good example of this is a prosopographical database of women

MPs at Westminster: the student ploughed through all the relevant volumes of Dod's *Parliamentary Companion* to get the basic dataset, and then other reference sources, like *Who's Who*, to find further information on the lives of the women involved. Opportunities for careful research of this kind are not often provided by conventional first year courses; perhaps they should be. Time constraints dictate that the majority of first year projects are not as ambitious as this. But although the databases are seldom large, it should not be imagined that they are inconsequential; still less that the exercise of source selection, database construction and ultimate analysis was of little value. Comparatively modest datasets can, after all, provide intriguing databases if they have a sufficiently intricate data structure and consist of a good mix of data types. Moreover, quite apart from the inherent historical interest of such database work, these projects represent a psychological and practical preparation for work in the second and third years. In particular, they provide a means of mastering the essentials of database design, and constitute what is essentially a dry-run for a more serious project which students may choose to undertake in their final year.

Only so much is possible with a conventional flatfile database, and we believe it important that the foundation course include an opportunity to explore more sophisticated database software such as that offered by a textbase. Of fundamental importance in a textbase is that the source is preserved entire. There is no extraction of selected items into a data matrix; instead, the text is 'structured' by means of a framework of coded markers. With the textbase software which has been developed at Hull for the Domesday project at their disposal,[6] students are able to explore the vocabulary and formulae of the Domesday text (which have always been at the centre of scholarly debate) or the numerical values, or to combine these two approaches with the utmost flexibility. The textbase software includes a suite of standard analytical tools, but perhaps most attractive are the integrated mapping facilities. Presenting the features of the Domesday text in cartographical form is potentially a very fruitful area of research and one in which our students are able to become actively involved. The foundation course can do no more than provide an indication of the enormous potential of mapping. Although as yet available for only Domesday and eighteenth-century electoral data, it is hoped before too long to provide a mapping dimension to other databases integrated into the history syllabus.

The first year foundation course should be viewed as a single component of a broader strategy which aims at a thorough integration of databases into the undergraduate history syllabus.[7] If the course is intended to demonstrate the potential of historical computation, then it is also designed as a practical and intellectual preparation for database work during a student's second and third years. This work may have two distinct dimensions: the interrogation of databases as part of essay and seminar preparation, and a serious database project leading to a final year dissertation. The strategy of database integration seeks to make computerised materials available for all suitable courses throughout the history syllabus and, moreover, to encourage a climate in which the databases are perceived by students as a natural study resource. For this to be achieved, the department must be in possession of an adequate collection of databases, but equally important is the preparation of the students' minds. This, indeed, is an important function of the foundation course. Although compulsory itself, the foundation course is designed to convince students of the benefits of computation, so they may continue to use databases as an everyday study technique when they are no longer compelled to do so. The advantages of a natural environment of database usage are quite clear: regular contact with source materials should deepen understanding and encourage students to project their thoughts beyond the artificial limits set by lectures and secondary sources. This healthy relationship with the sources, initiated by the database projects for the foundation course, is brought to an appropriate climax for those students who choose to write a dissertation based upon analysis of a substantial database in their final year. If past experience is a useful guide, such pieces of work will frequently contribute very favourably to overall performance in final examinations.[8]

Notes

1. The grant enabled the History Department to acquire 12 networked PCs, together with printers and software, and to employ support staff for the first year; the University has provided additional funds to pay for further hardware and to cover staff costs for a second year. The director of the CTI Project in history at the University of Hull is Dr John Palmer.
2. See Roderick Floud's review of Reflex in *Computing and History Today*, 1, 1987, pp. 22-3.
3. Apart from microlab classes, the foundation course is taught by means of lectures (to introduce source materials), seminars (for group discussion of results) and essay tutorials.
4. For example, three 'teaching databases' concerned with maritime trade are: English Medieval Wool and Cloth Trade; Baltic Trade in the 16th and 17th Centuries British Overseas Trade in the 19th and 20th Centuries.
5. Based on the appendices and text of J M Lockhart, *The Men of Cajamarca*, Austin, 1972.
6. For the textbase software see George Slater, 'The Hull Domesday Textbase: a programmer's view', *University Computing*, 10, 1988, pp. 2-8. The most recent discussion of the Hull Domesday Project is: J J N Palmer, 'The Hull Domesday Database Project', *Humanistiske Data*, 1987, pp. 4-22.
7. For a more detailed discussion of our strategy of database integration, see this author's paper in the proceedings of the 1988 Cologne Computer Conference.

8. For example, out of 40 students who, since 1980, have taken the third year special subject 'Domesday England' — a course which requires each student to create a database from a portion of the Domesday text — seven have gained first-class grades for their dissertations and 75 per cent upper second class grades or higher.

19 *Thomas Munck*

Counting Heads: Using Small Datasets from Eighteenth-Century English and Danish Census-type Sources in Undergraduate Teaching

If the student of nineteenth- and twentieth-century social history is almost too generously served with primary source material potentially suitable for systematic analysis, that is hardly the case for the early modern period. Even for the eighteenth century, when increasingly detailed and numerically specific information was collected by governments for a widening range of purposes, the sources are still frustratingly sparse and inconsistent in a number of important respects. For Britain this shortfall is most clearly illustrated by the absence of consistent census materials of the kind that exists for at least some continental countries during the last decades before the French Revolution. In this and in other ways British public administration was rudimentary; yet even the records of the more autocratic bureaucracies of Europe present enormous problems of interpretation and analysis.

Nevertheless, there is much to be gained from making some of this material available for undergraduate use. Compared with the broad generalisations about pre-industrial or proto-industrial community patterns found in secondary works, exploration of small datasets accurately transcribing a historical source can give a far more direct 'feel' for the structure of a particular community or communities. The computer in this respect does nothing that could not in theory be done manually with card files, but it does enable students to explore different questions and methods of analysis so quickly and efficiently that source analysis becomes manageable even within the constraints of broad introductory courses. Whilst the two datasets discussed here are in no precise sense typical of early modern Europe, students have gained from the project in two major ways: firstly in acquiring a much more tangible understanding of certain common aspects of pre-modern urban societies, and secondly in observing at close quarters some of the limitations of the historical source material itself. Neither of these could have been achieved effectively at this level without computers.

As part of the syllabus of a second-year survey course at Glasgow University covering early modern Europe, an exercise was set up designed to take the student into the computing lab for a total of six hours. These lab sessions were timed for the third term, when students had already covered most of the outline material and had completed their conventional essay and seminar work. Students not interested in database work were given alternative choices, and in either case the report they submitted on their option was assessed directly as part of their degree work rather than examined conventionally. In practice it has been found that upwards of half the class will take the computing option even though it involves more classroom time than the alternative.

Initially just one database was offered, namely an edited version of the 'census' of Wetherby, Yorkshire, compiled by the Reverend Kay in 1776 and transferred, partly from a nineteenth-century copy of the original, to machine-readable form by the Cambridge Group for the History of Population and Social Structure.[1] This listing is in British terms unusual for the period, in that every inhabitant of the market town is itemised in a way comparable to post-1840 censuses: it is in other words three generations ahead of its time. By continental standards, however, it is not remarkable. Denmark had a full nationwide census in 1787, giving for each individual information very similar to that in nineteenth-century British censuses.[2] The apparent similarity of the Wetherby listing and the Danish census made a juxtaposition of the two in a double exercise seem worthwhile. The fact that Wetherby was available on the British side was fortunate from the point of view of the course as a whole. A small placid market town on the London-Edinburgh road, beyond the reach of the growing Yorkshire textile economy, Wetherby was quite unremarkable. Its low-keyed urban economy mixing freely with an agrarian hinterland posed no great problem for the selection of an equivalent Danish community. The town of Varde was selected, and the data was entered directly from a microfilm of the original, reasonably legible enumerator's list. The information on Varde's 811 inhabitants distributed over 175 families (compared with Wetherby's 915 in 218 families), was entered in Dishdata[3] in such a way that the structural form of the two datasets was as nearly identical as the original material allowed.

The aim was to record *verbatim* all information contained in the original, except for marital condition (rendered accurately by abbreviation); in addition, codified fields based solely on internal evidence were inserted to facilitate analysis. For each inhabitant, therefore, the following information headings were included (fields added editorially in either or both datasets are indicated by *):

Family number in sequence
Address
Record number*
Size of household*
Size of family*
Forename

Surname
Age
Sex*
Marital condition
Occupation as given in source
Occupation translated into English (Varde only)*
Occupational code*
Relationship to head of household
Relationship code based on source (Wetherby only)*
Editorial relationship code*

As we shall see, the two sources differ considerably in the way some information is recorded. The two relationship codes for Wetherby, for example, are a reflection of considerable latitude in how certain relationships were recorded: internal evidence sometimes clearly indicates that a son is in fact a son-in-law or perhaps a step-son, and a granddaughter might be noted as daughter even if neither of her parents was head of the household. The Danish source, compiled by an administration with previous census experience, seems more consistent.

It was recognised from the start that direct comparison would in some respects be quite inappropriate. Whilst detailed instructions to the Danish enumerators exist, there is little certainty about why, how, or for what purpose Kay compiled his Wetherby listing.[4] A series of questions about each source on its own, designed to encourage students to formulate their own ways of questioning and checking the datasets, therefore seemed the most appropriate starting point. Fundamental features like age distribution, predominant household structures, occupational patterns, and the general economic orientation of each community are clearly discernible from either database. Whilst recourse to other source material would be essential for satisfactory analysis of childbearing trends and dependency ratios, discussion of such aspects could readily be initiated on the basis of the data in its existing format. For example, the relatively late age of first marriage is suggested by the number of men and women under twenty-five recorded as unmarried, compared with the rarity of older unmarried individuals. Whilst there is no indication in these sources of wealth or migration patterns in early modern society, the importance of the household as an economic unit is at least hinted at in the prevalence of complex households with resident servants, apprentices and journeymen. It is interesting to note how few families in either community appeared to have remoter relatives in residence; in Varde, even three generations of linear descent living in the same household (a stem family) turned out to be an extremely rare occurrence. So, while each user would need to be clearly aware of the limitations of the source and of the 'sample', careful analysis of the material could prove rewarding.

An examination of the two datasets together, however, does trigger some important questions. Whilst the Wetherby data suggest very clearly that the town was left untouched by incipient changes in textile production, apparent in communities not very far to the west, it gives only a very approximate indication of the economic life of its inhabitants. Only heads of households were accorded an occupation, and if the head happened to be a woman the information was left out in all but two cases (a glover and an innkeeper). For Varde, however, the rubric headed 'Title, office, business, craft or means of subsistence' sometimes contains a variety of information for several members of the same household, giving a better indication of the economic structure. And, more important for undergraduate students of early modern society, the frequent registration in Varde of several widely different occupations attributed to a single person suggests a truer reflection of reality than the single occupation given by the Reverend Kay for each head of household.

Originally, the occupational code was left blank in the Wetherby dataset, and students were asked to suggest ways of classifying and codifying the information that they found under 'occupation'. The difficulty of achieving a satisfactory coding system, however, became clearly apparent on examining the descriptions given in the Danish source. What, for example, should the historian make of someone who was 'Byskriver, hospitalsforstander og kirkeverger i Varde, og herredskriver i Vester, 0ster — og Norre herreder' — which might be rendered as 'Town clerk, hospital superintendent and church warden in Varde, and district court clerk in [three local courts]'? The issues of social rank, honorary office holding and actual breadwinning become inextricably but revealingly intertwined.

In other respects, too, juxtaposition of the two sources proved fruitful. The Reverend Kay gave no indication of the existence of illegitimacy or of unmarried mothers. In only one instance is the question hinted at, obliquely, in that one young mother living with her parents is described as being of unknown marital condition. In the Danish source however, there are signs of disarming frankness on this subject. The information on marital condition is much more detailed; second and subsequent marriages are clearly indicated, as are the number of marriages contracted by widows and widowers and the union to which each resident child is to be ascribed. More importantly, in comparison with the Wetherby list the Varde census also gives a clear indication of which children were born out of wedlock, and in some cases where paternity was attributed. No doubt premarital conceptions cannot be identified on this basis, but at least there is some indication of the scale of extramarital childbearing.

Despite these complexities, the vivid juxtaposition of the two communities in the exercise stimulated many of the students to think comparatively, transcending the national boundaries which naturally often loom large in their thinking. Moreover, the exercise helped to emphasise and illustrate generalisations in the course concerning the demographic characteristics of those parts of early modern Europe as yet untouched by sweeping economic change.

Comparative history is notoriously difficult, whether across national boundaries or (especially in the early modern period) even between regions of different economic orientation. It is easy to see the dangers of using small datasets in the way described here. Not only is the historical context of at least one of the datasets unclear, but there are also obvious differences of religious environment, administrative framework and economic potential not accurately reflected in this one-sided type of material. No historian would want to formulate broad conclusions on a basis as flimsy as this.

However, the experience of the course under discussion in this essay suggests that the risks are outweighed by the gains. Consistent data for the early modern period is scarce, and the historian has to accept imperfection if any attempt is to be made to get below the surface of generalisations. For students new to the early modern period, the two datasets described here triggered discussion and analysis unthinkable in the run of a normal outline course. In addition to investigating the general validity of their specific findings, many also went in the opposite direction, probing details of a microcosm out of intrinsic interest. In the process, it was difficult for them to avoid gaining insights into the demographic and occupational patterns of these two pre-industrial communities, and above all into the limitations and slanting inherent in apparently simple primary source material. At a practical level, the computer gave students the opportunity to make full use of source material in a language (and script) which would otherwise have been inaccessible to them. More important, in speeding up the search procedures immeasurably, the computer enabled students easily and quickly to return to (and reassess) their own previous findings once they had become aware of some of the implications inherent in a particular source. In these ways, the source-based comparative teaching method outlined in this essay helped students to deepen as well as broaden their knowledge of the relevant course material.

Notes

1. A copy of this data was kindly made available by Dr Kevin Schurer.
2. Folketælling 1787, Rigsarkivet (Danish State Archives); see also H C Johansen, *Befolkningsudvikling og Familiestruktur i det 18. Arhundrede*, Odense, 1976, pp. 11-23 and *passim*. For Britain, see: E A Wrigley (ed.), *Nineteenth-Century Society: Essays in the Use of Quantitative Methods for the Study of Social Data*, Cambridge, 1972; R Lawton (ed.), *The Census and Social Structure: An Interpretative Guide to Nineteenth Century Censuses for England and Wales*, London, 1977; E Higgs, *Making Sense of the Census: the Manuscript Returns for England and Wales 1801-1901*, London, 1989.

3. Dishdata is a flexible data entry and editing package designed by the DISH Project at Glasgow University specifically for use on historical sources with their frequent irregularities and often missing information. It allows easy transfer of data to most common database management systems.

4. For a discussion of the Wetherby listing, see R Unwin, 'An eighteenth century census: Wetherby 1776', *The Yorkshire Archaeological Journal*, 54, 1982, pp. 125-37, and *Wetherby: The History of a Yorkshire Market Town*, Leeds, 1986.

Prosopography and Proletarian Government: Using Mainframes, Complex Software and Research Databases in Undergraduate Teaching

In the age of microcomputers, educational packages and tailored teaching datasets, it is often supposed that computer-based undergraduate history teaching should avoid the mainframes and the research databases which were characteristic of the pioneering teaching experiments of the 1970s. This article, however, discusses how a very large mainframe database on Soviet government officials was effectively implemented and adapted for use in undergraduate teaching at the University of Glasgow.

The database, The Soviet Data Bank (SDB), was compiled by a team led by J Arch Getty (University of California, Riverside) and William Chase (University of Pittsburgh); it covers 28,000 officials active during the period 1917-1941, and in its basic form is suited mainly for advanced research.[1] Nevertheless, the team working at Glasgow University implemented the SDB for teaching using the Scientific Information Retrieval (SIR) database management system on the University's ICL 3980 mainframe computer.

The Glasgow University project had several starting points. The first was a long-standing research and teaching interest in 'Kremlinology', the study of personnel changes in the Soviet government, as one of the more fruitful ways of looking at this secrecy-shrouded institution. In teaching terms, it was desired to give history undergraduates a better sense of how Moscow's political system worked. Students were to be encouraged to move away from a treatment of the Soviet governing elite as faceless, interchangeable automatons, and from simplistic approaches stressing Stalin, totalitarianism or 'the bureaucracy'. In previous years students had been presented with paper lists of the Soviet top elite, and there had been some attempt to analyse personnel changes, but this had always proved awkward. A second starting point was a heightened interest in, and practical experience of, computing techniques within Glasgow's Modern History Department, thanks to the inception of the DISH Project,[2] funded by the Computer Board. The appearance of the American-based SDB in 1986 was the third and decisive development. Work had begun on home-grown small-scale teaching databases, but this was superseded when the much more comprehensive SDB became available, revolutionising the possibilities for teaching.

No detailed evaluation of the SDB will be attempted here,[3] but a general description is useful. The SDB includes 13 data files (or record types) containing the basic information in the database, and 29 codebook files. The data files are:

ARREST:	Incidents of arrest
BIOGRAPHY:	General information
EDUCATION:	
EXPULSION:	Expulsion from the Communist Party
KINSHIP:	
MILITARY:	Military offices held
OCCUPATION:	Pre-revolutionary jobs
OFFICE:	Office-holding in party and/or Soviet state
OPPOSITION:	Opposition to party leading group
PARTSTAZH:	Party membership
PREREVACTS:	Pre-1917 revolutionary activities
PRISON:	
REVACTS:	Revolutionary activities

The 29 codebook files are used to convert the numerically-coded information in the data files into text (e.g. from 003091 to 'Stalin, Iosif Vissarionovich'). Conceptually, each of the data files can be seen as a separate database; The one common element which the data files have is that one of the fields (variables) in each is the 'identification number' of an individual. Arrest can be taken as an example of one of the data files. The Arrest data file contains a large number of records, each of which gives details of one case of arrest; individual persons could have more than one Arrest record if they were arrested more than once. Multiple records are possible for individuals in all the data files except Biography.

Vast amounts of information can be held in the SDB. In the 13 data files there is a total of 104 different fields about each individual. These include values ranging from where and when individuals were born, to what faculty of what education institutions they attended, to when they were politically 'rehabilitated'. In many cases the number of fields can be much greater; someone might, for example, have held several jobs, so for an individual there are several values for the jobs field, one for each Occupation record.

* * *

The first task was to establish how best to use the SDB. The computing experience of the Modern History Department was growing very rapidly, but at the time we acquired our copy of the database this experience had mostly been based on relatively small and simple databases using the Quest[4] database management system and some locally developed software. Teaching had been done 'in-house' on the local area network

(LAN) of the DISH Project, using DISH's own programmer and lab manager. This arrangement had the advantage of assuring us direct access to expert advice and a teaching environment effectively free from breakdown. The size and nature of the SDB however, meant that the LAN route was not possible. The whole database takes up about 16 megabytes of filestore, and the different record types make it a relational database requiring sophisticated software. At the time the SDB was acquired the storage space available within the DISH network was limited and the most relevant available database management system, Superfile, was inappropriate for the purpose.

The Glasgow Computing Service, when consulted in the autumn of 1986, recommended the relational database management system SIR, a powerful and comprehensive package. We decided to begin with the SIR/SQL+ module. Many research projects use the database management system module of SIR, but this is not easy for beginners. SQL+, a version of Structured Query Language, is an interactive system allowing easy retrieval of information from the database using 'English-like' phrases.[5] We opted for the mainframe version of SIR rather than a micro-based version because of hardware compatibility problems and the desire for quick response. Students used their networked microcomputers in the DISH Lab as mainframe terminals.

A simple SIR/SQL+ query asking for selected information about all those born before 1881 would be:

```
SQL>    SELECT  NAME  BORN  BIRTHENV
        NATION  DEATHCAUE-
SQL>    FROM BIOTAB-
SQL>    WHERE YRBIRTH LT 1881
```

The above is from one of the teaching exercises that were eventually developed. SQL> is the SIR/SQL+ Query-Mode prompt. Name, Born, Birthenv, Nation and Deathcause are names of fields (variables) and LT stands for 'less than'. Biotab is a SIR 'table'[6] pre-created from the SDB, in this case with basic biographical data on all members of the Communist Party Central Committee in 1919 and 1939; there were nine Tables in our final teaching data subset. (Each segment of the query is put on a separate line as this makes it easier to follow and edit queries.) The result is given in Figure 1.

Retrievals involving aggregates can also be carried out, such as:

```
SQL> SELECT AVG (BORN)-
SQL> FROM BIOTAB
```

to get the average age of the sample. Another example is:

```
SQL> SELECT NATION COUNT(NATION)-
SQL> FROM BIOTAB-
SQL> GROUP BY NATION-
SQL> ORDER BY COUNT(NATION) DESC
```

which would tell how many in the sample population belonged to each particular national group (e.g. Georgians) and would group the result in descending order of size.

The basic implementation of the SDB with the SIR database management system, carried out by the Computing Service, was a major task. The SDB's size and complexity meant that the definition of the database structure (the SIR Schema) was a considerable task on its own.

```
NAME                BORN  BIRTHENV    NATION      DEATHCAUSE
------------------  ----  ----------  ----------  --------------------------
DZERZHINSKII, FEL   1877  **********  Polish      Natural
IAROSLAVSKII, EME   1878  Urban       **********  Natural
KALININ, MIKH. IV   1875  Village     Russian     Natural
LENIN, VLAD. IL.    1870  Urban       Russian     Natural
LITVINOV, MAKS. M   1876  Urban       Russian     Natural
LOZOVSKII, SOLOM.   1878  Village     **********  Arrested, died in prison
MURANOV, MATV. KO   1873  Village     **********  Natural
POTEMKIN, VLADIM.   1878  Urban       **********  Natural
RAKOVSKII, KHRIST   1873  Major City  Bulgarian   Arrested, died in prison
STALIN, IOSIF VIS   1879  Urban       Georgian    Natural
STASOVA, E. D.      1873  Major City  Russian     Natural
STUCHKA, PETR. IV   1865  **********  Latvian     Natural
TOMSKII, MIKHAIL    1880  Major City  **********  Suicide
TROTSKII, LEV. DA   1879  Village     Jewish      Assassinated
VLADIMIRSKII, MIK   1874  Urban       Russian     Natural
ZEMLIACHKA, ROZAL   1876  Major City  **********  Natural


Row 16/16, Col 1:5/5  DISPLAY >
```

Figure 1: Display of a Typical SIR/SQL+ Retrieval. (Details of members of CPSU CC [1919 or 1939] Born pre-1881)

Yet making the SDB available on Glasgow's mainframe was only a first step, as it would be impractical simply to give students mainframe user numbers and let them log into the raw SDB. First, it was necessary to put at least some of the data in textual rather than numeric form.[7] This can be done from the SDB itself but only with two record types at a time (typically a data file and a codebook file) and with some extremely ponderous relational joins involving several thousand records on each side. Part of the teaching operation, then, was to pre-create what are called in SIR 'Tables'. Tables are the results of retrievals from the original 'Record' (and can include the results of earlier joins between record types). The end product of this process gave students the SDB data, where relevant, as text rather than numbers.

More intellectually important was the task of creating sensible teaching datasets. Although in an ideal world students would be presented with an historical source and left to ask their own questions, in practice a good deal of guidance is necessary, especially as those enrolled would have only a few workshop sessions on the SDB in the computer lab. In addition, it was necessary to reduce the size of the database in order to minimise response times. To keep size down, our pilot exercise took only a few thousand records covering an elite within an elite — 100 people who were members of the Communist Party's Central Committee (CC); to give intellectual coherence we chose CCs at the beginning and end of our period, 1919 and 1939.

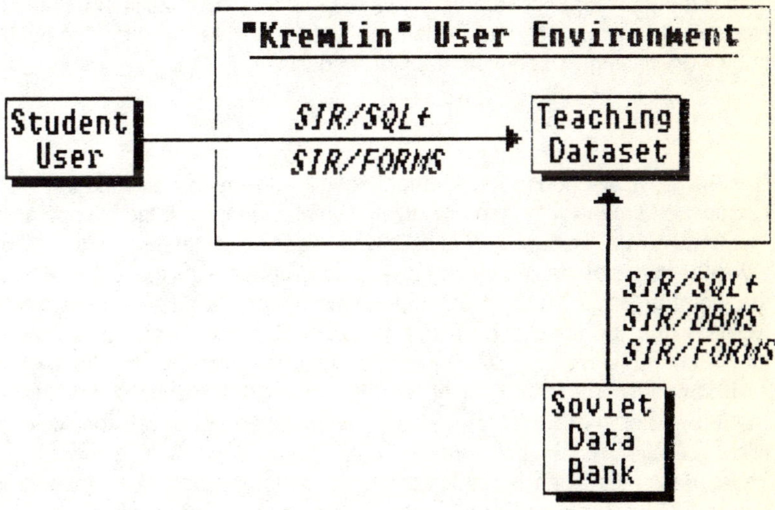

Figure 2: Overall Concept of the Glasgow Use of the *Soviet Data Bank* with *SIR* in the *Kremlin* User Environment

Yet how were students to access these data subsets? The obvious method would be to give students access to the original SDB and various 'Table Files' (Tabfiles), but this was slow, and there was the danger of corrupting any central database made available. It was equally an impractical luxury to give each student a complete copy of the 16 megabyte SDB, so we decided to produce within each user number a file containing a data subset (a Tabfile).[8] In the end, each user was given his/her own user number including a group of nine tables. Each user was also given a SIR 'Workspace' including certain selection parameters and built-in paths.[9] Finally, in order to simplify the process of accessing SIR and the SDB, the Computing Service created the 'Kremlin' user environment, which in its initial form gave a menu for accessing SIR and the SDB, for quitting and for changing passwords. Figure 2 attempts to diagram the overall concept.

An important part of the series of workshops was the provision of background handouts and worksheets. Bearing in mind that students in most cases were being thrown into the deep end of the computing pool (non-swimmers in the depths of a mainframe relational database), it was necessary to explain various concepts. They also had to learn part of the vocabulary of SQL+. The idea was to teach them the vocabulary and syntax of SQL+ through examples and then take them through a series of exercises which gradually added on layers of complexity. The object was that the students should understand what they were doing and not simply plod through exercises. In order to avoid unnecessary details, and to focus student attention on the historical issues involved, the computing knowledge was given on a 'need to know' basis.

* * * *

Despite a few 'bugs' the computing side worked reasonably well, Response times with the relatively small sample tables compared favourably with those experienced with teaching datasets on the LAN. Over 20 hours of class time there was no problem with the availability of the mainframe. The minority of students who had previous experience with Quest found the simplified version of SQL+ that they were given easier than Quest to learn and use. Most important, the pilot exercise, looking at and comparing the character of the 1919 and 1939 Central Committees, yielded — for the students — rather unexpected historical conclusions. (The details need not concern us here but they show more proleterianisation than bureaucratisation.) What needs to be stressed is that the computer allowed the students to demonstrate to themselves how these conclusions were reached.

A basic problem with our teaching was that it was too compressed to be fully efficient. Students rapidly mastered the simplified version of SQL+ on offer and the basic points of the SDB data subset, but the five-hour module within a conventional course was not long enough to get the bulk of participants beyond closely structured exercises. The objective now is to move towards open-ended work where the students use large samples, work on their own on particular subsets of the population, and ask questions which seem relevant to them.

Our particular purpose in this article has been to show that mainframe environments, powerful database management systems, and complex research databases (all 'off the shelf') can be pedagogically effective if they are carefully adapted to the computing skills and timetables of students. Naturally these tools will not be suitable in all computer-based history classroom situations, and the time and expertise required to adapt them will often not be available. The bulk of this article has been about computing techniques and not about the subject area of the Soviet elite. Although we are aware of the danger of the computing tail wagging the historical dog, our aim (like that of historians using simpler data and software) has been to create tools that encourage students to think about an historical problem in new and more profound ways.

Notes

1. The Departments of Modern History and Politics at Glasgow University have, since the paper on which this article is based was presented, begun 'The Soviet Elite Project', ESRC-funded research on the Russian political elite from 1917 to 1991, using the SDB as a starting point.

2. DISH stands for 'Design and Implementation of Software in History'. See: N J Morgan *et.al.*, 'The Design, Implementation, and Assessment of Software for Use in the Teaching of History', *Historical Social Research,* 38, 1986, pp.105-11, and the article by R H Trainor in this volume.

3. An extended review of the SDB by Evan Mawdsley appeared in *Soviet Studies*, 40, 1988, pp. 683-87.

4. The organisation which produced Quest is now called the Advisory Unit for Microtechnology in Education. Its address is: Endymion Road, Hatfield, Hertfordshire AL10 8AU.

5. The '+' in SQL+ includes valuable display facilities, paths helping link the various record types in relational joins, and a powerful command editor.

6. For an explanation of tables, see below.

7. It was possible to use printed handouts giving codes, but this is awkward and bulky; printouts of the identification number/name codebook are the size of a telephone directory. Value labels could be written into the Schema, but only for a small number of values (say 35), and in any event this would only work in our version of SIR from the original records, not from tables.

8. Considerable technical problems were encountered in setting up a tabfile without a related main database.

9. Paths simplify relational joins. For example, they enable the user to take values from the Biography and Education Tables (Biotab and Edutab) with the SQL retrieval 'Select Name Born Faculty From Biotab Edutab' without needing to specify the condition 'Where Biotab Name = Edutab Name'. Without the path the simpler command would have resulted in a full relational join and a nonsensical (and very large) result.

21 Richard Trainor

Improving and Expanding Computer-Based History Teaching for Undergraduates

Convinced that information technology will enable their students to learn about the past in deeper and more complex ways, a significant and rapidly increasing number of historians on both sides of the Atlantic have begun to use the computer in teaching.[1] Starting such instruction is in itself a difficult process, requiring considerable enthusiasm, appropriate hardware and software, support from heads of department, and back-up from computing services and departments of computing science.[2] Yet launching such teaching should be only the beginning of a complex, long-term process of development in which the initial computer-based instruction is both improved and expanded. This article will make the case for a developmental approach to computer-aided teaching in history, and discuss relevant problems and possible solutions, with particular reference to the experience of the University of Glasgow's DISH Project, which has significantly revised, expanded and diversified its teaching since its foundation in 1985.[3]

Especially careful preparation is essential in the computerised classroom, in partial contrast to more conventional teaching. Few university teachers can claim never to have led a class discussion on an impromptu basis. Likewise there can be few historians who have not *ad-libbed* at least parts of lectures. Yet Glasgow's experience suggests that this flexible approach, dangerous even in 'traditional' teaching formats, courts disaster when computers are involved, especially in the early stages of student familiarity with information technology. In a computerised setting elaborate precautions must be taken to minimise the frequency with which students grind to an impotent halt — which they seldom do in conventional history classes. Also, if students are to take an active, creative role in their computerised learning, they must be allowed to proceed at their own speed, trying different solutions to the problems posed. Yet such an approach means that the instructor cannot provide help to everyone simultaneously in the manner appropriate to a class discussion. Thus well prepared, carefully structured exercises are required as an aid to student self-reliance, especially when students are new to computer-based teaching.[4] Moreover, students tend to cope best when paper-based or on-screen exercises are available well in advance of the computer session itself.

Nonetheless, preparation cannot eliminate the need for changes both during and after computer teaching sessions. Even when students have become familiar with manipulating keyboards and coping with software, their reactions to on-screen, written or verbal directions often expose ambiguities and problems lurking in the instructor's teaching plan. Thus the historian must be prepared to alter aspects of an exercise during the class session itself, if necessary by means of hurried announcements! Other shortcomings will occur to the instructor as the 'workshop' session proceeds even if they are invisible to the students. Computer-based instructors are well advised to use a red pencil on their own work during a computer teaching period. Otherwise these insights will be forgotten once the intense experience of the session has ebbed, and the mistakes will be repeated next time the course is run. In my course 'Elites in Nineteenth-Century British Society'[5] I have found that, quite apart from typographical and other minor errors, the tendency to make exercises overly long and elaborate often requires that they be modified during the class session. Likewise, the exercises have altered considerably from one year to the next as a result of reactions to particular workshops and in response to innovations in hardware and software.

This revision process must take account of student reactions, so elaborate mechanisms for 'feedback' are also advisable. In writing up exercises students should be given an opportunity to evaluate the structure and content of particular workshops. Moreover, in light of the experimental nature of such teaching, and the intricate interaction which occurs between the teachers and students involved in it,[6] students must have the opportunity to comment on the computerised part of the course at the end of the term or year. Formal discussions among colleagues in collaboratively taught computerised courses also have an important place, both immediately after a course has ended and before it is repeated in a subsequent year. In addition, evaluations by outside experts can play a significant role in fostering improvement. All these devices have proven useful at Glasgow, helping the DISH team to overcome the temptation to conclude that, given the large amount of effort that goes into the preparation of computerised teaching, a particular exercise which avoids disaster will suffice next time around as well. Thus, in our interdepartmental short course 'Computing for Historians', successive processes of feedback, discussion and evaluation have resulted in an approach which attempts to cover fewer computing skills than formerly but in a more thorough fashion. These processes have also led to the course culminating in a student project and a certificate of completion. These alterations have increased the satisfaction of instructors and students alike.

Important as improvement is, the process of developing computer-based teaching should also include the expansion of the amount of such instruction, both within particular courses and throughout an institution's history curriculum. Naturally, information technology must be used only when it is suitable to the historical material and course in question. However, the modest amount of computerised teaching appropriate when individuals and departments are beginning to use 'the machine' in their teaching will seldom exhaust the potential of information technology to bring substantial educational benefits.

Where computers are being integrated either into existing courses or into new courses primarily concerned with historical periods and themes rather than with computers, the number of computerised sessions can be gradually increased over a period of years. An incremental approach may also be appropriate for new methodology courses in which computers play a significant role from the outset: after a year of cautious experimentation, it may be appropriate to increase the amount of time that students spend on the computer both in class and in project work. In all these contexts, expanding the computer element will allow instructors and students to increase their returns from the very considerable investment they make in becoming familiar with hardware, software and data.

Such expansion is not educationally costless, of course; there will always be a trade-off with conventional teaching. Yet, integration of the computer with traditional sources and methods will minimise this problem.[7] Also, it may be possible to substitute computer workshops for those conventional discussions or even lectures which work least well. In my 'Elites' course, for example, computerised tutorials on household structure and on the distribution of wealth have proven far more effective than the previous discussion classes on these subjects. Nevertheless, even when computer sessions become a major and accepted part of a course, they should not be expected to demonstrate their own worth. The relevance of these sessions to the course material as a whole, and to the examination process, should be carefully explained to the students. Also, the instructor must re-examine constantly the extent to which the computerised segments of a course serve the latter's overall aims. The computerised historian must be willing to discard particular exercises entirely, or even to reduce the total amount of computing in a course, if it seems pedagogically appropriate.

Additional colleagues and courses should be involved as soon as possible after computer-based teaching has begun in a department. The need to demonstrate adequate use of expensive machines, difficulties posed by sabbaticals and staff turnover, and the heavy demands on academic time of preparation and teaching: these problems mean that additional recruits may be necessary to sustain even one course using the computer. Moreover, if the computer is to make a significant impact on a department's teaching, a single participant will certainly be inadequate, whatever the range of his or her computerised teaching, and even a small group of enthusiasts will not suffice in the long run, if only because students who invest considerable time and effort in computing will expect to be able to use it in a substantial proportion of their coursework.[8]

How can colleagues be enlisted? Proselytising may have some impact; the demonstration effect of successful computer-based teaching will probably be even more useful. However, the process will almost certainly also require providing some training. While manuals are notoriously inappropriate for novices, introductory instruction provided by computing centres can be useful. Nonetheless, more specific training in appropriate hardware, software, data and teaching methods will also be needed. Because of the specialised nature of this material, most of the training will have to be provided by the initial enthusiast(s) in the department. Finding the time to mount such instruction may require prior success in convincing a department both that computer-based instruction is desirable and that preliminary training is a valuable service justifying remission from other duties.

The recruitment of colleagues may also be aided by approaching them in ways which take account of the genuine difficulties confronting the new computer-based teacher. For example, rather than force newcomers to integrate the computer individually into courses of their own, it may be advisable to encourage them to begin their computer-based instruction by taking a relatively small part in collaborative teaching. Thus, Glasgow's original team of four quickly expanded to more than two dozen by persuading colleagues to do a few hours' teaching in the 'Computing for Historians' course. Several of those who joined DISH by that route are now conducting, or actively planning, independent computer-based teaching ventures.

Enthusiasts should also emphasise to colleagues that the computer may be used in many different ways to assist historical teaching. For instance, textual analysis may interest many historians who are averse to databases.[9] Regarding the latter, the computer's utility for the study of collective biography appeals to 'traditional' historians of various themes, periods and countries.[10] Likewise, colleagues should be reassured that historical computing does not necessarily entail advanced statistical analysis. Many historians are unaware that software no longer requires data to be entirely numeric, and they may not realise that retrieval and linkage are often as important to historical computing as is counting. Likewise, it may be useful to emphasise the utility for the latter of simple descriptive statistics such as means and frequency distributions. Even more fundamentally, colleagues concerned about extra demands on their scarce academic time should be exposed to the argument that computer-based teaching can be useful for aiding (as well as exploiting) many different types of computer-based research.[11]

If willing colleagues can be found, the enlarged teaching team should resist the temptation to restrict computerised teaching to a ghetto within the curriculum as a whole. Enthusiasts and their recruits should reject arguments that computer-based teaching is appropriate only to methodology courses or to particular categories of history, whether defined by period, country, approach, or type of technical skill. The Glasgow experience suggests that this is not a utopian prescription. Here, although computerised history teaching concentrated at first on modern British social history, it has expanded into medieval and early modern history, into courses on America, Russia and Western Europe, and into political and economic themes. Likewise an initial focus on alphanumeric databases has now been supplemented by experiments with textual materials. Similarly, the computer's role has expanded in content-defined as well as methodology courses.

Historians should also avoid allowing computer-based teaching to be confined either to advanced or to introductory instruction, though it may be wise in the early stages of a programme to concentrate on one or the other. Computerised teaching is not appropriate merely for special subjects and dissertations; even students new to a discipline can cope with a well structured exercise, as indicated by DISH's success in extending instruction from initial experiments with third and fourth year students to first and second year courses. At the other extreme, enthusiasts must resist any assumption that computer-based teaching is suitable only for elementary instruction; the computer has proven an ideal tool for encouraging students to explore the more advanced parts of history, both in courses and in independent projects.[12] Eventually, extensions into fully examinable courses on historical computing itself and into postgraduate work may also be appropriate.[13]

Inevitably, the expansion of computer-based teaching within a history department accentuates the problems of assessment, curricular integration and resources posed by initial pedagogical experiments with information technology. At first, formal assessment of the computing elements of courses may deter student enrolments and discourage the cooperation of nervous administrators. During a transitional phase, pioneering instructors can reward those students who do well on the computing aspects of a course by appropriate methodological and content-based questions in a traditional written examination.[14] This tentative approach to assessment of computerised material is even easier to implement in courses which rely wholly or in part on 'continuous assessment': students can be encouraged to use the computer for data collection and analysis in essays, term papers and projects. Nevertheless, if historical computing is to be fully integrated into courses, it should be more directly assessed, at least by the award of some 'credit' for exercises handed in, probably also by marks on computer-based projects forming a substantial part of the final grade. However, timed examination exercises at the keyboard seem inappropriate in a subject such as history, especially as they would tend to reward disproportionately the best typists and 'mouse' handlers.

The integration of computing into the curriculum also requires careful tactics. Colleagues' fears of too much computing too soon will quickly be laid to rest as even the most enthusiastic historians experience difficulties in launching and expanding such instruction. Yet choosing which courses, and parts of courses, to target requires subtle historical and pedagogical judgement. For example, while extra-curricular courses may be a useful first step, it may prove difficult to convert them into part of the normal curriculum. However, if those interested in computer-based teaching adopt the catholic approach to content and methodology outlined above, information technology should acquire its own momentum within a department.

Resources are the most significant obstacle to improvement and expansion. The full development of computing in a history department will require more than, say, occasional access to a cluster of microcomputers in another part of the university: acquiring facilities at the departmental level or, at worst, sharing them with a group of cognate departments must be a high priority. Similarly, departmental budgets may need to be supplemented for computer consumables, software purchase and hardware renewal. Likewise, labs need technical support of the kind that departments in the humanities and social sciences traditionally have not enjoyed. Any substantial facility requires at least a part-time lab manager to cope with the plethora of difficulties which computer-using staff and students generate. Assistance from such a manager will also be necessary for the preparation of computerised teaching materials, even if a department wishes to do no more than mount computerised data from its own research files for use with standard software. Any aspirations to software development, even if merely to devise congenial 'front ends' to available packages, will in addition require programming support. Most fundamentally, computerised teaching devours academic time; if such instruction is to be successful this problem must be recognised by departments, at least by giving individuals some relief from other duties when they begin to introduce the computer into their teaching.

Yet it would be wrong to end this discussion of the improvement and expansion of computer-based history instruction on a negative note. Time can be saved, expertise pooled and, to a lesser extent, resources saved by collaboration among departments and by links with secondary schools.[15] The number, variety and vitality of the teaching experiments represented in this volume suggest not only that there is real scope for such collaboration but also that the potential educational rewards justify the effort required to overcome obstacles to the successful development of information technology in undergraduate history teaching.

Notes

1. P Denley and D Hopkin (eds.), *History and Computing*, Manchester, 1987, section 3; R H Trainor, 'History, Computing and Higher Education', in Denley *et al.* (eds.), History and *Computing II*, Manchester, 1989, pp. 35-42; *Historical Methods*, 21, 1988, special issue on history, microcomputers, and teaching.

2. See: article by Phillips in this volume; Trainor, 'Implementing Computer-based Teaching and Research: The Need for a Collaborative Approach', *Computers and Education*, 12, 1988, pp.37-41.

3. DISH stands for the Design and Implementation of Software in History. The Project was established under the UK Computer Board's Computers in Teaching Initiative, and has subsequently been funded by the University, to introduce the computer into history teaching and to develop the links between such teaching and computer-based research (see articles by Trainor and N J Morgan in *History and Computing*). The author, currently director of the Computers in Teaching Initiative Centre for History based at Glasgow (see note 15), was director of DISH 1985-9.

4. See Morgan and Trainor, 'Liberator or Libertine? The Computer in the History Classroom', in D S Miall (ed.), *Humanities and the Computer: New Directions*, Oxford, 1990, pp.61-70, on the need for a synthesis of freedom and discipline in computer-based history teaching.

5. This course, which incorporates traditional printed sources as well as computerised databases, and which uses conventional lectures and class discussions as well as computer workshops, covers most aspects of nineteenth-century British social history and is available to third and fourth year students, some of whom are doing only half their coursework in history.

6. Morgan and Trainor, *op.cit.*

7. For a discussion of DISH's workshop method see *ibid.* and the articles by Munck and by Mawdsley and Whitelaw in this volume.

8. These expectations are rising at Glasgow; see also the Ayton article in this volume.

9. See the articles by Nenadic, Newton and Spaeth in this volume.

10. See the articles by Dupree and Greenstein in this volume.

11. For the link between teaching and research, see Trainor, 'The Interaction between Teaching and Research in Computer-based History', Proceedings of the 1988 Cologne Computer Conference.

12. For a more general argument about the educational utility of the computer see Trainor, 'The Role of the Computer in University Teaching: Potential and Problems', in S Rahtz (ed.), *Information Technology in the Humanities: Tools, Techniques and Applications*, Chichester, 1987, pp. 31-40.

13. Thus DISH introduced in 1989 an interdepartmental undergraduate course in historical computing, which students can include as one of the eight papers on which they are examined at the end of their fourth year, and an M.Phil. in History and Computing.

14. Students in the 'Elites' course are more prone to use their computerised material in substantive than in methodological answers, perhaps because they are less comfortable with methodological questions.

15. Trainor, 'Implementing Computer-Based Teaching and Research'. In the UK this process has now been facilitated by the establishment, at the University of Glasgow, of the Computers in Teaching Initiative Centre for History (CTICH), whose role is to act as a national clearinghouse for information about computer-based history teaching in higher education. For an example of successful collaboration between universities and schools see J M McArthur (ed.), *Databases in History Teaching*, Glasgow, 1986.

V.
Research

Computerising the Godly: The Application of Small Databases to Anecdotal History

This article reflects the two different directions from which I approach history and computing, as an historian of early modern Britain and as the computing adviser in an Arts Faculty.1 It is intended to be read by historians with little or no computing experience, who are wondering if there might be ways they could use computers in their research besides word-processing.2 Most of the people I advise are in this position. One keen literature lecturer asked me whether the Basic programming language which came with her Amstrad PCW could help her with her research. Others are convinced that computing holds out nothing for them. A history lecturer recently told me, for example, that he has no plans to use a computer for more than word-processing because his research involves the analysis of textual material, such as correspondence and minutes, in order to determine individuals' opinions and actions, but does not require any statistical calculations to be done. This confusion of historical computing and quantitative history is still all too common. The goal of this article is modest: to demonstrate, using my own research experience, how small, specialised databases3 can be used in simple ways to link descriptive evidence.4

At the conferences of the Association for History and Computing (AHC), many of the papers have described ambitious computer database creation projects, containing all surviving records from a region in a particular period or all information from a single voluminous series of documents.[5] In reaction against the 'bad old days' of historical computing, when the rich variety of historical data was forced into the straitjacket of precise numerical codes, there has been a move towards transcribing complete documents into computer files, with as few modifications as possible. This virtually eliminates the possibility that the researcher will have to return to the original source to recover information lost by selective note-taking and makes the database a resource for other historians besides the creator.

At the 1986 AHC conference Manfred Thaller argued that the document is sacrosanct; researchers should be able to depend upon the computer version of a document to be as complete as a published edition.[6] But the construction of such databases is an enormous undertaking. Although completeness is indispensable in 'published' databases, clearly it may not be appropriate to all projects and sources. Court records, for example, contain a large amount of formulaic verbiage and procedural detail.[7] There is little point in keying in the complete text of every charge or sentence. An historian of religion, reading through ecclesiastical court books for an occasional description of religious behavior, is unlikely to want to devote the time to record enough information to be of use to an historian of legal procedure.

Before embarking on the creation of a large database, it is important to be clear how the information will be used, rather than to hope that once the data is entered the computer will help find both the questions and their answers. Otherwise a vast amount of time can be wasted entering data unnecessarily. I will describe an alternative approach, namely the creation of a number of small specialised databases, each fulfilling limited objectives. These files are simply computerised cardboxes, with the advantages of rapid sorting and record linkage which a computer gives.

Between 1668 and 1676 the villagers of Somerford Magna, Wiltshire, and their rector, the Rev. Nathaniel Aske, were locked in bitter conflict. Soon after the minister's induction, he sued the wife of his predecessor in an attempt to get her to pay for repairs to the rectory. When a local farmer called him names for behaving so meanly Aske sued him too, for slandering the clergy. In 1673-4 the rector prosecuted 16 villagers for failing to attend church or receive communion. The defendants accounted for half of the adult male population of Somerford Magna and included two of its wealthiest inhabitants and at least three one-time churchwardens. Aske seems to have thought that they were nonconformists, but this seems unlikely. The village had only half this number of dissenters in 1676, and there is no evidence in other records that they held a meeting. On the instruction of the Bishop of Salisbury, most villagers did appear for communion on Christmas 1673, but the rector refused to certify their obedience, and on the following Whitsunday the churchwarden prevented communion from happening by providing too little bread and wine. Aske used his sermons to threaten his congregation, and he prosecuted two men for allegedly failing to pay their tithes and yet another for slandering him. Ill-feeling did not even die with the rector in 1676, as the published funeral sermon testifies.[8]

This incident was one of many episodes of lay-clerical conflict which erupted in England in the century after the Stuart Restoration of 1660. In Wiltshire, the focus of my research, such conflict occurred in half of the county's parishes at some time or another in the period. Disagreements broke out over a variety of religious and secular issues, including non-payment of ecclesiastical taxes, the treatment of nonconformists, the neglect of religious duties, the correct performance of rituals and, as in this case, the scandalous behaviour of the minister. Relations between clerics and their congregations were poised on a knife-edge, and while some incumbents threatened their parishioners others lived in fear of them. This state of affairs does not fit in well with our usual image of the rustic placidity of village life supervised by squire and parson in the pre-industrial age. More important, these conflicts can tell us much about lay religious beliefs. In Somerford Magna, for example, the villagers were, with one or two exceptions, not nonconformists but conforming Anglicans who asked for no more than a respectable cleric to administer the sacraments to them and who refused to receive them from a scandalous and litigious one.[9]

The incidents at Somerford Magna and elsewhere were re-constructed from the type of descriptive sources very familiar to historians of early modern England: records from the ecclesiastical courts of the diocese of Salisbury, from Quarter Sessions and Assizes, and from the Court of Exchequer, including Act Books, indictments, depositions and court papers; churchwardens' presentments at visitations; parochial records for names of churchwardens and church rates; central government records, including hearth tax returns; as well as religious censuses and reports of Quaker sufferings.[10] The 'computerisation' of some sources, e.g. lists of rate or hearth tax payers, was the work of a few minutes involving the transcription of the material directly into a file, one line per ratepayer, for sorting and printing. I used the 'sort' command supplied by the operating system of my mainframe[11] but the same thing could be done with the DOS 'sort' command on an IBM-compatible,[12] in a spreadsheet package (which could also perform simple calculations, e.g. decimalising pounds, shillings and pence) or even in some word-processors.

The computer has largely played the role of a card-file in my research. The data could equally well have been recorded on record cards or slips of paper and filed manually. Just such a system was advocated in 1977 by Alan Macfarlane in *Reconstructing Historical Communities.* Macfarlane described how the history of a village could be built up by extracting and filing all personal and topographical data from the relevant sources. His system involved the use of at least ten different indexes: a source index, which contained complete transcripts, organised chronologically; a personal name index, on small coloured cards; a separate name index for each source; a place index; a subject index, also with full transcripts; a court index, again with full transcripts; plus four others. Each reference was to be transcribed in full, and extra carbons made for indexes.[13] It is difficult to believe that this book was written a mere 13 years ago, but in its details it has been overtaken by technology. As Macfarlane noted himself, indexing by hand is extremely time-consuming. It can be done much more easily on computer. All of these separate cardboxes could now be merged into one or two databases. Separate source, name and place indexes are no longer necessary; instead the main data files have source, name and place fields, and sorting or searching can be done on any field. Nor are multiple copies of the full transcripts necessary, since a file containing these can be linked to any other.

Because different records organise information in different ways, I have tended to create a new database for each type of record. Most of my work is based on five databases. Conflict contains information on all suits brought by ministers against villagers or *vice versa*, in ecclesiastical courts or at Exchequer.[14] Clergy lists the institutions (i.e. the bishop's appointment) of all incumbent ministers and the subscriptions of all curates to the Thirty-Nine Articles and Act of Uniformity, based on the registers and subscription books of the Bishop of Salisbury. The Quaker *Great Book of Sufferings* and several manuscript accounts are the basis of a third file, Quakers. Another file, Dpw, contains information about dissenters' places of worship licensed after 1689. The master file is Parish, which contains a large number of descriptive fields for each parish in Wiltshire, covering such areas as geology, agriculture, industry, religious censuses and clerical income. Besides acting as a reference tool, this latter file has provided the data for statistical analysis done with SPSS. The databases were designed specifically to resolve questions arising from my own research and probably would be of little interest to other historians. They are by no means perfect and are supported by personal notes on how I have categorised particularly troublesome records.

The main purpose of these databases is to link scattered information. Court books, such as bishop's Act Books and Exchequer Bill books, record cases chronologically in the order they appeared before the court rather than by place or name as the historian might like. The ordering of other sources seems largely random. The quickness of sorting makes it possible to take many views of the data with the minimum effort. Sorting the Conflict file by parish helps identify villages where lay-clerical conflict took place, while sorting by plaintiff's name points to clerics who were so litigious that they ran into trouble in more than one village. A similar process compensates for inadequacies in documents. There are several sources for Quaker sufferings, which largely, but not entirely, overlap. By sorting chronologically and by place it is possible to eliminate duplicate incidents.

The Somerford Magna affair was brought to my notice, not by the computer files, but by my handwritten notes from letters from the rector and petitions from the villagers, and these were the basis of many descriptive details, such as the rector's use of his sermons to threaten his parishioners. A look at the Conflict file turned up the court cases which the rector brought for non-payment of tithes and other matters. The Parish file contained the information on dissent which established that it was not strong in the parish, and there was no record in the Quakers file of sufferings of any Somerford Quakers, suggesting that no Friends lived in the village. The Clergy file provided the institution dates of the rector and of his successor. Fortunately, Somerford Magna is one of the few parishes in Wiltshire for which hearth tax returns survive, and these were quickly keyed in and sorted by the number of hearths.

As this account makes clear, many of my notes, such as lengthy transcripts from petitions and churchwardens' presentments, are still on paper rather than on computer disc. When I did the bulk of my record office work in 1981-2, I did not have a portable computer to record my notes in the record office, and later I could not justify the time it would have taken to copy my handwritten notes into computer files. In any case, in 1983-4 when I first analysed my notes and wrote up the thesis I knew of no software which could handle textual material easily. It was still the orthodoxy that such information should be categorised and given numerical codes. When I tried to create a database from my notes on churchwardens' presentments, I found that even an intricate system of codes lost too much of the wealth of detail to make the exercise worthwhile. The revolution in hardware and software over the past five years will allow me to work very differently on my next research project. Portables are now affordable, so that notes can be entered directly in the record office,[15] and a number of software products are available to handle free-form text.[16] The core of a good text-base program is its ability to index each document on *all* words which occur, as well as any additional keywords one chooses to enter, so that all documents referring to a particular name, place or subject can be located quickly.

The computer applications described in this article only begin to touch on the ways historians can use computers. Researchers are using expert systems to identify medieval Parisians automatically, complex relational databases to study gravestones, and textual analysis to reconstruct personal relationships in eighteenth-century England, to name only a few examples.[17] Often, the most innovative projects involve co-operation with other disciplines, such as computer science, cognitive linguistics and geography. But historians need not fear that computers will force them to abandon their current research interests and methodology, beyond using a keyboard to take notes rather than a pen or pencil. As this article has shown, traditional historical subjects based on the careful analysis of textual evidence can be aided by the computer's facility at sorting, searching for and listing notes. There is no type or field of history which could not make use of a database or textbase.

Notes

1. Donald Spaeth was the computing adviser in the Arts Faculty at Leeds University 1987-9. He is now the research officer of the Computers in Teaching Initiative Centre for History (CTICH) which is based at the University of Glasgow.

2. See also Derek Andrews and Michael Greenhalgh, *Computing for Non-Scientific Applications*, Leicester, 1987; Lou Burnard, 'Principles of Database Design', in *S Rahtz (ed.), Information Technology in the Humanities: Tools,*

Techniques and Applications, Chichester, 1987, pp. 54-68; Ian Lancashire and Willard McCarty, *The Humanities Computing Yearbook 1988*, Oxford, 1988.

3. Strictly speaking, a database is a group of related files of data. However, in this article the word is used in its less precise sense to refer to a single data file or dataset.

4. The product of this research was Donald A Spaeth, 'Parsons and Parishioners: Lay-Clerical Conflict and Popular Piety in Wiltshire Villages, 1660-1740' (Unpublished Ph.D. thesis, Brown University, 1985), which I am currently revising for publication as *Parsons and Parishioners in Restoration Wiltshire* by Cambridge University Press.

5. See for example, Josef Smets, 'South French Society and the French Revolution: the creation of a Large Database with CLIO', in Peter Denley and Deian Hopkin (eds.), *History and Computing,* Manchester, 1987, pp. 49-57. This was one of several research projects being prepared with the assistance of Clio, at the Max-Planck-Institut (see: Manfred Thaller, 'Methods and Techniques of Historical Computation' in *ibid.*, pp. 147-55; 'CLIO/C: A Data Base System for the Historical Disciplines at the Max-Planck-Institut für Geschichte, Göttingen', unpublished typescript, 1985.) An English example of a complete-source database is Andrew Ayton and Virginia Davis, 'The Hull Domesday Project' in Denley and Hopkin, *op.cit.*, pp. 21-27.

6. Thaller's paper at the conference was entitled 'A *Candide* Approach to the Best of All Possible Worlds in Software'.

7. For examples, see: E R Brinkworth, (ed.), *The Archdeacon's Court: Liber Actorum, 1584*, Oxfordshire Record Series 23, 24, Oxford, 1942-46; Dorothy M Owen, *The Records of the Established Church in England excluding Parochial Records, Archives and the User No.1*, London, 1970.

8. This incident is discussed in more detail in D A Spaeth 'Common Prayer? Popular Observance of the Anglican Liturgy in Restoration Wiltshire', in S J Wright (ed.), *Parish, Church and People: Local Studies in Lay Religion 1350-1750*, London, 1988, pp. 125-31. I discovered the funeral sermon more recently: John Clark, *A Sermon Preached at the Funerall of Mr Nathaniel Aske, Late Rector of Somerford-Magna in North Wilts*, London, 1676; Wing C4477.

9. Spaeth, 'Parsons and Parishioners', *passim*; *idem*, 'Common Prayer' pp. 130-1.

10. Spaeth, 'Parsons and Parishioners' pp. 368-76. The Wiltshire Record Office has published guides to county and ecclesiastical records edited respectively by M G Rathbone and Pamela Stewart.

11. The bulk of my computing was done on an IBM 370 running under VM/CMS, using Information Builders' Focus for database work and SPSS for statistics. More recently, I have imported my data into Prime Information.

12. For more details on facilities provided by DOS, see Michael Greenhalgh, 'PDB — The Poverty Database', *Computing and History Today*, 1, 1987, pp. 22-30.

13. Alan Macfarlane, in collaboration with Sarah Harrison and Charles Jardine, *Reconstructing Historical Communities*, Cambridge, 1977, pp. 89-92. See also pp. 38-80 for descriptions of the records. Macfarlane argued that 'for many types of search the human mind and eye are more efficient than a computer', *ibid.*, p. 90.

14. The diocesan records of the Bishop of Salisbury are far from complete. Of the two series of Act Books, the Instance books only begin to give the specific charge in the 1670s and the Office books are missing for 1680-1708.

15. Before purchasing a portable computer it is a good idea to check that the record offices and libraries you plan to use allow portables. Other workers may find the clatter of keys distracting, and power sources are not always available.

16. At this writing (January 1989), examples include: on IBM compatibles, Nota Bene's textbase and Notebook II; on Mainframes, Status (a micro version is also available, but is expensive); and on Apple Macintoshes, Texas, a public domain 'stack' used with HyperCard.

17. See Caroline Bourlet and Jean-Luc Minel, 'A Declarative System for Setting Up a Prosopographical Database', in Denley and Hopkin, *op.cit.*, pp. 186-91, and their article in this volume; Judith Dunk and Sebastian Rahtz, 'Gravestone Recording' in Peter Denley *et al*, (eds.), *History and Computing II*, Manchester, 1989; and Stana Nenadic's article in this volume.

23 *Allan I Macinnes*

The Treaty of Union: Influencing the Scottish Vote, 1706-07

Winding up the last session of the Scottish Estates on 25 March 1707, James Douglas, Duke of Queensberry, affirmed that the Treaty of Union would prove a visionary act of statesmanship. Rather than accept this pious prediction from the Queen's commissioner, historians would do well to scrutinize Queensberry's political role as head of the Court Party determined to retain office by accomplishing an incorporating union at the behest of the English ministry.

The Treaty of Union creating the United Kingdom of Great Britain came into effect on 1 May 1707. Since its making was for Scotland a self-inflicted act of political laceration which sacrificed national independence for material advancement, critical attention must be directed to voting influences in the last session of the Scottish Estates. Spread over five months from 6 October 1706, this last critical session accomplished a British constitutional option actually rejected by the Scottish Estates in 1702.

A variety of important influences were undoubtedly at work in favour of an incorporating union prior to the last session. Diplomatic brinkmanship, military intimidation and political manipulation on the part of the English ministry of Queen Anne were compounded by economic defeatism, financial chicanery and, above all, by political ineptitude on the part of the Scottish Estates. However, the immediate political influences in the last critical session have not hitherto been measured analytically to explain how the Scottish Estates voted themselves out of existence.

Using our locally created data-entry package, Dishdata, a 50 field database has been constructed, principally from primary sources. This provides a comprehensive picture of political behaviour in the last parliamentary session, based on recorded voting divisions, notional party affiliations, protests and procedural manoeuvres, constituency petitions, placeholding and monetary inducements. A separate record has been created for each of the 230 members cited in the parliamentary rolls — that is, the 76 nobles summoned individually to parliament, the three gentry attending *ex officio* as leading officers of state together with the 84 gentry attending as shire commissioners, and the 67 burgesses commissioned to represent the royal burghs. The 33 shires sent from one to four commissioners, the representation of each depending more on fiscal potential than geographic size. Each royal burgh was represented by a single commissioner, except Edinburgh which was accorded two burgh commissioners on account of its unrivalled wealth as well as its status as the capital.

The Estates sat separately within the unicameral Scottish parliament but combined to support or oppose the passage of Union along party lines. Only the Court Party had declared its intention to support an incorporating parliamentary union prior to the opening of the last session of the Scottish Estates. Support was sought but not guaranteed from the *Squadrone Volante* (Flying Squadron), a party formed as recently as 1704 by close political associates in pursuit of office. Opposition to an incorporating union was virtually the only common political ground of the party groupings who formed the confederated Opposition: the Jacobites, who sought the restoration of the exiled house of Stewart; the Countrymen, dominated by frustrated and disappointed placemen; and the Constitutional Reformers, who, as radical proponents of political and social reform, were deemed anti-aristocratic. The nominal strength of these three principal groupings among the Scottish Estates was, respectively, 106 members for the Court, 27 for the *Squadrone Volante*, and 97 for the confederated Opposition.

As well as fields separately itemizing for each member name, constituency and any remarkable features influencing voting, coding has been used for estate membership, parliamentary status, notional party affiliations and the regional location of constituencies. This latter field has proved notably useful in identifying territorial influences in a parliament for which the franchise was inherently feudal. For example, Alexander Murray, Lord Elibank and Sir Kenneth Mackenzie of Cromartie have long been identified as nominal members of the Opposition, bribed £50 and £100 respectively to support the ratification of an incorporating union. However, the database shows that both consistently voted with the Court in the last parliamentary session. Elibank's consistency accords with his close voting identification with Border associates, while Mackenzie's voting identified with that of his father, George, earl of Cromartie (an opportunist stalwart of the Court).

Because the Union was carried in the teeth of public opposition, the receipt of petitions from 15 out of the 33 shires and 21 out of the 66 royal burghs is denoted in the database not only by a separate field, but also by the insertion of a coded character covering the next recorded voting division. Blatant disregard for the wishes of their constituents is the most identifiable response of the shire and burgh commissioners.

Only two commissioners who had followed their nominal party affiliation in favour of the first vote on Union on 4 November 1706, actually refrained from voting for its final ratification on 16 January 1707 after receiving petitions to the contrary from their constituents. Another three commissioners affiliated to the confederated Opposition, having abstained on the first vote, did vote against the ratification after receiving petitions.

Conversely, only 10 members of the confederated Opposition who were against the first vote on Union abstained on the final vote despite receiving petitions; the ten included principal Jacobites like George Lockhart of Carnwath who had co-ordinated petitioning from the constituencies. To underline the marginal influence of constituents' wishes, all but four of the 15 members cited continued to indulge in selective cross-voting after receiving petitions against the Union.

As with petitioning, a character has been inserted into the relevant voting field to denote the timing of protests. Separate fields itemize the number of (and coding for) protests against specific articles, amendments or procedures. Protests mounted overwhelmingly, but not exclusively, by the Opposition in their efforts to negate, alter and delay the passage of Union, serve as useful indicators of who the party activists were. Only 80 members out of 230 failed to participate in protesting — although 78 members protested on only one occasion, the vast majority (64) in a counter-protest at the blocking tactics of the confederated Opposition.

Separate fields have also been created to itemize the holding and spoils of office, principally by members of the Court and the *Squadrone Volante* — the parties supporting an incorporating union. The predominance of members of these parties on the commission negotiating Union prior to the last session was carried over to the parliamentary committee charged with redrafting or amending articles referred from the floor of the house.

The monies advanced covertly by the English treasury, reputedly to meet arrears of salary, are itemized with respect to individual claims and actual payments. The £20,000 (£240,000 Scots) so advanced prior to the opening of the parliamentary session was used less to persuade members to abandon their opposition to Union than to shore up the votes of the Court and the Squadrone. Although Queensberry as Queen's commissioner did not have a vote, he received £12,325 — the bulk of the covert funding — which he certainly deployed to pay spies and *agent provocateurs* to enhance the aura of menace surrounding the last parliamentary session.

Figure 1: Party Office Profile

	ALL	COURT	SQUADRONE	OPPOSITION
OFFICE	106	71	8	27
ARREARS	65	46	5	14
PAID	27	18	6	3

Of the 27 members known to have received monies, only five without recorded arrears or office can be deemed to have been bribed. Of those in receipt of arrears among the 27, only John Murray, Duke of Atholl, the parliamentary leader of the Jacobites, was an active opponent of Union: in any event, as he consistently voted and petitioned against Union, his abstention on the ratification can be attributed less to his receipt of £1,000 (from claimed arrears of £1,500), than to his growing disillusionment with the feeble leadership of the confederated Opposition.

Particular attention has been given to the votes of each member for and against the 30 recorded divisions on articles, amendments and procedural disputes between the first vote on Union (4 November 1706) and that on its ratification (16 January 1707). Voting records reveal that only ten members failed to vote in any division; two were present throughout the parliamentary session but were constrained by office from voting, and the attendance of another two was excused on account of illness. Although a further nine members abstained on both the first vote and ratification, they participated fitfully in the interim voting divisions. The salient point about the voting record of the Scottish Estates was the high degree of participation. The vast majority of members (174) voted in over 20 divisions. An elite band of 71 voted in over 27 divisions. That none of the 31 members who voted in all 30 divisions identified with the confederated Opposition serves as a pointer to party performance.

No party had an absolute majority in the house, a situation which undoubtedly served as a political stimulant to the high degree of voting participation. The Court, as the party in office, controlled the order of parliamentary business. Yet, even though the Court combined consistently with the Squadrone to effect the passage of Union, they achieved an absolute majority (i.e. 116 or more votes) on no more than six occasions. Of the eight recorded divisions on constitutional issues, only the first vote on the principle of Union and that regulating the succession had an absolute majority; the vote on ratification did not. Of the eight recorded political (non-constitutional) divisions, an absolute majority was accorded only to the proclamation discharging unlawful meetings (this was occasioned by rioting against the Union in Edinburgh and the west of Scotland). Only three of the 14 recorded divisions on economic issues had absolute majorities — the vote in favour of free trade and two votes on the Equivalents designed to compensate Scottish interests adversely affected by integration with England. Conversely, the confederated Opposition mustered support sufficient merely for one amendment (carried from the floor by one vote) — that on maintaining and augmenting differential tariffs in favour of domestically produced salt.

The sorting of votes into constitutional, economic and political divisions, when combined with the voting record of each member, has facilitated the identification of party consistency and cohesion as well as cross-party voting. Albeit no more than 14 members can be deemed to have crossed the floor consistently (voting against their nominal party in at least 15 divisions), there was much occasional cross-voting. The Court and the Squadrone clearly outperformed the confederated Opposition by maintaining higher party discipline, by securing a higher proportion of members in the elite band (who voted solidly for their nominal party on more than 27 occasions) and by indulging less in occasional cross-voting.

Figure 2: Party Voting Profiles

	COURT	SQUADRONE	OPPOSITION
NOMINAL STRENGTH	106	27	97
NON-VOTING	5	0	5
CROSSED-FLOOR	6	0	8
ACTUAL STRENGTH	103	27	90
SOLID PARTY LINE	66	20	38
SOLID PARTY (20 + VOTES)	60	20	23
SOLID PARTY ELITE (27+)	40	16	5
OCCASIONAL CROSS-VOTING	29	7	46

Interrogation and interpretation of voting patterns by Quest is cumbersome, inflexible and, with respect to the associated graphics illustrated by Quanal and Qutils, two-dimensional. Nonetheless, Quest provides a useful basic introduction to interrogation techniques for teaching purposes. The linking of nominal party affiliation to the fields governing participation in protests, officeholding, membership of parliamentary committees and receipt of arrears provides an innovatory insight into party cohesion. The Court would appear to have maintained its party dominance as well as its close association with the Squadrone by spreading around the spoils of office, rather than concentrating political rewards on powerful nobles and relying on their territorial influence over shire and burgh commissioners. Conversely, 23 members affiliated to the Court and Squadrone voted consistently and without any tangible inducement in favour of Union in more than 20 recorded voting divisions. To regard all 23 as principled proponents of Union would be naive. But to regard them all as placemen would be unwarrantably dismissive.

Denied ready access to the spoils of office, the Opposition had demonstrable difficulties in holding together as a confederation. The 19 members identifiable as Jacobites did not vote against the ratification of Union. They exhibited a high indulgence in occasional cross-voting and a limited enthusiasm for parliamentary protest (as distinct from extra-parliamentary protest). Undoubtedly the most principled group in the Opposition was the rump of 15 members identifiable as the Constitutional Reformers; these maintained a high parliamentary profile by consistently voting and protesting against the Union. The remaining Opposition (56 activists) can be deemed the Countrymen, all but 11 of whom indulged in cross-voting as befitting an aristocratically dominated group of frustrated placemen. Nonetheless, that the 11 exceptions were nobles who identified closely with the voting and protesting profile of the Constitutional

Reformers serves to indicate that the Countrymen were not entirely devoid of principle.

As the database demonstrates, the hitherto accepted assessments of party affiliations and principled commitment for and against the Union are both quantitatively inadequate and historically misleading — at least with respect to voting influences in the last session of the Scottish Estates.

Notes

1. The principal source for the construction of this database, known as Trunvote, is T Thomson (ed.), *Acts of the Parliament of Scotland*, vol.XI, Edinburgh, 1824.

2. Supplementary sources used in the construction are: A Aufrere (ed.), *The Lockhart Papers: Memoirs and Correspondence upon the Affairs of Scotland from 1702 to 1715, by George Lockhart, Esq. of Carnwath,* vol. I, London, 1817; W A Shaw (ed.), *Calendar of Treasury Books*, vol. XXI, part ii, 1706-07 and vol. XXII, part ii, 1708, London, 1952 and 1953. Nominal party affiliations are based on P W J Riley, *The Union of England and Scotland*, Manchester, 1978, appendices.

A Database for Historical Reconstruction: Manchester in the Industrial Revolution

The Construction of the Database

The design of a database will only be as good as the data fed into it. This creates particular problems for historical reconstruction, where long data runs are the exception rather then the rule, and where the quality of the sources is often dubious. For the reconstruction of a local economy such as Manchester's, what is required is a data source providing detailed information across a range of business categories. Ideally we might want to know: (a) the type of business activity being performed; (b) the approximate magnitude of the activity; (c) the place where it is located; (d) a description of the property in which the activity is conducted; (e) the level of property utilization; and (f) the pattern of change in these variables over time.

The principal source used for our study was the Township of Manchester Poor Rate Assessment Books[1] which, with a few minor exceptions, rated all the property in the city. Apart from the rateable values (RV), which offer an estimate of size,[2] the books provide information on property type (factory, warehouse, foundry, bakehouse etc.), location of property, name of property occupier and pattern of property utilization. This material was then cross-referenced with data from local trade directories, which described the type of business activity conducted in the property. Thus the ratebook informs us that Mr Samuel Sinister occupied a warehouse at 4 Wrights Court in 1815 rated at £30, and that it was fully occupied. The trade directory shows that Sinister was a cotton twist and weft dealer. The data from these two sources generated the following fields:

a) Name of property occupier
b) R V of property
c) Location of property
d) Utilization of property
e) Type of business activity
f) Type of property occupation (single or multi- occupied)
g) Miscellaneous 1 and 2

The data was processed on an ordinary PC using dBase II.[3]

Prior to the input, clarification was required for one methodological issue: how to conceptualize the basic data. In the case of Manchester the main source, the ratebooks, simply provided raw data on a wide range of different property types such as factories, warehouses and slaughter houses. It became vital to use a common conceptual notion for the different property types, thus enabling subsequent aggregation, disaggregation and comparison. This common basic unit of data abstracted was termed a 'property asset' (P/A), which is defined as the spatial representation of a property right possessing both a function (i.e. a designated economic activity) and a value (i.e. it is open to transaction on the market).

There are a number of other attributes of a P/A, but two in particular are worth emphasising in the context of the Manchester database. First, the utilization of an asset is as variable as its designation. That is, over time it may be put to a range of different functions, at varying levels of capacity usage. Thus in Manchester private dwelling houses were not infrequently converted for use as warehouses. It follows that an analysis of Manchester's business structure over time requires consideration both of the growth (or contraction) of P/As and of changes in their composition.

The second important aspect of a P/A is that while it may be located *in* a building it is not necessarily *identical to* a whole building; it may comprise space rented within a given building. The spatial dimension of the concept is crucial, for subletting was a widespread practice in Manchester, and this was the case for factories, as well as a range of other P/As. For example, in 1815 some 66.6 per cent of Manchester spinning factories were multi-tenented,[4] while in Cannon Street, the centre of the town's largest warehouse district, 57 warehouses were occupied by 106 separately rated tenants.[5] P/As are the basic building-block of the database, and for 1815 alone 17,230 P/As were compiled. What then are the benefits of the database; what does it tell us about Manchester's economy?

Manchester Business Structure c. 1815-1825

All P/As in the town were divided into 12 different business categories based on the Standard Industrial Classification and were further divided into 55 sub-categories.[6] Figure 1 shows the distribution of the 12 major categories in 1815 and 1825; three main conclusions may be drawn.

First, it is high fashion at present to be skeptical of an Industrial Revolution based on steam, the factory and machine technology. Writers as diverse as M Fores, Raphael Samuel and J C D Clark have been dismissive of the classical Industrial Revolution.[7] A first reading of the empirical material generated by the database would appear to confirm the skeptics' case. Category 1 only forms a small proportion of total property valuation, a fact even more damning when it is recalled that this category includes at least some activities more associated with traditional modes of production than those normally linked with the Industrial Revolution. In fact, cotton spinning factories account for only 6.1 per cent of the total valuation in 1815, compared to 48.1 per cent for warehouses and 8.9 per cent for public houses and inns. Such data hardly confirms Manchester's status as a factory town at the end of the Napleonic Wars. Cottonopolis it certainly was, but the smokestacks of Ancoats (the main factory district) were swamped by warehouses located at the very core of Manchester's business system. Nevertheless, a degree of caution is called for before we abandon Manchester and the classical Industrial Revolution as historically redundant.

Figure 1: Distribution of Property Assets in Manchester by Business Category

TABLE 1

Category	Total R.V. of assets (£) 1815 a	% of Category value to total R.V.	Total R.V. of assets (£ 1825 a	% of Category value to total R.V.
1 Production general	18,307	11.96	36,050	19.9
2 Building trade	1,662	1.09	2,888	1.59
3 Food and drink processing	399	0.26	581	0.32
4 Retail/general	26,231	17.14	30,145	16.15
5 Retail: drink trade/hostelry	14,996	9.78	17,628	9.73
6 Wholesale/distribution	77,650	50.73	77,348	42.7
7 Finance/commerce/services	3,050	1.99	4,500	2.48
8 Transport services	5,172	3.38	5,725	3.16
10 Public Utilities/leisure	3,512	2.29	5,366	2.96
11 Extractive industries	280	0.18	218	0.12
12 Land and agriculture	1,836	1.20	649	0.36
Total	153,065	100.00	181,078	100.00

A Category 9 is housing - at this date it has only been collected for 1815 when its total R.V. was £144,620

Source R Lloyd-Jones and M J Lewis Manchester and the Age of the Factory: The Business Structure of Cottonopolis in the Industrial Revolution (1988) p.105

The second conclusion follows: while the database clearly targets warehouses as key business components, we know little of their function in Manchester's business system or the form of their relationship with the factory. A consideration of these questions is vital, if we are are to locate Manchester's role in the Industrial Revolution; it is not enough to rely on the initial empirical findings. That is, the database is beginning to beg a number of questions and to suggest new areas of research. A detailed examination of warehouse function has shown that warehouses were not just part of a distribution chain but were key nodal points in a widespread system of cotton textile manufacture.[8] As the organizing agency of the manufacturing putting-out system, they were the receivers of the vast volume of yarn produced by the new cotton spinning factories. Factories paradoxically, at least up until the 1820s, helped expand the warehouse putting-out system and provide an example of the parallel development of new and traditional forms of production in the classic Industrial Revolution. Factories did not follow a single technological trajectory but simultaneously impacted on new and old forms of production. The warehouse system in Manchester was in fact an infrastructural system supporting manufacturing putting-out, with the whole edifice ultimately dependant on the factory. The dynamic of the factory should not be separated from older structures of manufacture, any more than the Industrial Revolution should be defined in narrow technical terms. This simply produces an inverted form of technological determinism.

Thirdly, a comparison of the 1825 structure with that of 1815 shows a dramatic shift in the contribution of the factory to the overall structural pattern of Manchester's business system. Cotton factory R V rose by 141.6 per cent from c.1815 to 1825, while warehouse RV fell by 5.1 per cent; consequently factory share in total valuation more than doubled over the decade. This shift in the structural balance between factory and warehouse entailed changes not only in the business relationships of these two components but in the overall political economy of Manchester in itself. From the 1790s to the time of Peterloo there is evidence of sharp antagonism between factory and warehouse interests. The conflict ranged from economic to moral issues but was essentially focused on the threat that the factory allegedly presented to the overall stability of the cotton trade. Although the factory stimulated warehouse growth, the operators of the latter component feared that the expansion of the factory would undermine the manufacturing interest by encouraging the growth of foreign cotton production via the rapid acceleration in the export of yarn. In addition the vast increase in factory output associated with the excessive use of child labour would create both production gluts (further stimulating yarn exports) and an immoral and enfeebled population. The whole interest of the trade would be unbalanced in favour of the factory spinners.

The leading representative of this view was one of the largest merchant manufacturers in Manchester, Nathanial Gould, who, with his brother George, ran a fustian manufacturing business from their large warehouse in Peel Street. Nathanial Gould was a leading figure in the Northern anti-factory movement and an indication of his hostility to the factory was the fact that he supported Peel's Factory Bill to the tune of £20,000.[9]

Yet by the early 1820s the schism in the cotton trade receded as the Manchester business community came together around a coherent set of business policies. This in part is explained by a growing convergence of factory and warehouse. The database shows that while only 15.5 per cent of Manchester factory firms utilized warehouses in 1815, by 1825 this figure had risen to 46.3 per cent. The trend towards the integration of spinning and weaving in individual enterprises accelerated markedly in Manchester in the decade after Waterloo.[10] This growing convergence was accompanied by a series of other trends associated with greater business coherence: the establishment of the Manchester Chamber of Commerce and Manufactures in 1820, the growing demand for free trade (especially in the 1820s), the fear instilled by Peterloo when social unrest began to be connected with economic distress, and the increasing tendency for both factory and warehouse businessmen to become actively engaged in joint extra cotton pursuits.[11] This is not to say that there were no business disagreements in Manchester; the hostility of factory masters to the export of machinery is an obvious example of a simmering dispute within the trade. Nevertheless, the convergence of factory and warehouse components demonstrated by the database is clearly associated with a more coherent and visible business strategy in Manchester in the 1820s and is a reminder again that the factory did not follow a single technological trajectory but was part of that combined development so characteristic of the first Industrial Revolution.

The database has demonstrated that while warehouses must be recognised as key components of Manchester's business system this does not detract from the dynamic role of the factory or lend support to the present fashionable sport of Industrial Revolution bashing. Rather it is towards the patterns and forms of relationships (economic, social and political) generated by business systems that research should be directed. Databases, we are confident, will play a key role in this endeavour.

Notes

1. Poor Rate Books are located in the Archives Department, Manchester Central Library.
2. The RVs have been correlated against independent property valuations for 1812. For warehouses they give an r2 of 0.933 and for factories 0.994.
3. Data for factories in the period c. 1807-1841 is held on the mainframe computer at Sheffield City Polytechnic.
4. R Lloyd-Jones and A A LeRoux, 'The Size of Firms in the Cotton Industry: Manchester 1815-1841', *Economic History Review*, 33, 1, 1980, Table 4.
5. R Lloyd-Jones and M J Lewis, *Manchester and the Age of the Factory: The Business Structure of Cottonopolis in the Industrial Revolution*, London, 1988, p. 34.
6. *Ibid.*, Appendix 1, p. 213.
7. M Fores, 'The Myth of a British Industrial Revolution', *History*, 66, 1981; R Samuel, 'The Workshop of the World: Steam Power and Hand Technology in mid-Victorian Britain', *History Workshop*, 2, 1977; J C D Clark, *English Society 1688-1832*, Cambridge, 1985.
8. See Lloyd-Jones and Lewis, *op.cit.*, Chapter 4.
9. *Ibid.*, p.76.
10. *Ibid.*, Chapter 7.
11. *Ibid.*, Chapter 8.

25 Nicholas Morgan

The Glasgow Valuation Rolls Database: Sources and Strategies

This article describes part of the work of an ESRC-funded project at Glasgow University into property ownership in Victorian and Edwardian Glasgow.[1]

* * *

> [Councillor James Gray] May I ask you what class of people usually own houses of one, two, and three apartments; are they often people who have saved a little money, tradesmen and others in comparatively small circumstances?
> [Matthew Gilmour] You get them of all sorts. That very often happens. A tradesman who has been thrifty and well-doing and has saved a little can go in for a single tenement or two; but it is not an exceptional thing at all that they should be owned by a better class of owners as well.[2]

Matthew Gilmour's subjective opinion of the nature of property-ownership in Glasgow has informed the views and writings of urban historians studying that city for the past 30 years. Gilmour was speaking to Glasgow's Municipal Commission on Housing, an impressive but largely ineffectual investigation into housing in the city, convened at a time of growing ratepayer alarm about the alleged intention of the City's Improvement Trust to begin widescale building of working-class housing.[3] Gilmour, a house-factor (or property-agent) with a large practice mainly on the south side of the city, was one of a large number of interested parties who appeared to give evidence before the commission. Like many others who gave evidence, he was concerned to protect the position of the private landlord against the threat of municipal enterprise. James Gray, his questioner, was no less partial; a wholesale hat and cap manufacturer, he was exactly the type of small property owner that his question had encouraged Gilmour to caricature. He was, unusually in Glasgow, an owner-occupier, with a small house in the village of Strathbungo in the south of the city; however as an investment he had purchased a tenement in Kelvingrove Street, in the city's West End, which with eight houses provided an annual rental of £216.[4]

Together, by accident, design, or good fortune, Gilmour and Gray contrived to present to the Commission a favourable picture of landlords: decent hardworking men and women, possessed of all those virtues of thrift and respectability that the majority of the Commissioners thought were so patently absent from the occupants of the city's poorer houses. The landlords were not exploiters of the poor, they were rather exemplars to all of what could be achieved through sobriety and industry; how could the Commissioners support local legislation that would harm the interests of such worthy citizens? As the emasculated report of the Commissioners shows only too clearly, the views of Gilmour, Gray and others were accepted almost without question by the Commissioners.[5] The subsequent historiography of housing in Glasgow illustrates that the majority of writers have been equally unquestioning of the material contained in this most partial of sources, with the result that the structure of property ownership in Glasgow remains unexamined and misunderstood.[6] The particular case of Glasgow and its housing reflects a wider malaise in nineteenth- and twentieth-century scholarship. The vast resource of printed documents, local enquiries such as Glasgow's Commission, or more obviously the Parliamentary Papers, used frequently unquestioningly by historians, have hidden from researchers the real primary record sources they should be addressing.

In the case of Glasgow, and Scotland more generally, there is little excuse for such neglect. Scotland's centralised legal system and its feudal land tenure have combined to leave a massive array of records, of which the Valuation Rolls are the most relevant for the study of property-ownership. The Scottish Valuation Rolls are a unique source; although frequently described as such they are not the same as English rate-books.[7] For the local authority the Valuation Rolls underpinned the system of local rating by providing the basis for the calculation of the multiplicity of assessments to which the landlord and his tenant were liable (in Glasgow, for example, by 1911 there were some 22 separate assessments, 15 payable by owners and occupiers, two by owners and five by occupiers).[8] The rolls were not themselves, however, rate books. Duplicate copies of the annual valuation rolls were used to compile separate series of assessment registers, or rate-books, of property owners and occupiers. First compiled under the terms of the 1854 Act for the Valuation of Lands and Heritages in Scotland (17 & 18 Vict. c.91) the roll contains details of the yearly rental or value of all lands and heritages within the county or burgh for which it was kept. Compiled annually (in or by August) the roll was by law the 'final and conclusive' arbiter on 'all questions of value' of buildings and land.

The roll was to contain the following particulars: yearly rental of all lands and heritages calculated according to the notion of market value — as opposed to a hypothetical value (railways and canals were excluded and dealt with by a separate assessor); a description of all separately valued lands and heritages; names and designations ('designation' was changed to 'occupation' in the set form distributed for completion by the assessor) of the proprietors of lands and heritages; names and designations of tenants; names and designations of occupiers. In addition the rolls contained the name and address of the factor, accountant or lawyer acting as manager of the property (where appropriate). Additional information was added to the roll relating to Inhabited House Duty and the amount of payment due in respect of feu duty or ground annual (burdens created over property under the feudal system).

Data for the Valuation Rolls was collected by the assessor in two ways — property owners who had appeared in the previous year's roll were sent schedules to complete setting out their property holdings, and officials carried out a door to door investigation to obtain names and occupations of tenants and verbal confirmation of the property owner's identity and factor. The data were entered into survey books (by the turn of the century for Glasgow over 900 volumes annually) from which the roll was compiled.

After the roll had been completed and adjusted it was kept by the local authority, being made available for public inspection, until it ceased to be in force in the following year. The non-current rolls were retained by the assessor, being transmitted every six years to General Register House in Edinburgh for preservation. As a result of this statutory obligation the Valuation Rolls, unlike English parochial valuations or rate books, have survived intact. The survival of the Rolls has been crucial — many Scottish local authority rating records have been kept as badly (or worse) as those in England. In Glasgow, for example, in 1917 the Corporation's General Finance Committee agreed 'to authorise the City Assessor to dispose of the old survey, etc., books in his office for the years prior to 1911'.[9] In addition, because public scrutiny was integral to the process there are no restrictions on the use of this material.

The Scottish Valuation Rolls do, however, present one enormous problem; how can a researcher make sensible use of such voluminous material? Just to take the example of Glasgow, the Valuation Roll for 1861 comprises 12 bulky folio volumes, for 1881 14 volumes, and for 1911 45 volumes. Access by the casual enquirer seeking information on a street or a particular property can be difficult enough in the frequent absence of indexes, but for the researcher engaged on a comprehensive study of a town or city over a number of years the time involved is penal. 'The data collection', says George Gordon of his research on Edinburgh, in a masterly understatement, 'was time-consuming'; 'the main problem of using the rate books is clearly not the necessity of any sophisticated technique. The problem is rather that the extraction and analysis of the material is tedious and time-consuming,' complained Martin Daunton.[10]

The obvious solution to the problem of storage, access and analysis rests in the extensive and imaginative use of computing techniques. The use of computers by urban historians is not of course new. Some of those who have worked with rate-books and Valuation Rolls have converted their data to a machine-readable format in order to expedite analysis. However the majority have used computers as little more than high powered adding machines They have assumed that data had to be converted to a standard format, more often than not numerical, in order to suit the computer. In the process scholarly standards were compromised, and the data became impenetrable to all but its creator. At the same time one of the vital components, the individual person or property, was lost sight of.

One of the priorities behind the structure of the Glasgow Valuation Rolls database was that it should be accessible both to the casual enquirer and to the analytical researcher. Nonetheless scholarly priorities were foremost: what was intended was an examination of the implications for the urban fabric of the nature, status, continuity and size-distribution of property or house owners in Glasgow. This in turn was intended as a first step in a wider study of the operation of the housing market in the nineteenth-century city. Data was extracted from the Valuation Rolls for all owners of residential properties in Glasgow at the years 1861, 1881 and 1911.[11] The decision to exclude commercial and institutional properties, and information relating to occupiers and tenants, was dictated by the availability of resources and the project's particular research orientation. However, this compromised the integrity of the source that had been computerised; consequently care was taken to design a simple but flexible file, record and field structure to allow the subsequent addition of these missing items by other projects.[12]

Information was manually transcribed onto data-sheets from microfilm copies of the Valuation Roll. From here it was entered onto a microcomputer prior to direct transfer to Glasgow University's (then) ICL 2988 mainframe. Only one form of standardisation was imposed on the information: a rationalisation of the various abbreviations used for types of street name, common terms being agreed for descriptions such as 'Crescent' or 'Drive'. Beyond this, all information was entered in the spelling given in the source, even when this was patently incorrect. At this stage a simple classification of the owner's occupation was added. Hard copies were generated from the mainframe for checking and editing against both transcriptions and microfilms. Once this stage was completed files were retained online for processing into the main database.

The process of data-capture, data-entry, data-classification and data-editing took in all slightly over two years. The completed data files contained some 66,000 records (occupying around 15 megabytes of mainframe storage), each representing a separately rated (although not always a physically distinct) residential property. There were 16,973 records for 1861, 19,957 for 1881, and 29,683 for 1911. Each record took the following form:

DATE	1881
NUMB	111
VREF	285/
PADD	GREAT HAMILTON ST 126
WARD	4
POWN	BINNIE DAVID
OADD	QUEEN MARY DRIVE PARK VILLA
TOWN	GLASGOW
OOCC	BUILDER
CODE	1101
OWNO	N
FACT	N/A
FADD	N/A
NHSE	1
COMM	Y
RENT	18.00

Most of the fields are self-explanatory: Vref indicates the original volume and folio reference for each record; Ward the municipal ward in which the property was located; Owno the tenurial status of the property (Y for owner-occupied, N for rented); and Fact and Fadd the name and address of a property manager. Nhse contains the number of houses in the property (typically in Glasgow between six and eight); Comm, whether or not the property shared a residential and commercial function (such as 'house and bakehouse'); and Rent the total rental of all the houses in the property.

As the data files were constructed a variety of software options were evaluated. The final choice however was a proprietary ICL hardware product, Content Addressable Filestore - Information Search Processor (CAFS-ISP).[13] CAFS combines high speed searching facilities with sophisticated tools for textual retrieval. It offered an ideal solution as a searching engine capable of quickly identifying individuals or properties by single criteria or by a combination of both precise and uncertain criteria, linked by standard logical operators. A search like 'find me someone who might have been called Binne, Bine, Binnie, Binie, Binny or Bennie who owned a tenement in 1861 in Great Hamilton Street or Abbotsford Street or Abbotsford Place', would look as follows:

DATE	: 1861
PADD	: Great Hamilton St|Abbotsford!
POWN	: B*n?ie|B*n?y
NHSE	: >4

and would be executed in less than six seconds; the complexity of the search criteria makes no difference to speed. The user can choose from a variety of options for output (either a simple hit count or all, or selected, fields), and data can be sent to a file for processing by a statistical or graphics package.

The ability to retrieve information at the level of individual properties is not sufficient. More often than not the historian is interested in information recorded at the level of units of ownership. He or she wishes to know how many properties, and at what value, a particular individual, or type of individual, owned. In order to ease this process the data for properties was aggregated into units of ownership using a simple record matching program.[14] The program currently operates according to a strict matching criteria of name and address — the first occupation for any matched set of records is written out into the new record for the property-owner.

In order to ensure its value for others, the properties database was constructed with data as far as possible *in the form in which it was given in the Valuation Rolls.* The structure and content of the properties database is intended to reflect the structure and content of the original source. As a consequence many of the historian's problems of interpretation are simply transferred from manuscript to micro-chip. Elaborate checks have shown that the number of units of ownership are clearly overstated at this preliminary stage of analysis, and their size and value understated. A detailed check of owners identified by the programs for Ward 15 of the city (the Gorbals) in 1861 indicates the scale of the problem. The matching programs found some 476 owners — checking revealed at least 28 cases where two owners were in reality one, and one case where three owners were one. In all, this represents an error rate of around six per cent. Generalised programs currently under development at Glasgow for the matching of historical data are being designed to overcome many of these problems, and once complete the data will be aggregated against a more flexible matching pattern.

The files produced by the matching program have been processed to form a second database file of property-owners, searchable by CAFS through the same interface as the properties database file. The files contain 23,279 records (or matched units of ownership), occupying around 2.3 megabytes of disc-storage. A copy of this file has been downloaded to a PC and can be searched at relatively slow speeds on a microcomputer using any commercially available database management system (in this instance Superfile). The Owners file looks as follows:

```
DATE    1881
NUMB    1678
POWN    BINNIE DAVID
OADD    QUEEN MARY DRIVE PARK VILLA
TOWN    GLASGOW
OOCC    BUILDER
CODE    1101
PROP    9
NHSR    61
NHSC    2
RNTR    791.75
```

RNTC	35.00
NHST	63
RNTT	826.75

It contains additional numeric files indicating the number of properties and houses owned, and their total rental.

Conclusions

The result of this project has been the creation of an invaluable and enduring resource for both casual enquirers and the researcher, that will be comparable in its utility to the scholarly edition published by a county record society. It has created a database that will form the first step in the transformation of our knowledge and understanding of the nineteenth-century city by unlocking a record type that was previously inaccessible. At the same time the techniques employed demonstrate clear alternatives to the computational methodologies of the number-crunching self-styled 'social science historians' of the late 1960s and 1970s.

However it is clear that there is an inherent tension between the objectives of long-term projects such as this — where the creation of an enduring resource is as important as the subsequent analysis — and the short-term needs of funding bodies to produce published analytical results in order to justify expenditure. It is argued here that in the case of this project the failure to meet these short-term objectives should not be allowed to overshadow the longer-term fulfillment of the project's aims. Moreover the experience gained can serve as a working guide to others embarking on such a venture. One lesson in particular stands out: in such an ambitious venture of data collection it is easy for all those involved to lose sight of the original problem, no matter how simple and clearly defined; data, files, and megabytes become ends in themselves. The obsession with data, and increasingly ingenious means of processing it, should not force us to lose sight of those basic historical questions, posed by statements such as Matthew Gilmour's to the Glasgow Municipal Commission on Housing.

Notes

1. ESRC grant D00232126, 'Property ownership in Victorian and Edwardian Glasgow'. I am grateful to Robert Turner, research assistant on this project, for his invaluable contribution to the work.
2. Glasgow Municipal Commission on the Housing of the Poor, *Minutes of Evidence taken before the Municipal Commission on Housing*, Glasgow, 1904, q. 7474, Matthew Gilmour questioned by Councillor James Gray.

3. These concerns are expressed in, for example: Arthur Kay, *The Corporation of Glasgow as Owners of Shops, Tenements and Houses*, Glasgow, 1902; William Smart, *The Housing Problem and the Municipality*, Glasgow, 1902.

4. Scottish Record Office, VR 102/682,684. Gray's varied duties for the City had included acting as Convener of Finance for the City Improvement Trust; see George Eyre Todd, *Who's Who in Glasgow in 1909, Glasgow, 1909*, pp. 83-4.

5. Glasgow Municipal Commission on the Housing of the Poor, *Report and Recommendations together with Appendix and Summary of Proceedings...*, Glasgow, 1904.

6. See, *inter alia*, John Butt, 'Working Class Housing in Glasgow , 1851-1914', in S D Chapman (ed.), *The History of Working Class Housing*, Newton Abbot, 1971; Sydney Checkland, *The Upas Tree*, Glasgow, 1976; Sean Damer, 'State, Class and Housing: Glasgow 1885-1919', in Joseph Melling (ed.), *Housing, Social Policy and the State*, London, 1980; Andrew Gibb, *Glasgow, the Making of a City*, London, 1983; Richard Rodger, 'The Victorian Building Industry and the Housing of the Scottish Working Class', in Martin Doughty (ed.), *Building the Industrial City*, Leicester, 1986.

7. For standard texts explaining the legislative and administrative background to the valuation and rating system in Scotland see J R Fiddes and Joan Smith, *Guest on Valuation*, 2nd ed., Edinburgh, 1954; J P H Mackay, J J Clyde and J A D Hope, *Armour on Valuation for Rating*, 4th ed., Edinburgh, 1971. Much of what follows is based on the ESRC end of grant report D00232126, 'Property Ownership in Victorian and Edwardian Glasgow'; an earlier version of some of this material can be found in Nicholas J Morgan, 'Valuation Rolls, Rate Books and the Urban Historian', in David Reeder (ed.), *Archives and the Historian*, Leicester, 1989.

8. The rating system in Glasgow is explained in: Alexander Walker, *Lecture on City Rating in the Burgh of Glasgow*, Glasgow, 1911; John Mann, Lecture on the *Organisation of the Collector's Department in the City of Glasgow*, Glasgow, 1912.

9. Corporation of Glasgow, Minutes of the General Finance Committee, 4/5/1917.

10. George Gordon, 'Rateable Assessment as a Data Source for Status Area Analysis: the Example of Edinburgh 1855-1962', *Urban History Yearbook*, 1979, p. 93; Daunton, 'House-ownership from Rate-Books', *Urban History Yearbook*, 1976, p. 23. See also John Foster's comment on Oldham rate-books: 'where rates are listed by street and occupier, making the calculation of any one man's aggregate liability almost impossible'. John Foster, *Class Struggle and the Industrial Revolution*, London, 1974, p. 271.

11. Scottish Record Office, VR 102/74-85, 269-81, 648-93.

12. Data concerning occupiers has now been added to copies of the original files by Dr Callum Brown, Professor John Butt and Robert Turner of the University of Strathclyde as part of an ESRC-funded project on residential segregation in Glasgow.

13. For CAFS see *CAFS in Action*, London, 1985; Lou Burnard, 'CAFS: a New Approach to an Old Problem', *Literary and Linguistic Computing*, 2, 1987.

14. These programs were first written in Fortran 77, and later re-written in C by John Wood, whose assistance and tolerance are gratefully acknowledged.

Census Studies, Comparatively Speaking

The Irish Census

In Ireland, censuses were taken from 1821 to 1911 in exactly the same years as in Great Britain and by a similar administrative machinery. For varying historical reasons very little of the original nineteenth-century records survive — those for 1861 to 1891 were pulped in the early twentieth century to save storage space, and those for earlier years were destroyed by fire in the early 1920s. However, the census enumeration schedules for 1901 and 1911 survived both attacks and, after the establishment of the Irish Free State, remained archived in Dublin where they escape the '100 year rule' currently applied in Great Britain.

The 1911 census of the whole of the British Isles is known as the 'fertility' census because it asked some unique questions concerning age at marriage, fertility and child mortality. The published aggregated statistics of the census at enumeration district level have helped form many of the assumptions concerning the relationship between socio-economic change and fertility patterns in Great Britain. In Ireland, the analysis at nominative level of the 1911 census schedules enables assessment of the extent to which demographic differences have contributed to the historical development of the two communities, Protestant and Catholic, in present day Northern Ireland.

The research described below is based on a sample of households in Derry city and County Londonderry in 1911.[1] The city of Derry had a population of about 40,000, 55 per cent of whom were Catholic, and an extensive shirt industry using outworkers as well as factories. The county population was about 100,000, 43 per cent of whom were Catholic, and its main economic activity was farming. The city and the county offered potential contrasts in class, religion and fertility patterns (as we shall see, this required flexible file handling). The sample was a stratified one of two per cent of households in the county and four per cent in the city, which can be weighted together or analysed separately.

The Data Structure

The database was constructed so that analysis could take place over several levels in a way which retains relational and hierarchical characteristics between records; the SIR database management system was used.

There are three defined levels in the database: household, family and individual. SIR allows the user to develop 'ownership' relations between the records in the database; these ownership relations are then used as guides for retrieving and manipulating data items. Thus each household record is assigned a unique identity number which is tagged onto each family and individual record. Record, relational and individual identifiers are part of the coding frame at the data input stage and so enable efficient navigation (in terms of both human and computing time) of the hierarchy. This procedure permits retention of all the information from the origin census record — up to five pieces of information for each household, two for each family group or set of non-related persons within it, and up to 18 pieces of information for each individual.

Figure 1: Example of File Structure Based on 1911 Census Enumeration Schedules, Ireland, defined under SIR. *(Personal Details are Fictitious)*

```
FILE NO     HHD ID                      PAR
   01         652       52      31      45        DERRY LONGMORE ROAD
                     FAM ID
   02         652       1
   02         652       2
   02         652       3
                     FAM ID             FAM REL                    RELIG  LIT   SEX   AGE
   03         652       1       1         1      RUTH COLLINS        1      2     2     60
     MAR ST   MAR YRS   BPLACE              OCCUPATION
       3        42      43                    NO OCCUPATION
```

Figure 1 combines extracts from the three files to illustrate the extent to which the historical record can be retained. (Note that in this example several variables are missing, having no values; among them are disabilities, and also information on numbers of children born and surviving, which was not recorded for widows.) The household numbered 652 at Longmore Road in Derry city comprised three families. Information on the head of the first of the families, who is also the household head, is given in file 03. She is Ruth Collins, a Catholic widow aged 60, born in the city, with no listed occupation. Some information is already numeric, e.g. position in household list, age, marriage duration. Precoding is kept to a minimum — for the attributes of religion, literacy, sex, marital status and birthplace. This semi-coded transcript retains the names, addresses and occupations of each individual, a decision taken in the interests of sharing the data with other researchers.

The three families in Household 652 (see Figure 2) were defined in terms of the Cambridge Group's typology of conjugal units[2], and comprised a complex structure of 11 people in all, each of whom was related to all the other people in the household. Each of these familial and household relationships is retained as a variable. Thus the head's unmarried teenage son is also recorded as the uncle of the other children in the household, who are all aged under ten years. Equally these children are grandchildren, nephews, or offspring, depending on context.

Figure 2: Structure of Household 652. (*Personal Details are Fictitious*)

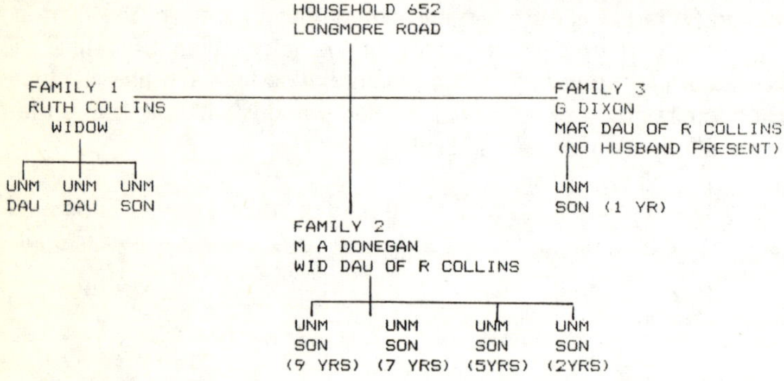

Data Enrichment

A major advantage of SIR is that it can not only cope with relational analysis, but also manipulate a data set to 'enrich' its information — without altering the original. The main way in which this has been done in the present study is by using SIR's Retrieval Update procedures; these permanently add transformed values into the database in dummy variables.

An example of this concerns occupational data. As with personal names, occupational titles were transcribed into the database in full (there were about 450 separate occupational titles covering 3500 people; more than half were in two categories, 'scholars' and 'housewives'). They were then sorted alphabetically and numbered sequentially. An occupational coding classification was devised which was based on the published 1911 census classification in Ireland. This was the same scheme as had been used in England and Wales between 1891 and 1911, so it permitted comparison with research in progress on the nineteenth-century British censuses. The scheme was based on a four digit code of 24 groups (see Figure 3, stages 1 and 2). Codes were assigned manually and input through a series of SIR Recode statements, as a Retrieval Update. In addition, two other parameters of occupation were devised to add, where feasible, the dimensions of (a) economic activity and (b) hierarchy in employment (see Figure 3, stage 3). These dimensions of an occupational title can be combined to select for analysis, for example, 'dock labourers' or 'retired farmers' as opposed to 'labourers' or 'farmers'.

The advantages of having created a computerised occupational dictionary are several; firstly this tool can be used with other sets of census data. New occupational titles can be incorporated into the dictionary with decreasing labour (there is an eventual rate of decline in the occurrence of new entries). Secondly, because the raw data have been retained, alternative and additional classification could be used, to take account of, for example, numbers of employees at an individual's place of employment or value of business property.

Figure 3: Extracts from Occupational Dictionary Compilation of 1911 Census Data, Ireland

```
Stage 1. Raw data (sorted in alphabetical order).

 Variable: IND19   (6)ACCOUNTANT (7)AGL LABOURER
     (8)AGRICULTURAL LAB

Stage 2. Sorted data given a four digit code based on 24
groups, including a unique two digit code for each
occupation within each group. (accountant = group 5, number
10, agl labourer = group 7, number 15.)

 New variable: I01=IND19(6=0510)(7,8=0715)

Stage 3. Coded occupation given a single digit hierarchy
code, where appropriate. Hierarchy code value 8 = labourer
or porter.

 New variable: HIER=IND19(7,8=8)
```

The database was also extended by using SIR to create additional variables. New variables have been inserted at the household level by aggregating up the hierarchy both household size and number of co-resident children. Similarly, new variables can be constructed concerning the presence or absence of certain structural features, such as household composition (for example, households where the head has no resident offspring); using the Retrieval Update procedure these can be distributed down the hierarchy to individual level.

It is important to note that these transformations enlarge the range of existing data in the historical record but in a completely unambiguous way. Moreover, they provide a much more analytically powerful version of the data without losing any of the original.

The advantage of this 'enrichment' of the database lies, of course, in the creation of 'context' variables arising out of specific research interests. Thus a path of analysis on my part which assembled basic tabulations of household size and wives' ages at marriage, led to a construction of their ages at the birth of their first children, and this latter variable was then stored as a new structural variable at family level. Other interests could equally be accommodated by the provision of additional new structural variables inserted in the dataset in the same way. Individual ascriptions can be assigned to household level or vice versa (for example, households where the head is a female Catholic). This also leads to much faster execution of results. Finally, although these data are analysed on the three levels of one source, it is always possible to add, as an additional record type, another documentary source such as electoral or civil registers.

Conclusion

In an earlier report the methodological aims of this project were described as twofold: to test the applicability of SIR as an easily available package for the analysis of census data, and to develop a standardised set of procedures with which the research can be extended geographically in Ireland.[3]

Certainly SIR has proved capable of constructing a flexible database. Its report writing facilities are more cumbersome, and for this reason the original intention was to transfer certain sections of the data into SPSS Saved files. However, all research to date has been carried out on the SIR files, as transfer would involve some loss of flexibility. SIR's Schema Definition and Retrieval Update procedures have proved very robust in coping with most contexts of the enumerated returns, primarily because of the continuing modifications possible between the coding frame and data capture.

Implicit in my original aims was the question of making these data, as well as the results, publically available. In the short term, questions of confidentiality of a twentieth-century census may well make this a non-starter; ethics rather than legal guidelines are the best dictates of behaviour. There is the possibility of omitting personal names and addresses, but this might undermine the nature of the historical interpretative process and, moreover, might be ineffective in relatively stable communities where names and addresses (and descendants) can be guessed from context. In the longer term (i.e. after 1992 when any surviving people named in the census will be over 80) ethics may be replaced by discretion. Meanwhile, the management of these data surely confirms the point made by Bob Morris of the necessary distinction between a learned edition and a popular story; each may draw a separate audience, but both have their place in evaluating where the past meets the present.[4]

Notes

1. This project was financed by the ESRC under the title 'Fertility, Religion and Social Class in early Twentieth Century Ireland', reference number G00232224. The 1911 census enumeration schedules of Ireland are housed in the National Archives, Dublin.

2. See P Laslett, 'The History of the Family', in P Laslett (ed.), *Household and Family in Past Time*, Cambridge, 1972, pp. 1-89.

3. Brenda Collins and John Power, 'Families, Individuals and Fertility in Ireland: the FIFI Project', in P Denley and D Hopkin (eds.), *History and Computing*, Manchester, 1987, pp. 271-4.

4. *Computing and History Today*, 4, 1988, pp. 5-9.

27 *Stana Nenadic*

Identifying Social Networks with a Computer-Aided Analysis of Personal Diaries

Introduction

This article outlines some of the ideas and methods that have formed part of the pilot stage of a study of social networks in the eighteenth and nineteenth centuries. The theoretical foundation of these ideas and methods is informed by socio-linguistic studies of language change and 'speech communities'.[1]

The project employs a computer-aided analysis of diaries and is intended to address two aspects of social experience. The first concerns the evolution and use of particular words and phrases.[2] It is based on the premise that certain social groups defined by status, occupation or gender (in addition to regional origin) are characterised by identifiable linguistic and word use patterns that reflect the attitudes and experiences of members of those groups. A good illustration and one that generated contemporary comment, is provided by the conscious rejection of the Scots idiom in favour of standard English forms of language by socially aspirant professional and business groups in the major Scottish cities of the eighteenth century.[3] Anecdotal evidence suggests that women were an important element in the adoption of this 'prestige pattern' of language, a tendency that conforms with studies of language change in modern western societies[4] and lends force to the notion that these groups in Scotland were among the pioneers in the process of social modernisation.

The second aspect of the project and the one addressed here is concerned with changes in the structure of the social and communication networks that characterised social groups.

Social Networks

From a socio-linguistic perspective an important distinction is sometimes drawn between social networks that have 'multiplex' structures and those with 'uniplex' structures.[5] Individuals who belong to relatively closed, dense multiplex networks have many strong social links between the domestic and economic areas of their life. Such networks are typically seen among the aristocracy, among people who live in isolated rural communities, and in stable industrial working-class districts. They are associated with a tendency towards norm reinforcement, limited capacity for innovation (in word use or in attitudes and activities). They are also associated with particular types of family relationship that give rise, for instance, to close contacts with wider kin and to high levels o independence within marriage. By contrast, open uniplex networks consist of many weak social contacts and the separation of the links that form domestic and employment experience. They are associated with high levels of interdependence within marriage and immediate kin but with limited contacts with the wider family. Such networks are commonly associated with geographically mobile urban populations where there is a marked separation of places of home and work. Studies of language change in contemporary communities suggest that the sparse and fractured ties that characterise uniplex networks are a better mechanism for transferring new word usages and ideas than strong and closed ties.[6]

The relationship between network structure and the capacity for innovation among professional and business groups in the eighteenth and nineteenth centuries is a primary area of interest in this project. The broad intention is to identify changes in network types and, in addition, to explore the character and significance of the 'events' from which social networks are constructed and via which new information and ideas are transferred.

In the context of the present project the term 'event' refers to any action that creates a link between two individuals; it might be a deliberate personal 'event' such as having a meal with a relative, a casual 'event' such as meeting an acquaintance in the street, or an indirect 'event' such as receiving a letter.[7]

The Diary as a Source for Network Analysis

Before considering the process of computer-aided analysis of diaries it should be acknowledged that the diary as a source presents significant problems. Diary records are obviously not the same as 'speech'. They are variable in quality and content, and many fail to record the detailed patterns of social contacts that are necessary for identifying a network structure. Information on day-to-day social 'events' is often limited, and certain diaries arise out of situations that are untypical of the individual's normal experience, such as journeys and tours. Finally, the availability of these records tends to favour studies of the nineteenth century and of relatively well educated social groups. But the source has positive features also, and as 'text' data is well suited to a computer-aided analysis. For although the diary is not 'speech', the immediacy of the record and the tendency to use vernacular forms of language give the source value when recorded speech is not available. In addition, the events recorded in diaries are usually presented sequentially through time, as they occur. This is important, since dealing with the temporal dimension of unstructured text has always been a problem of machine analysis of historical texts.[8] Finally, these texts have a semi-structured quality to them; they are day-to-day accounts with each day providing a logical break in the narrative of events.

Computer-aided Analysis of Social Networks

The machine procedures on which this project is based are not especially sophisticated: indeed they have something of a 'Heath Robinson' quality. At present they use a combination of standard micro packages, combined with tailor-made software (still in the process of development), run on an MS-DOS system.

The several stages of text analysis are illustrated with an entry from the diary of James Beattie, Professor of Moral Philosophy at Aberdeen University in the latter part of the eighteenth century. Beattie was a successful poet and essayist who made frequent visits to London, and with his wife spent several months in the capital in 1773 visiting friends and attempting to secure royal patronage.[9] The diary has been selected because it provides excellent details on the network of social contacts that Beattie employed while endeavouring, eventually with success, to generate a government pension.

Stage 1 — Text Entry

The text is entered manually using one of the standard word-processing packages, Wordstar. With a published diary it would be possible to use an optical character reader such as the KDEM system.

Stage 2 — Line Numbering

The Wordstar file is copied to a non-document format and then transferred to a small tailor-made program called FIXW3. This removes the unnecessary spaces and allocates a sequential number to each line of text, as shown in the diary extract in Figure 1.

Stage 3 — Content Analysis

The processed text file is then transferred to a tailor-made content analysis program called Mark3.[10] This has some of the facilities of standard content analysis software such as the Oxford Concordance Package, with other features that are designed to suit the purposes of the present project. It can undertake word, part-word or phrase searches and word counts and create full or preselected lists of word/phrase occurrences and locations. Word or phrase searches can be undertaken interactively or based on a

Figure 1

1 3/8/1773
2 Day warm. Wind SE. In the morning Sir William
3 and I went to London. I breakfasted with Mr
4 Gray in Conduit Street; but he had heard
5 nothing of my affairs, nor could I learn
6 anything at all concerning them, which
7 surprises me a good deal as I certainly had
8 reason to expect they would have been brought
9 to a conclusion before now. Received a letter from
10 Mrs Montague to inform me that her health was
11 rather better but that if it was not greatly
12 better she would come to town on Monday on
13 her way to Tunbridge, and would think herself
14 happy if Mrs B and I could go along with her.
15 I sat an hour for my picture to Miss Reynolds.
17 Paid Al Urquhart tailor one guinea for a pair
18 black cloth breeches. Dined with David Gordon
19 in a chophouse: not chusing to accept of Sir
20 Joshua Reynold's invitation, as he dines very
21 late. The monthly Review for the last month
22 contains a long account of the pamphlet lately
23 published against me, which account is as
24 favourable to me as I could desire, and indeed
25 favourable enough to the pamphlet too
26 considering its insignificance. Sir William
27 and I returned to Arno's Grove in the evening.
28 4/8/1773
29 Warm and clear. Wind SW. In the morning Sir
30 William sent me, by Miss Grahame, a present of
31 a very fine Cane, accompanied wt a droll Couplet
32 ....
38 ....
39 my power to accompany him. Sir W & Lady Mayne
40 Lady Erskine, the two Miss Burn's, and Mrs B and
41 I dined today wt Mr & Mrs Udny at their house
42 about a mile from Southgate. We returned to Arno's
43 Grove in the evening.

predefined list. It is possible, for instance, to construct a list of all the words/phrases that might be used to record an 'event' such as social eating. 'Breakfasted with' or 'dined with' are examples from the Beattie diary. All references to a particular individual, with the variations in name that are used for that individual, can be listed and searched. The program will also undertake contingency analyses of words/phrases within previously specified windows of text.

Stage 4 — Creation of a New Text Fil
The results of these searches come in the form of sections of text of adjustable character size with the searched words or phrases underlined and the line numbers in the original text indicated. These sections of text can be printed or copied to a new text file. An example is given in Figure 2. This records, in windows of text of 40 characters, the different 'events' associated with social eating that are mentioned in the Figure 1 extract. The 'events' file can be copied back to the word-processing package to be edited or 'cleaned'.

Figure 2

[3] I went to London. I *breakfasted* with Mr [4] Gray in Con

[18] ack cloth breeches. *Dined* with David Gordon [19] i

[20] s invitation, as he *dines* very [21] late. The monthl

[40] 's, and Mrs B and [41] I *dined* today wt Mr & Mrs U

This newly created body of text, recording all instances of a predefined activity, is a useful mechanism for enhancing an understanding of the types of personal link and 'events' through which social networks are created. The Beattie diary, for instance, shows the importance of 'breakfast' as an event at which men conducted business affairs and of dinner (a late afternoon meal) as a formal social event in which women played a significant role. Mrs Beattie is usually present at dinners.

A similar process applied to a specified individual can draw together all the events and situations in which the diarist and that individual came into contact (in person, by letter or via an intermediary). It can also indicate the events and situations in which that specified individual interacted with others who are mentioned in the diary. By way of example, the analysis of James Beattie's diary reveals the importance for Beattie of the Scottish migrant community in London. Most of the men mentioned in Figure 1 had close family ties with Scotland. Yet the links between Sir William Mayne (a Scottish-born landed gentleman and minor politician) and Mr (Alexander) Gray (partner in the firm of Ross and Gray, army supply agents) were limited. They formed elements in two different social networks with which Beattie had relatively weak connections and via which he was attempting to make contact with Lord North, First Lord of the Treasury and the government official whose patronage was being sought. In this endeavour it was the link with Alexander Gray, and the commerce-dominated social network with which he was associated, that eventually proved to be of the greatest value. Neither Sir William nor Mr Gray had any direct contacts with David Gordon (also mentioned in Figure 1), who was a former student of James Beattie from Aberdeen. The evidence of the diary would suggest that James Beattie's social network had a fairly uniplex structure. The diarist's close, interdependent relationship with Mrs Beattie would seem to reinforce this conclusion.

Further Developments

This set of procedures does not, of course, automatically construct a social network from a personal diary. As presently designed, it merely provides assistance in the manual exploration of network patterns. A further stage of analysis, that has yet to be implemented but is worth mentioning, will enhance the capabilities of the approach. It involves the transfer of Stage 2 and Stage 4 text files into one of the text database (or hypertext) software packages. In addition to database functions these packages provide word-processing and some content analysis facilities. An example is Apple's HyperCard, a text or graphics card file database with its own authoring language. HyperCard, employs the principle of 'screen defined' cards. The cards can hold text, statistical data, or graphics, any part of which can be defined as a database 'field'. The card also incorporates 'icon buttons' which allow access to other cards (or associated 'stacks' of cards) holding lower level data. It should be possible to transfer a diary file from Mark3 to HyperCard allocating the text from each day to a separate card and to construct subsidiary card stacks holding edited information on the 'events' of each day. It should also be possible to create associated stacks of edited information on the individuals mentioned in the diary and allow access from these individuals to others who form part of the diarist's network. Although such an application cannot automatically construct a network pattern, the ability to move with ease from the main diary to edited texts on 'events' or 'individuals' will be of considerable value.

Notes

1. L Milroy, *Language and Social Networks*, Oxford, 1980; also W Labov, *Sociolinguistic Patterns*, Oxford 1972; J P Blom and J Gumperz, 'Social Meaning in Linguistic Structures: Code Switching in Norway', in J Gumperz and D Hymes (eds.), *Directions in Sociolinguistics*, New York, 1972; J Boissevain and J C Mitchell (eds.), *Network Analysis: Studies in Human Interaction*, The Hague, 1973.
2. See S Nenadic, 'Illegitimacy, Insanity and Insolvency: Wilkie Collins and the Victorian Nightmares', in A Marwick (ed.), *The Arts, Literature and Society: Some Major Issues*, London, forthcoming 1990, for parallel points discussed with reference to the value of novels as historical evidence.
3. Sir W Sinclair (ed.), *The Statistical Account of Scotland*, Vol.19, Edinburgh, 1798, p. 182.
4. Milroy, *op.cit.*, p. 112.
5. *Ibid.*, chapter 3.

6. See note 1.

7. 'Events' can be categorised and ranked to give a measure of 'uniplexity' of network structure.

8. G P Zarri, 'An Outline of the Representation and Use of Temporal Data in the RESEDA System' (unpublished paper).

9. The manuscript diary is located in the University of Aberdeen Archives. There is also a printed edition with many useful annotations; see *James Beatties's London Diary 1773*, Aberdeen, 1946.

10. Mark3 and FIXWS are being developed by James R Cowie, Department of Computer Science, University of Stirling.

The Medical Profession in Scotland, 1911: The Creation of a Machine-Readable Database

Introduction

In a recent article and book Irvine Loudon pioneered the systematic examination of members of the medical profession in England in the middle of the nineteenth century by using individual level data from the *Medical Directory* of 1847.[1] However, there has been little systematic examination of the members of the medical profession in any part of Britain during the early twentieth century — a period which is particularly important for the development of 'scientific medicine', the 'welfare state' and the profession as a whole.

The purpose of this article is to report the methodology of a project which I have undertaken in collaboration with Dr M A Crowther of the Department of Economic History, University of Glasgow. The aim of the project is to make possible the systematic analysis of members of the medical profession in Scotland during this important period by creating, using readily available software packages, a machine-readable database of the profession based on a sample drawn from the *Medical Directory* of 1911.

The year 1911 is particularly strategic. It provides a profile of the profession on the eve of major national insurance legislation. Furthermore, it is a pivotal year from which we can go back into the nineteenth century and forward into the interwar years for additional samples. In addition, it is a census year, so it is possible to use the sample in conjunction with information from the published census.

Some medical historians have used the computer extensively in their research on asylum or hospital admission records and clinical hospital records.[2] However, our aim is to create a database which not only will be useful to us in pursuing our research interests, but also, and equally important, will be open to and useful to historians and students interested in a variety of problems. Furthermore, we hope that this project will serve as a pilot study: in the future we hope to add samples from the *Medical Directories* of 1891 and 1931 to facilitate the examination of change over time. In addition, the possibility exists of linkage with records such as later directories, matriculation records and obituaries to build up an unusually full 'group biography'. Although there has been skepticism about attempts to create databases for others to use,[3] this database can be seen as the extension and elaboration of what is already a useful research tool; it takes advantage of the superiority of the computer over the printed book for extracting and recombining information.

In what follows the source, the method of data input, and subsequent steps necessary to create the database are described.

The Source

The source, the *Medical Directory*, has been published annually since 1845, when it was first compiled and edited by 'a Country Surgeon and General Practitioner' who sought 'to promote union amongst all grades of the profession'.[4] Since the Medical Act of 1858 it has been 'compiled mainly from returns of the annual schedule which is sent to every member of the profession whose name, at the date of going to press, appeared in the Principal List of the Register kept by the General Medical Council'.[5] In other words, at a minimum the *Directory* includes all practitioners in the *Medical Register* and the information about address and medical qualifications found there. For most practitioners, however, there is much more information in the *Medical Directory* (see Figure 1).

Figure 1: The Source: An Entry From the *Medical Directory 1911*

ADAM, JAMES, Linnview, Hamilton, Lanarksh. (*Tel.* 197) & 4, Sandyford-pl. Glasgow (*Nat. Tel.* 634)—**M.A. Glas., M.D.** (commend.) 1900, **M.B., C.M.** 1887; **F.F.P.S.** Glas. 1894; (*Univ. Glas.*); Aural Surg. Glas. Roy.Infirm.Disp.; Med. Off. Rechabites; late Prosect. of Anat. Univ. Glasg.; House Phys. and House Surg. West. Infirm. Glasg., and House Surg. Glasg. Matern. Hosp. Contrib. "Chole-Pulmonary Fistula," *Brit. Med. Journ.* 1890; "Clinical Evidence for a Toxic Factor in certain Diseases," *Ibid.* 1903; "Hidrocystoma," *Brit. Journ. Dermat.* 1895; "Asthma, its Nature and Treatment," *Glasg. Hosp. Reps.* 1901.

For each doctor the *Directory* it gives his or her current address, qualifications (including the date and place they were obtained), medical school, present and in many cases past appointments and memberships, and publications. It excludes locum or acting positions. Thus, by taking a sample of the entries in the *Medical Directory* and putting the information into machine-readable form, it is possible to answer questions about the geographical distribution, the educational background, the variety and number of appointments held and in some cases the detailed career paths of members of the medical profession in Scotland. In particular, the sample can indicate how typical or representative were different patterns of education and types and numbers of appointments. Furthermore, even though the 1911 database is essentially synchronic, the date-of-degree information enables us to extend its time dimension.[6]

In 1911 there were 3,958 medical practitioners in Scotland or 10 per cent of the total number in the UK (40,642). Rather than include the information on all 3,958 we decided for two reasons to take a one in four systematic sample, which yielded 981 individuals. First, above about 1000 cases statistical significance increases very little with the addition of extra cases. Thus, for most purposes it is unnecessary to have more than a thousand cases. Second, data entry is time consuming and expensive. In the time it would take to do all 3,958 individuals for 1911 we will be able to take samples from other years such as 1891 and 1931.

Data Structure

The design of a structure for the database proved to be particularly challenging, primarily because career patterns vary in the number of qualifications and appointments for each individual or 'case'. This makes it impossible to use a simple rectangular or single flatfile data structure without having either a very large, inefficient size or an unacceptable loss of information. We would either have had to code the maximum amount of information for each individual and therefore generate much missing data, or we would have had to telescope the information and lose much potentially valuable data. Because the aim has been to create a database which will be open to and of use to historians interested in a variety of problems, it needed both to contain as much information and to allow as much flexibility for retrieval as possible.

The software package that seemed most appropriate was SIR — Scientific Information Retrieval System. SIR was developed in the United States and is widely available on both sides of the Atlantic; it was available to us through the Glasgow University Computing Service, both on the mainframe and in an IBM/PC version. SIR supports multiple record types and also multiple occurrences of the same record. Also, SIR makes it possible to restructure the database by dividing it either into subsets of the original or into a new database organized along different lines. It is relatively simple to add new types of records. It has its own structured query language (SQL) which makes it easy to ask questions of the database. Although it has only limited statistical capabilities, SIR produces files for easy statistical analysis in any of a number of widely available statistical packages, including SPSS.

SIR is especially appropriate for organizing databases of career information. It has been used, for example, to reconstruct the work histories of railway shop workers in the United States 1890-1967[7] and to develop a teaching database on the Soviet Elite of 1917-1941 from the Chase/Getty 'Soviet Data Bank'.[8]

For the Scottish doctors or Scotdoc database the data is organized so that each of the 981 individuals in the sample represents a case; the case ID is a number between 0001 and 0981 which was assigned to it when it was selected in the sample. Each individual or case has three record types — Person, Educ, Appoint. It is easiest to think of each record type as a data table with information arranged in rows and columns. Each horizontal line or row is also a record. Each vertical grouping or column provides one type of information about an individual and is therefore a field. Within each table, uniform information is given for each record, i.e. each record in a particular table is composed of the same fields. The Person table, for example, includes fields called: Sname, Fname, Sex, Address, Medsch. The fields for the tables are given in Figure 2.

In the Person record type or table there is only one record per individual. But for the other tables an individual can have more than one record. The only fields the tables have in common are the ID and Sname Fields. Thus, instead of one big table, the Scotdoc Database is made up of three tables. Tables contain many and varying numbers of records, but the records for each table have uniform fields.

Data Entry

The relevant pages of the *Medical Directory* of 1911 were photocopied, and the starting point for the sample was randomly chosen. The data was input directly from the photocopy of the source. Using the data entry software Dishdata (developed by Francis Candlin of Glasgow University's DISH Project), the data was entered in three separate files; each file corresponded to one of the three record types or tables — Person, Educ, AppoInt.

While we wanted to retain as much of the structure and information in the source as possible, some of the fields were also given numerical codes for ease of analysis. The lists of hospitals, asylums and medical societies in the *Medical Directory* of 1911 formed the basis of the code book, but an interesting and substantive result of the project is the large number of additions to these lists that came from the individual practitioners' entries. Thus, rather than 'pre-coding' before the data was put in or 'post-coding' after the data was put in, we coded during input.[9] We tried to make the codes as unique as possible so that users can easily recode information later depending on their research interests. Nevertheless, the information is also in the database in alphanumeric form, so it is possible to adopt a completely different coding schema and still use the database.

A useful feature of Dishdata is that the datasets can be formatted in a variety of ways for export. The data sets corresponding to each of the three tables were formatted initially for checking with the Quest database

Figure 2: The Structure of the Scotdoc Database

```
Table or Record Type 1. PERSON (basic individual data)

  Fields:  ID - identification number (including one column
                for the record type number, i.e. 1)
           SNAME - surname
           FNAME - first name
           MNAME - middle name(s)
           TITLE - title, e.g. Mrs, knighthood, military dec
           SEX - sex
           STREET - street address
           TOWN - town
           COUNTY - county
           TCODE - town code
           POP - population
           COCODE - county code
           MEDSCH - medical school listed in ()
           MSCODE - medical school code
           PUBS - publications listed?
           ASTERISK - asterisk present?

Table or Record Type 2. EDUC (educational data)

  Fields:  ID - identification number (including one column
                for the record type number, i.e. 2)
           SNAME - surname
           QNUMBER - qualification number
           QUALIF - educational qualification
           QCODE - qualification code
           PLACE - place of institution giving qualification
           PLACODE - place code
           DATE - date of qualification
           HONOURS - any honours rec'd with qualification?

Table or Record Type 3. APPOINT (appointments/memberships)

  Fields:  ID - identification number (including one column
                for the record type number, i.e. 3)
           SNAME - surname
           APNUMBER - appointment number
           APPOINT - appointment
           APCODE - appointment code
           INSTITUT - institution where appointment held
           INSTCODE - institution code
           TCODE - town code of institution
           COCODE - county code of institution
           TYPE - type of institution
           INDIV - individual number of the institution
           CURRENT - is this appointment current or 'late'?
```

management system and subsequently transferred to fixed format text files with each field on a separate line. Editing was necessary to shift the Rectype (record type) field onto the same line as the ID. When this was completed the files were read into SIR to create the Scotdoc database.

The Database

The Person table or record type 1 contains 981 records (i.e. one per case). The Educ table or record type 2 contains 2746 records (an average of 2.8 educational qualifications per individual). The Appoint table or record type 3 includes 3424 records (an average of 3.4 appointments or memberships per person), making a total of 7151 records in the database.

Use of the database has begun. An examination of the educational backgrounds of practitioners in 1911, for example, reveals both the increasing uniformity and the continuing variety of their primary qualifications. In addition, analysis of the appointments of practitioners in 1911 reveals a range and complexity of medical appointments which seriously complicates and calls into question the conventional distinction between hospital and general practice.[10] Also, the database has been used as the basis for a 'group biography' of two groups of graduates of Glasgow University who were practicing in Scotland in 1911. The information in the database was augmented by information from Glasgow University matriculation records, earlier and later *Directories*, and obituaries.[11]

There are plans to use the database in studies of the Highlands and Islands Medical Service and of general practitioners in Fife. The aim is to investigate the extent to which medical practitioners in these parts of Scotland differed from those in Scotland as a whole with regard to their educational backgrounds or the types and numbers of their appointments and memberships. Moreover, the database can be used to explore the extent to which medical practitioners in Scotland studied abroad as part of their training, and if so, where they went.

Finally, we welcome others to use the database. We hope this will increase further the value of what one President of the General Medical Council called the 'invaluable information' in the *Medical Directory*.[12]

Notes

1. I Loudon, '2000 Medical Men in 1847', *Bulletin of the Society for the Social History of Medicine*, 33, 1983, pp. 4-8; I Loudon, *Medical Care and the General Practitioner 1750-1850*, Oxford, 1986.

2. A Digby, 'Quantitative and Qualitative Perspectives on the Asylum', and G B Risse, 'Hospital History: New Sources and Methods', in Roy Porter and Andrew Wear (eds.), *Problems and Methods in the History of Medicine*, London, 1987, pp. 153-74, 175-203; J Howell, 'Patient Care at Guy's and the Pennsylvania Hospital, 1900-1920', unpublished paper presented at the Joint Conference of the British Society for the History of Science and the History of Science Society, Manchester, 11-15 July 1988.

3. Professor William Speck expressed such a view in his keynote address at the Association for History and Computing UK Branch Conference in Glasgow, 18th March 1988.

4. *Medical Directory of Great Britain and Ireland for 1845*, p. vi.

5. *Medical Directory 1988*, Part I, p. 1.

6. For a discussion of the strengths and weaknesses of the *Medical Directory* as a source, see: M A Crowther and M W Dupree, 'A Profile of the Medical Profession in Scotland in 1911', unpublished paper presented at the seminar of the Wellcome Unit for the History of Medicine, University of Glasgow, 11 October 1988.

7. J L Reiff and S Hirsch, 'Reconstructing Work Histories by Computer: The Pullman Shop Worker, 1890-1967', *Historical Methods*, 15, 1982, pp. 139-42.

8. See article by E Mawdsley and S Whitelaw in this volume.

9. For the distinction between 'pre-coding' and 'post-coding', see article by K Schurer in this volume.

10. Crowther and Dupree, *op.cit.*

11. A pilot study, 'The Background, Education and Careers of a Sample of Glasgow University Medical Graduates', has been completed by M Villiers of the Department of Economic History, University of Glasgow.

12. Longman Archives, University of Reading Library, 382/30, H L Eason to A W Churchill, 22 Feb 1944.

VI.

Conclusion

The Nature and Future of Historical Computing

Introduction

Few subjects are currently more fashionable than the history of history: a new self-consciousness has spawned ideas, books and articles, especially on the Victorian period, when professional academic historians first established themselves in Britain. Heyck, Goldstein, Slee, Levine and others have all written recently on this subject. At the same time there has been something of a resurgence in studies of historical purpose and method.[2] A good example is the appearance in 1987 of Lawrence Stone's *The Past and the Present Revisited* which examines in brilliant style the relationship between history and the social sciences and the supposed 'revival' of narrative as a mode of historical discourse.[3]

It is probably a fair bet that, in the not too distant future, we ourselves — members of the Association for History and Computing — will become the subject of serious historiographic enquiry. The great success of the Association's milestone events are sure to attract attention: future historians will wish to know just what drew us together, what happened between us, and what, at the end of it all, we achieved.

My hope is that when the history of the Association is written, later rather than sooner, due emphasis will be given to the essential simplicity of the shared perception and enthusiasm that drew people together: history, with its emphasis on working with large volumes of complex data, must somehow be modified, possibly quite radically, by the advent of cheap and generally available computing power. Enough work had already been done, by Bill Speck and other pioneers, to suggest what might follow in the future. And yet, at the time of the first Westfield Conference in 1986, it seemed that few people really understood what the implications might be if large numbers of professional historians were to embrace computer methods.[4] I am not sure just how much sharper our vision has become since then. My own experience is of being swept along; of coming to grips with new technologies, projects and methodological possibilities; of hardly having time to draw breath. When I was asked to prepare this paper, I resolved to stand back a little and give some thought to the wider significance of my own efforts and those of other historians working with computers.

The Nature of History and Historical Computing

It is worth noting, by way of introduction, how radically conceptions of the nature of history have changed since the advent of academic history in Britain in the second half of the nineteenth century. First, there were the great amateur historians like Macaulay, who, as legatees of Gibbon, saw in history a means of teaching moral philosophy by example, seizing the attention of the reader by emphasising the controversial and the picturesque. History was a story, a dramatic narrative, whose purpose was to support all deemed best in national life: unity, liberty, the rule of law, the triumph of good over evil.[5] Free reign was given to the imagination, and though efforts were made to conform to the known facts, little effort was made to supply new ones. The telling of the great human story was as much a literary as a scholarly task. The Macaulay approach, shared by Hallam, Palgrave and others, made for a good read, the most successful works selling in tens of thousands.

Then came the scholars, the professional historians who gained a foothold at the Universities of Oxford and Cambridge following the establishment of specialist degree courses in history (and law) in the middle of the nineteenth century.[6] These scholars shared the same high purpose and predilections of the German scientific school associated with Ranke: the duty of the historian was to conduct research, and to produce 'true and accurate' representations of the past that adhered strictly to the facts. In this way moral lessons could usefully be drawn which might help guide the affairs of men: history has a social purpose, according to the 'exemplar' paradigm, and this idea has often been used to justify its study. Sir James Stephen, Regius Professor of Modern History at Cambridge, told the University Commissioners that history 'should cater for the less able men, those incapable of high standards in classics or mathematics, but still men of whom it is unjust to despond and who might thus be rescued from the temptations of a misspent youth.'[7]

Thirdly, there is the view associated with the second generation of professionals who abandoned the exemplar paradigm of history in favour of the developmental. According to the developmental paradigm, the purpose of history is to study 'man in action'. It is, to quote Stubbs, 'the history of ourselves, of the education of our nation, of the development of our government, of the fortunes of our fathers, that caused us to be taught and governed as we are, and formed our minds and habit by that teaching, government and position.'[8] The legacy of Stubbs' position at Oxford was an emphasis on continuous history or, more precisely, continuous constitutional history. More widely, the developmental conception of history has endured in Britain, although it has been refined in subtle and important ways.

The most important refinement is that associated with the generation that followed Stubbs and his colleagues, of whom the best known are Bury and Tout. These men shifted the emphasis of history, from a concern with accurate representations of past realities to the process employed by historians to represent the past. History is seen as part process and part organised knowledge. Bury went so far as to say that 'History is science, no less and no more.'[9] And this view was later supported by the mighty Collingwood who, Carr tells us, is the only Briton to have made a serious contribution to the philosophy of history. To quote the great man:

> Every historian would agree, that history is a kind of research or inquiry ... It consists of fostering something we do not know, and trying to discover it ... science is finding things out, and in that sense history is a science.[10]

To rephrase this in modern terminology: history is a set of research methods applied to the building of models of past realities. The focus here is on process rather than outcome, a position later supported by E H Carr when, at the conclusion of his famous essay *What is History?* he wrote: 'It is a continuous process of interaction between the historian and his facts, an unending dialogue between the past and the present.'[11]

It is my contention that we have not moved far beyond this point in the last quarter of a century: the modified developmental paradigm of history rules, in Britain at least. Recent decades have seen a rise in theoretical awareness, and this has certainly enriched the dialogue between the historian and his facts, as the work of E P Thompson and others amply testifies. But theory has not revolutionised either our research methods or our mode of discourse. Thompson's rejection of 'intellectual Stalinism' in *The Poverty of Theory*, for instance, is indicative of the strength of support for empirical, scientific, developmental history in Britain.[12]

What is the importance of all this for historical computing? Does it help define the nature of the subject and its relation to the discipline of history? I think it does.

First, it should be apparent that the tremendous support for historical computing in Britain can be explained in no small measure by the national attachment to empirical, scientific history. Our first rule is that the historian must really know his sources; and what better tool to help in this process than the computer? We are already wedded to the database concept to a degree that was inconceivable even a decade ago.

Second, reference to our national paradigm helps explain what historical computing is and what it is not. Pre-eminently, historical computing must be concerned with the creation of models of the past or representations of past realities. It cannot, therefore, be defined simply in terms of areas of application: psephology, demography or whatever. In theory, at least, historical computing should be applicable to all fields of historical enquiry. Nor is it possible to define historical computing with reference to especially relevant branches of computing or applied information technology.

Database technology may be of tremendous interest at the moment, and expert systems might be thought to offer possibilities for the future, but there is nothing specifically historical about such things: they are general tools which might be applied to any number of subjects or problems.[13]

Historical computing can only be defined in terms of the distinctive contribution it can make to historical research. As a subject it exists on the methodological plane. It must be viewed at a high level, not in terms of grubby practicalities. It is the design of research procedures that counts, not hardware or software. The following are relevant questions:

> How do we define the historical issue under consideration?
> What are the characteristics of the available data?
> How do we manipulate, process, or interrogate the data to extract meaning, stimulate ideas or test hypotheses?

There are doubtless many other questions of equal relevance, but they must be of the same order, if they are to be embraced by the notion of historical computing, at least as I have chosen to define it. Back-projection, generalised inverse projection, family reconstitution, record linkage, social savings and notional corporate rate of return are instances of concepts that are the product of historical computing. There are many more, and others will follow as historians attempt to shed fresh light on the past (or, using our earlier jargon, create new historical models or representations of the past). None of these historical methods owes anything to computers as such: historical computing can be done without computers. Computers merely make operational the concepts and methods that are the product of historical computing.

To summarise: historical computing is best viewed as an approach to research; an approach that is formal, that requires data and algorithms to be made explicit, that gives full attention to documentation, and qualifies its results in an appropriately scientific fashion. Historical computing is part and parcel of a scientific history.

The Significance of Historical Computing

It is one thing to define historical computing; it is quite another to assess its significance for history as a whole. These are still early days. Some historians may have been involved with computing for many years, but as a general phenomenon historical computing is of recent vintage. We have comparatively little experience on which to base an assessment, and must tackle the problem from a different angle. A useful starting point is the identification of those features which, more than others, distinguish current historical practice in Britain.

First among these must be the importance attached to primary sources. This tradition dates back to the era of Stubbs and has been affirmed by nearly all senior historians who have written on historiographic matters: Bury, Tout, Pollard, Powicke, Collingwood and Elton are examples. Elton even managed to reach agreement with the cliometrician Fogel on this point in *Which Road to the Past?*

> Of all the elements that affect the quality of an historical work, none is more important than the thoroughness of the search for the evidence and the care that is taken in the investigation of the provenance, domain and reliability of the evidence. We take issue with those who argue that details are subordinate to interpretation, not because we celebrate the facts for their own sake, but because the quality of an historical interpretation is critically dependent on the quality of the details of which it is spun.[14]

The two go on to advise that history is often shaped through chance discoveries made whilst ploughing primary sources: Elton's Thomas Cromwell, for instance. They conclude:

> The one conviction that unites us is that there are far more things in historical evidence than are embodied in current interpretations of history.[15]

A second distinguishing feature of British academic history is the application, implicitly or explicitly, of scientific notions in historical construction. In the post-Stubbs era there has been a long-standing rejection of the idea that the 'facts should be allowed to speak for themselves'. Bury raged against this, arguing instead that the historian's task is to think his way into a past situation, reconstructing the scene, and validating or rejecting the construction through reference to the known facts.[16] Collingwood later took up the theme. For him, 'historical procedure, or method, consists essentially of interpreting evidence',[17] and of the interplay between evidence and imagination he writes, most brilliantly:

> The historian's picture of a subject, whether the subject be a sequence of events or a past state of things, thus appears as a web of imaginative construction stretched between certain fixed points provided by the statements of his authorities; and if these points are frequent enough and if the threads spun from each to the next are constructed with due care, always by the *a priori* imagination and never by merely arbitrary fancy, the whole picture is constantly

> verified by appeal to these data, and runs little risk of losing touch with the reality which it represents.[18]

Collingwood anticipated the quantitative historians of the post-war generation, whose whole thrust has been (a) to forge strong logical threads, through strict reasoning, between pieces of evidence, and (b) to verify observations through systematic use of the available data. Yet the main difference between quantitative and non-quantitative historians is mode of discourse, rather than the substance of the procedures adopted. Both qualify as 'historical scientists' as defined by Collingwood.

A third feature of British academic history, already mentioned, is the sense that it is a professional pursuit requiring specialist skills. These skills relate to knowledge of sources and the application of high-level interpretive skills already discussed. It is this sense of professionalism that distances academic historians from antiquarians and local history societies. The outward signs of professionalisation — journals, professional societies, conferences and research institutes — began in the late nineteenth century and are expressions of a community life, with shared values and standards. Participation in the community, through publication, giving papers, attending events, is very much a prerequisite of professional success.[19]

A fourth feature of the profession, already touched upon, is the intellectual distance that exists between historians and social scientists. To the historian, theory is a means of stimulating the imagination, of setting the research agenda; it is not the route to generalisation. Generalisation is the product in history of accumulated evidence and empirical observation — hence, in economic history, the likes of Rostow, Gerschenkron and Alfred Chandler are not theorists, though they have clearly been influenced by contact with theoretical ideas; they are grand generalisers, and it is this that makes their work acceptable, even inspirational, while the cliometric school has not found a welcome in Britain.

A fifth factor conditioning British historical practice is the means by which the subject is taught and the aims of the teaching. One aspect of professionalisation has been the prevalence of the idea that history is studied largely for its own sake, not for reasons of immediate utility or social value; all of which began with the rejection of the exemplar paradigm. Associated with this is the idea that the real value of historical study lies in the training offered to students. Tout and the Manchester school are usually credited with popularising this idea, which is still in vogue today. History, we assert, teaches students to reason, to evaluate evidence, to order information, and to appraise complex arguments, empirically and logically. We are back to the notion that history is scientific in method. In 1910, Tout made the case for well-resourced historical laboratories, as follows:

> Our primary business is to find out as much as we can about the past. Our methods, then, must necessarily be the methods of the observational sciences, and we require as much training in the technique of our craft as any other skilled worker. Nay, more, the educational value of our study lies not so much in the accumulation of a mass of unrelated facts as in training in method, and evidence, and in seeing how history is made. It follows, then, that the study of history should be largely a study of processes and method, even for those for whom history is not mainly the preparation for a career, but chiefly a means of academic education. No historical education can, therefore, be regarded as complete unless it involves a training in method. The best training in method is an attempt at research.[20]

This view has been terribly influential: at the undergraduate level it has been used to justify the special subject, the seminar method of teaching and, more recently, the undergraduate final year dissertation; at the postgraduate level it gave rise, after the First World War, to the Ph.D. It was also used as an argument for the establishment of the Institute of Historical Research.[21]

My argument, then, is that five main features — primacy of sources, scientific procedures, professionalism, the subordination of theory, and the emphasis given in teaching to historical method — are the clearest characteristics of British academic history today. What are the implications for historical computing?

Generally speaking, it is evident that historical computing represents no kind of threat to the existing order; rather, it reinforces existing tendencies or predilections. The logic of database-centred research, for instance, reaffirms the primacy of documentary research. The computer is seen as a supremely efficient investigatory tool, one that prompts interaction, the making of associations and an understanding of complex relationships. Moreover, the method of proceeding is scientific and distinctively historical. There is less room for fudge. Data and processing must be explicitly defined. And this type of activity can be seen as requiring specialist knowledge that enhances the standing of the profession. The case for history-as-training benefits immeasurably, and with the spread of historical computing laboratories, equipped for the teaching of advanced methods using primary sources, Tout's vision of well-equipped historical laboratories can be brought nearer than ever before to reality. Computing is experimental and practical, and reinforces the empirical inclinations of professional historians. Historical computing promises better practice and higher-quality research. The scissors-and-paste approach, so despised by

Collingwood, and still woefully present in certain branches of history, has nothing in common with historical computing.

It is not going too far to represent historical computing as one of the standard-bearers of historical science, just as quantitative history two decades or more ago pushed forward the ideal first expressed by Bury and his contemporaries. The subject is not revolutionary; it simply reinforces an existing paradigm, but it may put one or two more nails in the coffin of what remains of the intellectually debased school of selective narration.

Conclusion

It is fair to conclude that historical computing has taken root in very fertile soil: a fact which explains the large intitial membership in Britain of the Association for History and Computing, and the success of its conferences. It is very much to be hoped that the new skills the technology demands, and the higher degree of methodological sophistication that it encourages, will become commonplace, making for more and better history. We might expect a rise in professional standards and even in prestige.

The role of the Association for History and Computing is to encourage these developments. Its membership should not become a clique with its own pathetic jargon. It is born of a tradition, and does not exist to satisfy a passing fashion. Our goal should be a well-trained, methodologically acute profession. Once this exists, we might disband! However, before that time comes, there is important work to be done:

(1) In increasing awareness of the nature of historical computing; taking the debate away from the realms of hardware and software towards those of method, technique and data.
(2) In increasing awareness of the potential of historical computing.
(3) In encouraging sound technical practice.
(4) In demonstrating the requirements for success in historical computing, and the ways in which research procedures must be amended to achieve success, individually and collectively.

In the British way of things, we shall receive little help from government in carrying out this work. The community of historians must help itself, through the provision of training, conferences, advice and published materials. University departments must use historical computing as a means of pressing ahead with methods courses and project work. And we must ensure that the next generation of research historians is well trained, through the provision of Master's courses and training schemes for those preparing for a research degree.[22] The future is bright, but much remains to be done.

Notes

1. This article is the unmodified text of my closing address delivered at the First Annual Conference of the UK Branch of the Association for History and Computing held at the University of Glasgow in March 1988. The theme of the paper was inspired by the work of my former colleague Christopher Parker. I am grateful to Chris for guiding me through the literature. Any errors of interpretation, however, remain mine alone.

2. T W Heyck, *The Transformation of Intellectual Life in Victorian England*, London, 1982, pp. 120-51; D S Goldstein, 'The Organizational Development of the British Historical Profession, 1884-1921', *Bulletin of the Institute of Historical Research, 1884-1921,* 55, 1982, pp. 180-93; P R H Slee, *Learning and a Liberal Education: The Study of Modern History in the Universities of Oxford, Cambridge and Manchester*, Manchester, 1986; P Levine, *The Amateur and the Professional: Antiquaries, Historians and Archaeologists in Victorian England, 1838-1886*, Cambridge, 1986; G G Iggers, *New Directions in European Historiography*, revised edition, London, 1985.

3. L Stone, *The Past and the Present Revisited*, London, 1987.

4. More than 300 people attended the first Westfield College (University of London) conference on History and Computing. The conference led to the setting up of the Association for History and Computing, whose constitution was approved at the second Westfield conference in March 1987.

5. In the introduction to his *History of England*, Macaulay refers to the eight volume book as covering 'a single act of a great and eventful drama extending through ages': T B Macaulay, *The History of England*, London, 1849, vol. I, p. 3.

6. A more sophisticated interpretation of changes in British historical thought and methods is provided by C J W Parker, 'Academic History: Paradigms and Dialectic', *Literature and History*, 5, 1979, pp. 165-81.

7. Quoted by Parker in 'Paradigms and Dialect', pp. 168-9.

8. Quoted by Parker in 'Paradigms and Dialectic', p. 172.

9. H Temperley (ed.), *J B Bury: Selected Writings*, Cambridge, 1930, p. 4.

10. R G Collingwood, *The Idea of History*, Oxford, 1946, p. 9.

11. E H Carr, *What is History?*, London, 1961, p. 24.

12. For an interesting critique of Thompson's position, see S Hall, 'In Defence of Theory' in R Samuel (ed.), *People's History and Socialist Theory*, London, 1981, pp. 378-85.

13. A point made by several contributors to P Denley, S Fogelvik & C Harvey (eds.), *History and Computing II*, Manchester, 1989.

14. R W Fogel & G R Elton, *Which Road to the Past? Two Views of History*, New York, 1984, p. 125.

15. *Ibid.*, p. 129.

16. Temperley, *op.cit.*, pp. 6-22.

17. Collingwood, *op.cit.*, p. 10.

18. *Ibid.*, p. 242.

19. See Goldstein, *op.cit.*

20. T F Tout, *Collected Papers Volume I*, Manchester, 1932, p. 80.

21. C J W Parker, 'The Development of History Courses in British Universities, 1850-1975' (MA thesis, University of Exeter, 1976), pp. 67-81.

22. Master's degree programmes in historical computing have already been devised at the Universities of Hull, Glasgow and London. The last mentioned is based at the Institute of Historical Research.